The Germans and the Final Solution

B

JEWISH SOCIETY AND CULTURE

General Editor DAVID SORKIN

David Bankier *The Germans and the Final Solution*
Edited by David Cesarani *The Making of Modern Anglo-Jewry*
Artur Eisenbach *The Emancipation of the Jews in Poland (1780–1870)*
Ben-Cion Pinchuk *Shtetl Jews under Soviet Rule*
Peter Pulzer *Jews and the German State*
Simon Schwarzfuchs *A History of the Rabbinate*

FORTHCOMING

Tony Kushner *The Jews in Post-War Britain*
Frances Malino *Zalkind Hourwitz: A Jew in the French Revolution*

Jewish Communities of the Modern World

Esther Benbassa & Aron Rodrigue *The Jews of Turkey*
Todd Endelman *The Jews of England*
Paula Hyman *The Jews of France*
Hillel Kieval & Michael Silber *The Jews of the Habsburg Empire*
David Sorkin *The Jews of Germany*
Norman Stillman *The Jews of North Africa*
Steven J. Zipperstein *The Jews of Russia*
Jack Wertheimer *The Jews of the United States*

The Germans and the Final Solution

Public Opinion under Nazism

David Bankier

BLACKWELL
Oxford UK & Cambridge USA

First published 1992
Reprinted 1993

Blackwell Publishers
108 Cowley Road
Oxford OX4 1JF
UK

238 Main Street
Cambridge, Massachusetts 02142
USA

British Library Cataloguing in Publication Data
A CIP catalogue record for this book is available from the British Library.

Library of Congress Cataloging-in-Publication Data

Bankier, David.
    The Germans and the Final Solution: public opinion under Nazism /
David Bankier.
        p.   cm.–(Jewish society and culture)
    Includes bibliographical references and index.
    ISBN 0–631–17968–2
    1. Germany – History – 1933–1945.   2. Antisemitism – Germany
3. Holocaust, Jewish (1939–1945) – Public opinion.   4. Public
opinion – Germany.   I. Title.   II. Series.
DD256.5.B32   1992
943.086 – dc20   91–17503
                                                              CIP

Typeset in 10 on 12 pt Ehrhardt
by Graphicraft Typesetters Ltd, Hong Kong
Printed in Great Britain by T.J. Press Ltd, Padstow

This book is printed on acid-free paper.

Contents

Acknowledgements

This book could not have been accomplished without the material help of individuals and institutions. I gratefully acknowledge the financial support of the Memorial Foundation for Jewish Culture and the Deutscher Akademischer Austauschdienst, which provided me with a scholarship, a travel grant and research expenses in the early stages of the research. The continuation of this study was supported by a Hedwig Goldschmidt scholarship and its expansion by a scholarship from the Wingate Foundation, for which I would like to express my gratitude.

I am obliged to all archives listed in the Bibliography and particularly to the staffs of the Bundesarchiv in Koblenz, the Institut füt Zeitgeschichte in Munich, the Wiener Library in London and Yad Vashem in Jerusalem for their assistance in the research for this book.

I must thank colleagues for spending time reading my work: Otto D. Kulka, who suggested this topic for research and gave me valuable guidance and advice; George L. Mosse, with whom I enjoyed many invaluable conversations and always served as a model teacher and scholar; Shlomo Aronson, Walter Laqueur, Ian Kershaw and Christopher Browning, who read all or parts of the manuscript in draft and commented and suggested revisions; and Evelyn Abel, who worked on the text, making my views less obscure.

I am particularly indebted to David Sorkin, who, as editor of the series in which this book appears, spent a great deal of time on the manuscript converting it into a readable text. Thanks are also due to Longworth Editorial Services and to Graham Eyre's meticulous copy-editing.

I worked on the manuscript while on sabbatical at the University of London. I owe warmest gratitude to my colleagues and friends in the Hebrew and Jewish Studies Department of University College for creating the best possible conditions and atmosphere for my writing.

Finally more than anyone else my children – Ariela, Itai and Moshik – deserve my gratitude for their patience while I was working on this book, and this is why I dedicate it to them.

David Bankier
Jerusalem, 1991

Introduction

While one of the central tasks of historical investigation has been the examination of public opinion and the evaluation of its influence on policy-making, public-opinion researchers have not yet resolved some of the basic problems involved. What is an 'opinion'? What degree of constraint makes it impossible for public opinion to be genuinely independent? Is 'public opinion' identical to consensus, or does it simply mean the views supported by the majority?[1]

If there are no ready-made answers to these basic questions with respect to democracies, the problems raised are obviously far greater in relation to totalitarian regimes. Some scholars have even argued that there is no point in exploring this topic for such systems, either because public opinion does not exist in them or because they manipulate it to the point where it ceases to have any independent existence. In fact, in the immediate post-war literature on totalitarianism, we find almost complete agreement as to the effectiveness of the propaganda machinery in creating uniformity and absolute loyalty to the regime among the masses: interpersonal relations are broken down and previous social institutions and political cultures destroyed, with the result that society is transformed into an amorphous, classless mass devoid of independent opinions. Whether people willingly identify with the ruling ideology or are terrorized into accepting it, the result is the same: social atomization and the extirpation of critical and individual judgement. This analysis of the situation has been common since the 1950s, and still has many adherents.[2]

Many investigators of the social reality in Nazi Germany have likewise concluded that independent opinion gave way to an almost monolithic consensus of the population in favour of the regime.[3] In the present study we shall re-examine such views, drawing on documentary material from a wide range of sources for evidence of the public mood in the Third Reich. The very multiplicity of the sources provides a basis for comparison and invites critical examination of the evidence and of the conclusions to which it leads. Our discussion will focus primarily on the upsurge of revolutionary radicalism in the face of the consolidation of authority, and on the dialectical tension between the drive for institutionalization and the revolutionary potential embodied in the radical elements of the Nazi Party and its organizations. In this connection we shall also consider the reactions of the German public to attempts to revitalize Nazi ideology and mobilize the masses.

With specific reference to the Jewish question, the sources permit us not only to examine public reactions to Nazi antisemitism and their effect on policy-making, but also to compare them to reactions provoked by other issues of the time. This is important, because the German public responses to antisemitism cannot be studied in isolation from its attitudes to the regime's policies in general. During the preparation of this study it became clear that removing responses to the Jewish problem from their general context would be to lose a sense of proportion and run the danger of reaching the wrong conclusions. Thus, in examining the attitudes of particular social classes and ideological streams towards antisemitic policy, it is for example necessary to see those groups' relationship to German Jewry in its historical perspective. At the same time, however, it is clear that the Jewish theme has certain peculiarities that need to be considered separately.

A number of studies published in the 1930s were at variance with the official Nazi line on the Jewish question,[4] but the Second World War not surprisingly shifted the emphasis away from the differences between German society and the Nazi leadership to their monolithic unity. Thus, after 1945, because the German public had not actively opposed the Nazi regime, this earlier literature was regarded as irrelevant to the understanding of Nazism. Moreover, the awesome magnitude of the Holocaust and of German public acquiescence increased the reluctance to allow that Germans had varied in their reactions to persecution of the Jews, and this in turn bolstered the view that the unity of government and populace had been a major factor enabling the extermination to be carried out. It was to be expected that the relatively few works written after the war which touched upon the reactions of the German population to antisemitic policy did not challenge the accepted picture. They either ignored the subject almost entirely or made sweeping generalizations deriving from the current images of Nazi Germany. Only a generation later, with a new historical perspective based on systematic recourse to archival sources, did it become possible for historians to see the Third Reich as a multifaceted society replete with internal tensions. German historians in particular revealed the polycratic nature of government in the Third Reich.[5] A similar change occurred in the exploration of public reactions to the Nazi rule. In 1965 William S. Allen published his classic work on the town of 'Thalburg', paving the way for a more balanced assessment of popular opinion in the Third Reich.[6] Yet, even though most of his conclusions were to be confirmed by subsequent research, their immediate impact was limited by the fact that they were based on personal interviews and documentation restricted to one town only.

A major change in the study of the German public's responses to the policy of the Third Reich took place when researchers significantly widened their documentary base, resorting to reports on public mood compiled by the Nazi security services. At first, the new studies utilizing these sources touched upon the Jewish issue in passing, or not at all.[7] Not until the 1970s did historians make a breakthrough in this field by using such material to discuss the Jewish question. Marlis Steinert dedicated a few pages to this issue in her pioneering study on the war years, and Lawrence Stokes examined the extent of the German population's knowledge of the Holocaust. Otto D. Kulka analysed two cases in the 1930s and the war period. Ian Kershaw's studies and the documents published by Falk Wiesemann focused on Bavaria, while Sarah Gordon explored mainly the Rhine–Ruhr region.[8] Although research in this field has advanced considerably in recent years, there is still a need for a study applying a synthetic approach to German society in the Third Reich, its attitudes to the regime and to Nazi ideology, and hence its stance on antisemitism.

This study attempts to provide such a synthetic approach, locating the Jewish theme within the general context by examining a wide body of sources. The variety of reports available is far more comprehensive than the work of other scholars of the public mood in Nazi Germany would suggest, and embraces a wealth of documents from numerous archives. These include the reports of the Gestapo and those of district governors in Prussia and Bavaria, together representing the majority of the German population. Along with these documents we have regional and national reports of the SD (the security service of the SS) and numerous underground publications.

This book seeks to further research by giving a prominent place to the relationship between the concrete reality and the perception of it. Thus the study does not confine itself to the picture provided by the empirical data, but focuses on the meaning assigned to this picture by the regime and by the population at large. It appears that the public, on the one hand, and different sectors of the regime, on the other, interpreted the same reality in different ways. The population generally viewed the process by which the revolution was institutionalized as a positive indicator of the regime's consolidation, and reacted accordingly to the party's initiatives, including its antisemitic agitation. In contrast, Hitler and the Nazi radicals viewed the same processes of consolidation as a most dangerous manifestation of racial decay. These divergent interpretations generated contradictory reactions: the situation which the public perceived as a cause for demobilization and indifference to mass politics prompted in party activists and especially in Hitler a drive for renewed radicalization.

THE SOURCES

Modern political systems have increasingly involved the population in public affairs: more and more spheres of life have taken on political significance and become objects of open discussion. This fact also explains the sensitivity of the government to public opinion, not only in democratic regimes but also, as we shall see, in the Nazi dictatorship. It seems that, despite sophisticated methods of surveillance, repression and terror, the Nazi system was still unable to ensure complete social assent. Neither could it automatically mobilize the public to support its aims. As a result, a basic dilemma developed: how could one reconcile the abolition of freedom of expression with the need to know the mood of the population and the effect of government policy? It is therefore not surprising that a large number of agencies collected information on the public mood in Nazi Germany.

It was only natural that the rulers of the Third Reich wished to be informed of the public mood in order to be able to evaluate the effects of their policy. This does not mean, however, that the Nazi leadership was always willing to accept the conclusions derived from the information that the various monitoring-services had collected. The main reason for this was simple: all accurate reporting on public mood necessarily conjured up a picture which was at variance with the myth of a 'total state' embodying a monolithic 'racial community'.

The sources used for this book consist mainly of confidential reports on the public mood · – generally known as *Lageberichte* (situation reports) or *Stimmungsberichte* (reports on the public mood) – compiled by the German security services and the various state, party and administrative bodies. These surveys continued and broadened to an unprecedented degree the historical tradition of government surveillance, whereby the authorities kept close tabs on irregularities, oppositionist trends, subversive elements and disturbances to the public order.

Periodic reports on the public mood were not an invention of the Nazis: they had been produced in various European countries since the eighteenth century.[9] For example, the state archives in Munich hold a large collection of monthly surveys written by the district governors of the kingdom of Bavaria, along with weekly reports for the period 1850–9. Together these present a complex picture of social and political developments. The surveys were written in accordance with detailed instructions on how to report on the population's mood, taking into account what they thought of the royal family, how they stood on political and religious issues, what newspapers they read, support for democratic associations, and so on.[10] The abstracts of the Baden political police convey similar information.[11] The Third Reich continued this long-established monitoring-system. Thus Himmler, in his capacity as chief of the Bavarian political police, for example, set up a surveillance force based on the equivalent existing section of the Munich police. However, because of their totalitarian aspirations, the Nazis combined the previous administrative tradition with their new centralization policy, creating an unprecedentedly wide network of informers and refining the methods of reporting.

District governors' and provincial presidents' reports

One of the main sources used for this study is the monthly and bi-monthly reports of district governors and provincial presidents, compiled for the Ministry of the Interior between 1934 and 1936. These documents, which have been preserved mainly for Prussia and Bavaria, carry special weight because their information covers most of the Reich. With the aid of these sources we can trace the relations between the regime and the populace during the early years of Nazi rule. In addition, the analysis of this material makes it possible to evaluate the effect of various factors at the regional level in accelerating or retarding the consolidation of the Third Reich. These reports are particularly useful because they piece together a mass of information from local councils and police and gendarmerie stations, and include very few evaluations and summaries by the reporter or informer. To some extent the very nature of the information prevents it from being coloured by subjective or ideological bias and this in turn makes it easier to reconstruct the reality.

There were two main reasons for the intensified centralization policy and the establishment of a nationwide reporting-system in 1934. One was the political climate following the purges of the SA in June–July 1934 and the tightening of internal security. The other was the increased rivalry between the different authorities of the Third Reich. The Minister of the Interior, Wilhelm Frick, demanded reports on the mood of the population. By this means he hoped to take charge of internal security and counteract the Gestapo, which in September 1933 had begun to compile its own reports on the public mood.[12]

The district governors' reports were stopped by Goering in April 1936.[13] On the face of it, his order was intended to make the administration more efficient: passing to a higher level the authority to correct the situation would weaken the power of the reporting body. Nevertheless, if we read between the lines, we realize that Goering's real concern was that reports portraying the public mood as negative might damage the image of national unity that the Nazis sought to foster. In addition, this order reflected a struggle going on in government circles. Apparently as a result of Gestapo pressure, the strengthening of Himmler's influence and the Nazification of the administration, Goering was acting to curtail the power of the Ministry of the Interior by reducing the responsibilities of district governors.

Party reports

Another set of sources used in the present study is the reports of functionaries at various levels in the Nazi party – from *Gauleiter* and *Kreisleiter* at the top, to local officials dealing with education, culture, economic matters, and so on. Their surveys, which were sent to the office of Hitler's deputy, Rudolf Hess, contain a full picture of the relations between the party and the German population. Before the Nazis assumed power, a number of party agencies were engaged in gathering information on subjects likely to interest Nazi leaders. However, it was only after improving the machinery of control and the functioning of the competing surveillance agencies – the SD and the Gestapo – that the party's monitoring-system was institutionalized. At the end of 1934, again as a result of the power struggle between the various authorities in the Reich, Hess ordered monthly reports on the public mood, explicitly prohibiting their distribution to competing bodies.[14] A circular from the *Gauleiter* of Hesse–Nassau eloquently testifies to this friction: it prohibits any direct contact with the SD in this area, threatening the violator with dismissal.[15]

In their 1934 format the party reports already included dozens of aspects to be monitored. In 1939, as totalitarianism became further entrenched, even more areas were scrutinized.[16] The reason is obvious: capturing the allegiance of the masses remained the basic task of a party which sought to mould the character of the nation down to the smallest social units. Hence obtaining information on a wide variety of party activities, such as participation in political meetings, became essential for effective policy-planning. Since the reports were considered a device for monitoring the positive or negative effects of party policy on German society, they also had to provide extensive information on the moods and aspirations of the public. In his guidelines on writing reports Hess demanded accurate and reliable data on 'complaints and grumbling by the public, special events of political importance, rates of participation in party campaigns, the nature of common rumours and the status of the party in public life.'[17] However, despite the demand for objective information, these documents are obviously biased and have to be used with great care. The factual information they contain can be useful, but they need always to be checked against other sources to ascertain the degree of distortion.

Gestapo reports

At the beginning of November 1933, the Gestapo chief, Rudolf Diels, instructed all local stations to submit monthly surveys to the organization's central office in Berlin, the 'Gestapa' (Gestapo-Amt).[18] He strictly emphasized that the agents should report objectively, without doctoring the facts to produce a rosier picture. Unfortunately, hardly any Gestapo surveys have been preserved from these early days, at least in archives in the West. Nevertheless, in certain cases their gist can be learned from the abstract printed in the Gestapo's internal news bulletin. As with the district governors' reports the significance of the Gestapo surveys lies in their chronological and geographical continuity, making it possible to chart changes in public mood.

SD reports

The SD intelligence apparatus was founded at the end of the Weimar Republic. At that time a number of parallel information services operated independently of one another in the Nazi Party, advising its heads on political developments of special importance. Following his appointment as chief of police, Himmler decided to reduce the overlap between the SD and the Gestapo. At the end of 1934 an order was issued which assigned the SD, as opposed to the Gestapo, the task of tracing enemies of Nazism and directing the activities of the state police. This made it clear that, in addition to suppressing opposition elements, the SD had to keep a check on the mood of the German people and to furnish a picture of the political, economic and cultural situation. To this end, the SD operated a country-wide network of agents organized according to the regional divisions of the SS (*Oberabschnitt*, *Abschnitt*, etc.) and graded in five categories according to reliability:

V Leute (*Vertrauensleute*)   Reliable party members.
A Leute (*Agenten*)   Reliable informers, not necessarily party members.
Z Leute (*Zubringer*)   Paid informers on contract.
H Leute (*Helfer*)   Informers with personal motives.
U Leute (*Unzuverlässige*)   Unreliable collaborators, ex-convicts.[19]

All agents were instructed to keep watch on the public mood and to assess its character and strength, noting the influence of local factors. The data furnished by the regional SD stations were classified by subjects, each of which had its expert who processed and analysed the relevant data. The various subject analyses constitute the parts of the report, which received a final editing at SD headquarters. A wide range of officials served as editors: lawyers, judges, doctors, teachers, scientists, economists, journalists, and others.[20]

Otto Ohlendorf, head of the SD surveillance department, commented in September 1943 in a conversation with Himmler's personal doctor, Kersten, that the purpose of these reports was to examine the effects of government policy and find out which measures aroused opposition. Just as the general staff in an army needs a continuous flow of information in order to assess the situation at the battlefront correctly, so, in its way, does the political leadership: the party heads must know the results of every single political step, even when these are not to their liking.[21] Thus the information service of the SD was considered by those in charge as an objective instrument of the utmost importance. In Ohlendorf's view, the duty of an SD agent was not to denounce but to report, suppressing information motivated by personal interests. In addition, he said, the overall picture and not the small details interested the SD. A mosaic of agents' personal impressions became a significant survey only after the final processing of the information at SD headquarters. According to Ohlendorf, 'Without it, it is impossible to set up a totalitarian state which attempts to penetrate the complex web of modern society.'[22] The complexity of social relationships, the heterogeneity of citizens' activities, the impact of conflicting trends in public life – all required the establishment of an information service able effectively to monitor the needs of the different social bodies, and so help to shape life in the modern centralized state.[23]

Reporting had to be carried out without any bias in favour of Nazi doctrine, albeit serving its aims. This explains the tensions which arose between the SD's goal of preserving objectivity and the constant attempts to stop its monitoring-activities, or at least alter the guidelines of its reports. Ohlendorf commented on this pressure, 'What Himmler wants is an information service... which provides optimistic reports.... That's impossible. As the situation becomes more critical, the reports become more gloomy.'[24] At the end of 1944, Martin Bormann ordered an end to all co-operation with the SD. Having no alternative, Ohlendorf changed the line of the reports, avoiding open criticism of the situation in the Reich. It is important to notice that fact: despite the pressure to halt them, the reports continued because of their value to policy-makers.

Sopade reports

The reports published by the German Socialist Party in exile (Sopade), furnish surveys parallel to those of the Nazis but drawn from a totally different ideological and political perspective. The surveys mainly deal with economic matters and the living-conditions of workers under Hitler's rule, but they also contain special sections with abundant information on antisemitic terror. Between 1934 and 1940, supporters of the Socialist Party smuggled out of Germany tens of thousands of reviews, letters and other documents, which were collected, processed and finally edited in the party's headquarters in Prague and later in Paris. Hundreds of copies of this material, in its edited form, were distributed to the socialist underground in Germany and to statesmen, intelligence services and journalists in other countries. The Sopade survey for April–May 1934 sets out the plan for these reports. The editors asked their sources in Germany to furnish them with as much detail as possible, no matter how trivial, because single items that may seem unimportant to the informer may be significant for the editor who receives similar data from other areas.[25] These reports do indeed contain a multitude of details on the general situation in the Reich and thus provide a wide-ranging picture of the people's mood. They generally complement and corroborate the findings in the Nazi documents, and that the German security service appreciated and made use of them points to their reliability. In one of its reports on the leftist underground the SD admitted that the Sopade material gave an excellent picture of the state of affairs in Germany.[26] Similarly, a Gestapo report from Berlin for the first quarter of 1939 asserted that the copious and accurate data in the Sopade reports, on internal matters otherwise unknown outside Germany, indicated the socialists' excellent connections in factories and other organizations in the Reich.[27]

What problems does the use of this material pose? The major difficulty that arises is how to assess the influence of public opinion when drawing on sources which, by their very nature, do not reflect 'public opinion' in the conventional sense of the term, but rather the moods and attitudes of a population subject to state coercion. In addition, the scarcity of views stated in their original form only sharpens the methodological complexities, as does the state of the sources themselves, since entire collections have been destroyed and the quality of the material varies from place to place. None the less, it must be noted that, because of the sheer extent of the documentation, it can be broken down in different ways and various general conclusions drawn.

For a number of reasons we cannot create representative samples of population sectors from these sources. First, the number of known variables is limited; we have no way of ascertaining variables such as age, sex or occupation. Second, a sample should be a statistical model of the whole population and we have no way of sorting out the data to make sure that each element of the population is represented in its true proportion. These problems stem from the fact that the data were not compiled with a view to quantitative analysis and only occasionally include samples of any kind. Nevertheless, the use by informers of expressions such as 'widespread', 'representative' and 'typical' implies a degree of quantification on which certain valid generalizations can be based, allowing for appropriate exceptions. The classification of information makes it possible, if not to quantify attitudes, then at least to map out overall trends.

Another major problem is that informers rarely stated which sectors of the public actively supported the regime, accepted its aims and willingly participated in the antisemitic campaign. Whereas reports often do identify the opponents of the National Socialists' antisemitic policy, they generally fail to identify those sectors of the population making up the silent majority who consented to it. So to a certain extent this book is about the attitudes of the 'other Germany', those who were not committed Nazis and manifested their disagreement with particular aspects of the regime's policies.

A great deal of information on public opinion in the war years is provided by the SD surveys known as *Meldungen aus dem Reich*. However, the major difficulty in working with these sources is the paucity of documents for comparison. For the early years of Nazi rule we are able to juxtapose the SD reports to those prepared by the various state, party and administrative bodies, primarily the reports of the Gestapo and the district governors of Prussia and Bavaria. For the war years cross-checking becomes much more difficult, and, because the SD abstracts only occasionally differentiate the attitudes of particular social classes or religious groups, we have to look further ahead for relevant data.

Finally, as regards the reliability of the reports, it must be emphasized that to some extent it doesn't matter. *This was the picture presented to the regime by officials active in its decision-making process.*

THE INFLUENCE OF THE REPORTS ON DECISION-MAKING IN THE THIRD REICH

There is ample evidence that decisions made by heads of the German security services were directly influenced by information on the mood of the population. For example, Ernst Kaltenbrunner, head of the Reichssicherheitshauptamt (RSHA), the Main Security Office, testified in the Nuremberg trials that all the information of this kind that he received came from the SD and other surveillance agencies.[28] According to Walter Schellenberg, who was in charge of external affairs at the SD, Kaltenbrunner's decisions were based on these reports.[29] Furthermore, we know that Kaltenbrunner more than once considered suspending Ohlendorf's activities but refrained from doing so because he greatly valued the information he received from the SD.

Yet it was not only the security services who expressed an interest in this material. Other government offices constantly requested surveys of the public mood, in order to develop suitable policies in their respective fields. Alfred Rosenberg used them in his capacity as ideological educator of party members; he was especially interested in public reactions to his anti-Church policies.[30] Abundant evidence shows that the Ministry of Justice not only used the reports to gauge public opinion, but also took action in response to the SD's findings. Two examples will suffice. When the SD reported that the local court in Klagenfurt was thought to have been lenient in sentencing homosexuals, the Ministry of Justice immediately imposed more severe sentences.[31] The Ministry also intervened in July 1940 when the SD reported public disquiet that Jews could still inherit from Germans. The law was changed to make this impossible in future.[32]

The official in charge of labour relations (*Reichstreuhander der Arbeit*) was also on the SD circulation list. He had to ensure industrial peace in the Reich and to this end needed detailed information on the mood of the workers. On the basis of the data passed to him from various sources, he compiled monthly digests for the Minister of Labour. This material has not been preserved, but it can be partially reconstructed from the abstracts prepared by the Ministry of Labour and passed on to other Reich ministries.[33] The Economics Minister was likewise interested in public opinion, which alerted him to unpopular measures and helped him to draw up plans relating to employment, wages, prices and supply.[34]

It was, however, the Ministry of Propaganda that was most interested in survey material. It was clear to Goebbels that Nazi propaganda would not succeed in penetrating the masses unless it was based on accurate and objective information on public reactions to films, radio broadcasts and newspapers. He knew that no propaganda machine could operate without feedback, or afford to remain ignorant of the weak points in the regime's policy and accordingly insisted that, if reporting was found to be superficial or distorted, it should be corrected immediately.[35]

The direct link between reports, on the one hand, and decision-making in the Ministry of Propaganda, on the other, can be demonstrated by a number of representative examples. A significant part of Goebbels' meetings with German newspaper editors was devoted to reading and analysing surveys of the public's mood. At one meeting, for example, after hearing that increasing numbers of people were listening to foreign stations, Goebbels ordered the editors to publish examples of the punishments meted out for this offence.[36] One legal issue relating to the Jewish question appeared in an SD report of 26 April 1941 and was discussed in Goebbels' next meeting with the editors, four days later.[37]

Himmler also took note of these surveys. We know that he read with great interest the reports brought to his office, especially those from the SD,[38] though, like the other Nazi leaders, he was ambivalent towards them. He refused to accept their portrait of the public mood, since the reality stood in opposition to the myth of national unity so cherished by the Nazis. Thus, for instance, Ohlendorf claimed in one of his conversations with Himmler that reports from all over the Reich detected harsh criticism of a speech delivered by Hitler. Himmler, as usual, refused to believe this, claiming that the writers of the reports were exploiting them to voice their own defeatist attitudes and lack of faith.[39]

The most interesting question is whether the reports reached Hitler himself, and, if so, how far they influenced his decisions and policy-making. Some testimonies indicate that a wall of silence was erected around the Führer, hiding the true mood of the German public. Reports revealing fatalistic and negative attitudes did not reach him at all, and any information liable to contradict his basic conceptions, and thus to arouse his anger, was suppressed by his aides. Kersten writes that sometimes he would find Rudolf Brandt, Himmler's secretary, in utter despair, because Himmler had filed away the SD reports without bringing them to Hitler's attention.[40] Himmler used to do this whenever the surveys showed the German people getting gloomy. He claimed that such information, despite its importance, could be of no use to the Führer, whose duty was to lead Germany to victory. Anything which might interfere with this objective should be concealed from him.[41]

Ohlendorf was well aware that his reports were not reaching Hitler, and that information on the public mood was being censored by Bormann on receipt at the Chancellery. However, there is evidence that this was not always the case. In the memoirs of Fritz Wiedemann, who served as Hitler's military adjutant in the 1930s, we read that it was his duty to give Hitler an oral summary of the reports, since the Führer did not have the patience to read them himself. On one occasion in 1936, reports received from the Gestapo or the SD showed that the prevailing mood was negative. As soon as Wiedemann had read the first few sentences Hitler responded, 'The mood of the public is not negative. I know better. Those reports are what cause the worsening of the mood. I forbid any further presentation of reports of this kind to me in the future.'[42]

It seems, however, that from one source or another, information on the public mood continued to reach Hitler. In a report of his table talk we learn that in March 1942 he received a survey showing a decline in public morale, and that he added to it the handwritten comment, 'If the situation were what people say, we would have long lost everything. The true mood of the nation lies much deeper and is based on an inner strength. If this were not the case we could not explain the nation's achievements.'[43]

Hitler's reaction in this case is substantially the same as in 1936. From these two instances it would seem that he took no account at all of popular feelings, and continued his policy regardless of public opinion. Yet from some of his utterances we may infer that he was aware of the trends. Reports dating from the summer and autumn of 1938 depict widespread apathy and fatalism. Knowledge of this situation would appear to be the background to his call to party leaders to make sure that the mood was positive: 'Nobody should inform me that in his *Gau* or his *Kreis* or in his group or in his cell the mood is bad. You are the ones responsible for creating the public mood.'[44]

I shall try to show in the course of this study that one of the factors which decided the timing of Hitler's policy moves and sparked off his drive towards radicalization was his perception of this defeatist mood. This point will be explored in depth in chapter 4. In his speech on 10 November 1938, the day after *Kristallnacht*, Hitler revealed just how far public mood affected his decisions. Addressing nearly 400 journalists and newspaper editors gathered in Munich, he summed up the events of 1938 and outlined their significance for his policy. He openly displayed his dissatisfaction with the mood of the German public, revealing the methods he had employed in order to conceal his real aims. 'Circumstances forced me to speak only of peace', he said.[45] These circumstances were, among others, the public mood.

1

Image and Reality in the Third Reich

Unlike dictatorships of traditional elites which sought to neutralize the masses by preventing them from taking an active part in political life, the Nazi regime attempted to create a situation in which the public would be permanently mobilized.

Many researchers attribute the broad consensus behind the Third Reich to the readiness of almost all strata of the population to participate in the new order. They argue that a religious devotion gripped the masses, which spontaneously and willingly followed the party's lead. The picture which emerges is one of unequivocal support for the Nazi system and its political culture by most of the German public – a picture closely matching the one painted by Goebbels' propaganda media, and in keeping with what the regime hoped to achieve, rather than with any historical reality. In contrast to this idealized state of affairs, our sources reveal that, from as early as summer 1934, the euphoria which had accompanied the party's rise and accession to power was steadily on the wane.

THE LIMITS OF MASS MOBILIZATION

Once the party was entrenched in power, public attitudes were characterized not by mass revolutionary fervour, but by a growing distaste for political action, manifested in unwillingness to participate in mass-mobilization campaigns, and reluctance to support the rallies, parades and meetings organized by, or on behalf of, the party. Indeed, there was a marked tendency to political indifference, and official propaganda was often met with passive hostility. The Nazis' purpose in holding rallies and meetings was to get rational individuals to succumb to the spell of clichés and stereotyped slogans and undergo an emotional experience of collective awakening. It seems that this form of indoctrination often fell short of its target.[1]

Only a year after the party came to power, sizable sectors of the population began to criticize the mass mobilizations, though the criticisms were phrased with utmost caution for fear of reprisals. Early signs of the dwindling influence of Nazi propaganda can be traced in the April 1934 report of the district governor in Regensburg. Among other things, he pointed out that 'In the county of Deggendorf, the peasants complain about too many festive, political parades and too much canvassing; this discontent is, however, expressed very cautiously.'[2] Evidence from all over the Reich shows that little by little this disposition became a widespread phenomenon.

At first the surveys merely mention this new trend in a few casual sentences without any attempt at appraisal or interpretation, because the reporter regarded it as insignificant and transient. However, by summer of 1935 it had become so strong that many observers thought that the broad base of support for the regime might be cracking. From August 1934 the central authorities started to receive reports from all areas of the Reich noting increasing apathy and withdrawal from political life. The governor of the Aachen district, for instance, detected, 'more and more indifference...as far as political life is concerned.'[3] The optimistic and self-satisfied accounts that local party bosses submitted to the leadership, in order to consolidate their own positions, were contradicted by more objective surveys. In October the Düsseldorf Gestapo wrote in no uncertain terms of deep-seated apathy, political lethargy and lack of faith. Bowed down by pessimism the public tacitly rejected the daily press, particularly the party organs. The same Gestapo station even cautioned the decision-makers not to misinterpret the state of affairs in the Reich:

Even though the external image is one of quiet and equanimity, one cannot obtain an objective appreciation of the prevailing public mood when one realizes that the undercurrents mentioned are gaining in importance. The indifferent and often apathetic disposition of broad sectors of the population points definitely in this direction.[4]

In Münster the local Gestapo similarly noted that 'The true mood of the population is reflected in the passivity of great parts of the public towards the movement's activities. Only because of fear of reprisals has this attitude remained submerged.'[5] The Aachen Gestapo further warned that the rosy accounts purveyed at the national convention of party leaders in Munich should not be taken too seriously. Although the convention reported impressive achievements and an extraordinary rise in party popularity, the reality was rather different.[6]

A central reason for the public's apathy was the numbing effect of too much propaganda. There is little doubt that, after the Nazis had gained power and begun to consolidate their position, there were two opposing trends. Like other revolutionary movements which have succeeded in winning power, Nazism experienced a clash between the impulse towards permanent revolution and the forces of institutionalization. The Nazi ideal was itself a contradiction in terms: political stability achieved through, and expressed in, constant action. All the festivals and parades were part of an attempt to regulate the pace of life of the German nation, to overcome crises by diverting people and at the same time to maintain a high profile for the party. Dynamism was at the heart of Nazism, inherent in both its revolutionary nature and its vitalist philosophy, which it shared with all other fascist movements. Propaganda had an essential part to play here, both through indoctrination and through inculcating a heightened sense of political consciousness. Hitler himself pointed this out when he decided to establish a propaganda ministry: 'There will now have to be a large-scale campaign of propaganda and information in order that *no political lethargy* should set in.'[7]

The bulk of the population sought to institutionalize the achievements of the revolution and prevent dynamism from becoming the basis of day-to-day life. The party leadership, by contrast, sought constantly to reactivate the masses, to prevent ideological ossification and a loss of fervour. To this end it attempted to detach people from their traditional cultures and to prevent a simple 'return to normal'. The result was the opposite of the one intended: people became satiated with political activity and lost interest.

This was the background to the report of the Hanover Gestapo in February 1935, which commented that participation in party assemblies was declining everywhere owing to the abundance of such mass gatherings.[8] The governor of the Minden district had a similar tale to tell. Illustrating developments in his region, he mentioned that an order to assemble for a rally had met with an apathetic response. This he thought understandable, considering the fatigue engendered by years of consciousness-raising.[9]

It would be a mistake to assume that these attitudes were typical only of areas in which Nazism was less firmly entrenched. William S. Allen, using different evidence, arrived at similar conclusions: the marches, flag-waving and rallies induced and coexisted with public weariness, boredom and lack of involvement.[10] Moreover, our sources show that this was so even in areas with a political record of mass support for Nazism. Erfurt Gestapo reported in April 1935 that very few people attended the indoctrination evenings. The same went for all the rallies and ceremonies, which, in the view of the reporter, aroused absolutely no interest in the public.[11]

A study of the opinions of various social classes, taking into account geographical, religious and other variables, shows how widespread such indifference was. Let us look first at the bourgeoisie.

A good deal of material has been preserved about what the Nazis termed 'the better circles' – the bourgeoisie and intellectuals. In August 1934, the Trier Gestapo noted a significant drop in the number of better-off people joining the party; the writer added, referring to information he had from other Gestapo stations, that it would appear that this sector of the population was losing interest in political life.[12] While this picture relates to the bourgeoisie of a Catholic region, it is not essentially different from what we know of Schleswig-Holstein, a Protestant district where the Nazi Party had deep roots. A Gestapo report from Kiel notes the reluctance of the bourgeoisie to participate in rallies or use the 'Heil Hitler' greeting, and their increasing withdrawal from political life.[13] Statistical evidence of this was reported by another Gestapo station in the region: 'the split in the vote in the Lübeck area shows a drop in support for Nazism among the "better circles".'[14]

If these attitudes might have been expected among the educated classes, whose initial enthusiasm was dampened by Hitler's methods of repression and brutal terror, the phenomenon is also apparent among a sector of the population generally considered supporters of Nazism: the peasants, especially those of northern and eastern Germany.

From the start, the Nazis spared no energy in winning over the peasants. They promised comprehensive and far-reaching agricultural reforms, and mounted an intensive propaganda campaign aimed at the rural population. With Hitler's rise to power, Walter Darré, the Minister of Agriculture, embarked on a broad programme of legislation designed to transform agricultural production – for instance, through the Entailed Farm Law (*Erbhofgesetz*). In addition, the regime courted the rural public through its *Blut und Boden* ('blood and soil') doctrine idealizing the peasant as the fount of the Nordic race. How effective was this propaganda, and what was the response to it?

Most of the comments on the mood of the rural population speak of political apathy and fatigue. The governor of the Magdeburg district reported that the harvest celebrations in his area in 1934 had attracted little interest: at some ceremonies only the local peasants' leader and a few dozen farmers had turned up.[15] A propaganda campaign in the autumn failed to improve matters, and, according to the governor of the Koblenz district, was responsible for an increase in complaints. In his view, apathy and lack of concern had begun to give way to opposition: 'The farming public claims that so long as no significant changes have actually been instituted, despite the party's tales of constant improvements, there is no point in attending its meetings.'[16] The same reservations were evident in the Trier Gestapo's report in May

1935. Here an attempt was made to blame seasonal factors for the peasants' absence from parades: 'in the summer months the farmer puts in late hours in the fields and he is not interested in meetings after a hard day's work.' It seems, however, that the writer was himself unconvinced by this excuse, for he immediately added that party speeches did not interest the rural audience.[17]

Through its monopoly of the media the Third Reich reached the rural public, and demanded its active participation in the Nazi rituals; but people's attitudes were not to be changed so easily. Political indoctrination bored them and, despite the fact that some, particularly the young, stood to benefit from the new system, the bulk of the peasant population continued to have reservations. A major reason for this was the irreconcilable contradiction between the Nazis' promise to establish an agrarian state (part of the romantic–racial myth of *Blut und Boden*) and the industrialization which actually followed.

Another important group that the Nazis tried to win over was the industrial labour force. From its inception the party devoted considerable effort to canvassing workers, especially in the north, but when Hitler acceded to power the workers were not a significant component of the Nazi movement. In order to reach them and make them part of a general consensus in favour of the new system, the regime established 'temples' of the Hitler cult in factories; arranged for street-cleaners to be interviewed by the press, to make it appear that they were being taken seriously; and promised various rewards. The climax of the propaganda efforts came on May Day 1933, when the rector of Heidelberg University marched beside a common worker in a festive parade symbolizing the realization of the slogan 'The unity of the workers of the mind and fist'.[18]

To what extent were the workers won over by the propaganda campaigns? Some idea of this may be gained from the festivities of May Day, which the regime declared a 'national labour holiday'. The fact was that, as the Nazis recognized, workers were too attached to the traditional celebrations for them to be abolished outright; but, at the same time, efforts were made to give the holiday a new, Nazi content and significance.

Press articles on May Day conjure up a picture of mass participation and spontaneous enthusiasm that would appear to demonstrate the workers' identification with the holiday in its new guise. However, a look at other sources shows that this picture is basically distorted. Most reporters begin by noting the success of the party's propaganda and the high rate of participation in marches. Thus, in its report on the 1935 May Day festivities, the Münster Gestapo claims that the holiday was a great success: that there were public celebrations; that homes were adorned with flags and that people displayed many other signs of loyalty to the regime. Later, however, the report notes that there was a significant decrease in flag-waving in comparison to the previous year. Participation in rallies is declared good, but it is also stated that the rural population and the middle classes tended to keep their involvement to a minimum. Most enlightening are the report's concluding words:

The good participation at parades and rallies cannot serve as a true gauge of the public's real mood and we must not be led astray by what appears on the surface. The public mood has considerably deteriorated in recent weeks, particularly among the local workers. This negative mood has already manifested itself in various ways on May Day. According to reports which have reached me, the workers joined in parades and rallies under duress; at many sites they tried to abscond from the rallies as soon as they had received the beer vouchers which were distributed. This was particularly noticeable at the Gladbeck Stadium: immediately after the festive entrance they decamped *en masse*. This shows that some of the workers feel more or less compelled to participate in the rallies while in their hearts they do not exult in them.[19]

It is patently obvious here that the reality was not always what the regime made it out to be. The above example is, moreover, nothing out of the ordinary: in other localities we find a similar picture, even in the Nazi organizations themselves. Thus, for instance, the Bielefeld Gestapo commented on the May Day celebrations, 'Complaints have been received from various areas in the Padeborn district to the effect that the NS-HAGO [Nationalsozialistische Handwerks, Handels und Gewerbe Organisation: Nazi Craft and Commerce Organization] and the Peasants' Estate did not participate in the May Day festivities to the same extent as last year.' To substantiate this point, the station furnished concrete examples, quoting reports from various police stations.[20] We learn from the Herford police that at many factories nobody showed up, not even the factory leader on behalf of the party and the German Labour Front; and that, among the workers who did appear, there were signs of overt opposition to the regime: 'Some removed the German Labour Front insignia and swastika from their blue caps, and when the parade arrived at the assembly site they retired from it so that they would not be compelled to listen to the *Kreisleiter*'s speech.'[21]

Finally, it should be mentioned that the Berlin Gestapo explicitly stated that mass public participation in the May Day celebrations could not be taken as a measure of the public mood. To underline the point, it enumerated the means used to coerce people to attend rallies.[22]

That public attitudes were vastly different from what they are commonly assumed to have been can be further demonstrated by examining the public responses to mass rallies, for which the party set its mighty conscriptive machinery in motion. At Osnabrück, for example, the Gestapo reported that a rally addressed by the governor was poorly attended, because, as the writer admitted, the public was tired of parades and meetings.[23] The Aachen

Gestapo likewise reported that a party-conference rally for the entire Cologne–Aachen *Gau* attracted little support, and that the public in general demonstrated a basic lack of interest in political activity.[24]

A study of the public responses to other major campaigns organized by the party leads to similar conclusions regarding the failure of mobilization. In a community-affairs report for the Hesse–Nassau *Gau*, for instance, we find a note that the number of marriages in the region has risen surprisingly – in one district by 150 per cent over the previous year.[25] In a comparable report from the Cologne–Aachen *Gau*, we hear that marriages there have risen among the under twenty-fives, and this time the reporter adds significantly that the development should be viewed as an attempt to evade conscription for work service, to which all unmarried males under this age were liable.[26] This evidence of reluctance to perform work service contrasts with the familiar photographs of happy youngsters marching in ranks to build roads, and is confirmed by Gestapo surveys as well. The Düsseldorf report for September 1934 states that marriage is on the increase in the under-twenty-five age group, and surveys from Bielefeld, Kösslin and elsewhere say the same.[27]

It would seem that, after only one year of Hitler's rule, the willingness of various social groups to take part in the mass-mobilization campaigns was declining, producing a growing gap between the regime and the populace. This contention can be further substantiated by looking at another tool of indoctrination – the press.

THE LIMITS OF THE PRESS AS AN INSTRUMENT OF PROPAGANDA

The fluctuations in the circulation of the party press, subservient to Goebbels' propaganda machine, is a partial indicator of the degree to which many Germans responded to Nazi indoctrination. In order to obtain a fuller picture, we must compare the circulation rates of the Nazi press to that of the non-party periodicals published during the first years of the Third Reich. Our main emphasis will be on dailies, weeklies and periodicals which, despite the coercive policy of *Gleichschaltung* (forcing into line), continued to serve as a sounding-board for the right-wing conservatives and the churches.

In Nazi Germany, as in all totalitarian systems, the press played a vital role as an agent of political socialization – taking the lead in transmitting and instilling official ideology. When necessary, it churned out propaganda aimed at mobilizing the masses and channelling their activities in the interest of the government or the party. It is therefore hardly surprising that surveys of the public mood devoted a special section to the media – press, cinema and radio – keeping the state and party authorities up to date with the effectiveness of these propaganda tools in transmitting the ruling doctrine to the masses. These reports contain an abundance of information on the fate of the various press organs in Germany and the public response to what was printed in them. It stands to reason that this information was invaluable to policy- and decision-makers, helping them assess the influence of the propaganda machine on people's lives, and the degree to which people were susceptible to, or would tolerate, such indoctrination.[28]

It is commonly assumed, even by some researchers, that with the collapse of the multi-party system the German population became an amorphous and disorganized mass of individuals, devoid of political or social views. People lost all capacity for independent judgement and critical thinking, and submitted to the regime's pressure to conform. This in turn, the view holds, produced total loyalty to the system, and credulous acceptance of the regime's propaganda.[29] A critical look at the Gestapo reports, the district governors' surveys, and other sources concerned with the press and its influence suggests that the reality was quite otherwise.

These sources indicate that, at least during the early years of the Nazi regime, there was still a struggle between the party press and the various church journals. They continued to operate despite pressure from the regime for uniformity, and, for those who knew how to read between the lines, served as an alternative source of information. It would appear, then, that the notion that all Germans underwent a process of social atomization in the Third Reich is nearer to Nazi propaganda than to historical reality. Public receptiveness to press propaganda reached saturation point soon after Hitler came to power, and thereafter went into decline: it was not long before a trend of outright rejection became manifest. This process can be detected both in the general introductions to the reports and in the survey material on the media. It is also evident in the statistical data furnished by the summaries, which point to a steady decline in the circulation of party journals. This was undoubtedly part of the reaction noted earlier, that set in after the first year of Nazi rule, when the new system's inability to fulfil all its promises became apparent.

From the beginning of summer 1934 one finds neither the 'disappearance of faith in the ordinary reality, the pull towards indoctrination', nor 'the cancellation of independent views in the face of official propaganda',[30] but rather the reverse: a gradual widening of the credibility gap between the regime and those segments of the public which refused to bow to the tide of propaganda. Various commentators tell of critical responses among readers, and lack of confidence in the information published in the press. Thus the president of the Rhine province wrote in his report for September–October 1934, 'The little information that has been transmitted to the public has proved harmful, rumours are ever rampant. The press and radio are not considered reliable and two public opinion systems are developing: the one represented by the press and on the radio, and the one known as the "rumour press" which spreads quickly.'[31]

Equally illustrative of this state of affairs is the report by the Aachen Gestapo covering the same period. Among other things it states that, in response to articles praising the changes and improvements initiated in the country since the inception of the Third Reich, people say that about 50 per cent of what is written distorts the truth and should be discounted.[32] This report, of course, came from a Catholic region with a more liberal tradition than in some parts of the Reich, but reports from other regions tell a similar story. The same September the president of Westphalia said that people no longer believed what was written in the press,[33] and during the autumn and winter the credibility gap widened all over the country.

As can be seen from the surveys, the public adopted two main forms of response. One was to refrain from reading several newspapers daily, since, in the words of Oldenburg's Minister of the Interior, '[In the public's view] all newspapers say the same thing.'[34] The other response was to search out alternative information sources. Once a gap had been opened between their sense of reality and the picture presented by the media, people quickly learned to rely on foreign newspapers or on church periodicals, which managed to get round the *Gleichschaltung* policy to some extent. As a result the church press experienced a great surge of popularity. The Aachen Gestapo report for September 1934 indicates that people thought church periodicals more reliable than their competitors.[35] In the space of three months, the local church weekly increased its circulation from 65,000 to 100,000 copies.[36] The yearly summary for the same region is equally revealing. It states that this same periodical more than doubled its circulation during the year: from 38,000 to 90,000 copies on average. The Nazi who reported the success of this non-Nazi paper correctly attributed it to the ordinary reader's lack of trust in the party press.[37]

The foreign press enjoyed increased circulation in Germany for the same reason. The Swiss *Basler Nachrichten* was especially popular, and the Aachen Gestapo reported an increase of almost 100 per cent in the number of foreign newspapers found and confiscated by the security services.[38] While the actual number of foreign papers in circulation remained relatively small, the Düsseldorf Gestapo reported that the readership far outstripped the available copies:

We are aware that apart from constantly tuning to the foreign stations, [the public] is intensely reading the foreign press. The latter is sold as soon as it appears and is passed from hand to hand among friends and acquaintances until it is completely illegible, while with the local press an attempt is made to read between the lines.[39]

Of course, geography affected the availability of foreign papers: they were easier to come by in border regions such as the Rhineland, which received newspapers direct from Belgium and Holland. At the same time, many foreign papers penetrated further into the Reich, as the reports from such regions prove. After voicing the familiar claim that the population was critical of the press and complained of its one-sidedness, the governor of the Kassel district stated that the public was turning more and more to the foreign press.[40] The situation in the Minden district in August 1934 was described in the following terms: 'Reading the foreign press is becoming increasingly widespread, a fact which unequivocally shows that the population does not agree with what is written in the German newspapers.'[41] The same reporter noted that 'The people listen avidly to news broadcasts on foreign radio stations, and read the foreign press, chiefly from Switzerland.'[42] It could be argued that this was not so surprising in a district that, with industrial centres such as Bielefeld and Herford, had a high concentration of voters who had previously supported the leftist parties. However, in Protestant eastern regions known for their support of Nazism a similar picture prevailed, as may be seen from a Gestapo report from Frankfurt-on-the-Oder.[43]

Even on the Jewish question, the official version of events was not accepted as reliable. With regards to the antisemitic riots in Berlin in July 1935, it was reported from Aachen that 'The vague official news printed in newspapers on what is happening in Berlin is not deemed reliable by the public.' The same Gestapo station added that the public had lost all trust in the party press, and relied on foreign papers and broadcasts to find out what was really happening.[44]

This rejection of, and alienation from, official propaganda by large sectors of the population explains the steady decline in the circulation of the party press. Casual statements in various reports at the start of Nazi rule already point to this trend. To begin with, the Gestapo commentators noted the phenomenon but dismissed it as a local aberration since they were unable to see the picture for the Reich as a whole. A case in point is the governor's account from the Aurich district for the month of September 1934. The report states that the circulation of the only party paper in Emden, the *Ostfriesische Tageszeitung*, had decreased and that the public was searching for alternative information sources.[45] As in Protestant Friesland, so in the Catholic west: the governor of the Koblenz district, in his report for October–November, complained that the public was gradually cancelling its subscriptions to the local party paper, the *Koblenzer Nachrichtenblatt*.[46]

The vacuum produced by the declining circulation of the party press was quickly filled. Side by side with this decline, all reporters noted a steady rise, or at least no decline, in the circulation of church-connected papers. The governor of the Wiesbaden district wrote in his survey for February 1935 that, parallel to the decline in circulation of the party press, there had been a 100 per cent rise in sales of the *St Georg Blatt*, a church paper.[47] The situation in Aachen was much the same. Here the Nazi press enjoyed wide popularity in 1933, but in September 1934 the public, particularly the rural population, was switching to newspapers which took a bourgeois or Catholic line.[48]

Even the most important Nazi newspaper in the west of the country, Robert Ley's *Westdeutscher Beobachter*, was injured by the rise in circulation of competing newspapers.[49] Indeed, Goebbels' own paper, *Der Angriff*, suffered in the same way: its circulation fell from 94,200 in January 1934 to 82,996 in July, and to 61,000 in January 1935.[50] The decline was unsurprising. *Der Angriff* was sold only in the streets and not by subscription, and it was therefore more difficult to coerce people to buy it. Again, the process was not confined to a few regions. A Gestapo station in Protestant Lower Saxony, a stronghold of Nazism, reported that, 'Despite the pressure of the party, and despite the financial support extended through advertisements, the circulation of the National Socialist press is constantly declining.'[51] He went on to describe the fate of the local party organ, the Hanoverian *Niedersächsische Tageszeitung*. Similarly a survey from Speyer shows that there the party press had declined by one quarter.[52] This state of affairs was well known to exiles, who apparently had access to very reliable and accurate information sources.[53]

The changing fortunes of the press in the Cologne area is illustrated by the following table, which compares the circulation figures of a Nazi paper, the *Westdeutscher Beobachter* (*WB*); a bourgeois paper, the *Kölnische Zeitung* (*KZ*); and a Catholic newspaper, the *Katholische Kirchenzeitung* (*KK*).[54]

	WB	*KZ*	*KK*
Jan. 1934	202,657	104,190	80,939
Apr. 1934	191,416	99,181	83,822
July 1934	184,450	99,825	84,193
Oct. 1934	186,620	92,061	84,715
Jan. 1935	186,029	93,127	88,000

The increase in circulation of the foreign and church press, and decline in circulation of the party press, was accompanied by another manifestation of the reading public's resistance to indoctrination: conscious depoliticization. This found expression in a growing interest in strictly local events, and unwillingness to consider country-wide topics. Thus, for instance, we learn from the Gestapo in Hanover that people there wanted the press to increase coverage of local events at the expense of national affairs.[55] This is typical of public reaction to the press in dictatorial systems. While in regimes with a free press the individual can voice criticism of, or express his own views about, events of which he has no first-hand knowledge, in totalitarian regimes his personal experience necessarily becomes the most reliable information source, and it is by this that he judges what he reads. The reader assumes that reports on local events cannot be distorted, since he has some first-hand knowledge of them and has no need of an official commentary.[56]

From the point of view of the Nazi regime, distrust of the party media reached crisis level in early 1935. The Düsseldorf Gestapo report for February states in this connection, 'The National Socialist press is facing extremely serious difficulties and is hardly holding its ground. The number of readers is steadily declining for the newspapers do not interest them at all. Only an economic blow or the total destruction of the bourgeois press can change the situation.'[57] In March the Bielefeld Gestapo reported that in Padeborn the latest edition of the *Völkischer Beobachter* had sold only forty-five copies.[58] A month later the district governor announced that the local Nazi paper had closed down due to financial difficulties, and that the public was reading the Catholic press.[59] In the same month the Aachen Gestapo complained that the *Westdeutscher Beobachter* was losing its readers and that even party members were criticizing it.[60] There is no reason to suppose any inaccuracy here, since broadly the same picture surfaces from statistical data for other areas. The SD survey of the Bavarian press, and circulation statistics for the Rhineland and Stuttgart, confirm the trend.[61]

It would appear that, despite the blows dealt to the non-Nazi organs, the circulation of the party press did not improve. And, given that the regime could not afford to have propaganda weakened or contradicted by rivals, it could not remain indifferent to the situation. This type of regime, based on a delicate balance between coercion through terror and persuasion through propaganda, relies on the press to instil its message and encourage political conformity. It is therefore important that it should possess a reasonable level of credibility.

There seems little doubt that the decline of the party press was the chief motive for the measures adopted by the authorities in the spring of 1935 to curtail the freedom of the press. The notorious 'Amann regulations' of 24 April 1935 were directed at 'Revoking the licence of any publisher whose newspapers are detrimental to the honour of the press because of their sensationalist character or because of the moral harm they constitute to the public. Shutting down newspapers to stamp out unfair competition. Ensuring the independence of the newspaper industry.'[62] The unstated purpose behind these regulations was undoubtedly that of bridling the competition and halting the decline of the party press, in an effort to repair the widening credibility gap between the regime and the public. Beyond these regulations, the party did all it could to strengthen its own newspapers, weaken the competition and restrict the influence of papers which represented a non-Nazi stand. Along with the 'legal' and financial damage inflicted on the non-Nazi press came a vigorous propaganda effort to get more people to subscribe to the party papers.

On the face of it, the regime's measures worked. The Augsburg police reported that the local party paper had 3,000 new subscribers.[63] Police elsewhere in the same region inform us that, although the church press continued to be popular in rural areas, the party press managed to maintain its circulation rate as a result of the increased propaganda.[64] Statistical figures for the first and second quarters of 1935 in the Munich area reveal that, while the circulation of the church press remained stable, and that of the non-Nazi papers declined, the party press increased its sales.[65] It appeared that the regime had persuaded thousands of readers to switch to the party papers. We learn from Gestapo reports, however, that this was not the whole story. A careful comparison of statistical data from different regions of the Reich shows that the Amann regulations by themselves were unable to increase the readership of the party press. The regime knew very well that any rise in circulation was achieved mainly by coercing the public, not through any propaganda successes. The governor of Potsdam, for example, reported improved sales of the *Völkischer Beobachter*, but went on to admit that, in deciding to take the paper, people had been responding to pressure rather than exercising their choice.[66] From Aachen, too, we hear of readers taking out subscriptions to the party paper because of threats, and out of fear of reprisals. The reporter noted that the situation had come to light through the censors' reading of letters being sent abroad. The writers candidly revealed that they had taken out subscriptions under duress, and planned to cancel them at the first possible opportunity.[67] In July the same Gestapo station indicated that the central party organ in the Rhineland, the *Westdeutscher Beobachter*, had been unsuccessful in obtaining new subscriptions on its own merits, and that those it had secured had been obtained through coercion.[68]

It is safe to say that the central government in Berlin was well aware of this state of affairs and so of the inadequacy of its attempts at indoctrination. The governor of Bielefeld district commented that the authorities knew the danger of trying to activate the public during a crisis of confidence, and that in view of this the party's organizations had better stop soliciting contributions. Many refused to contribute, thereby dissociating themselves from the party's activities, and the exercise as a whole helped lower the party's popularity still further.[69] Given that in only one month people in Münster, for example, were asked to give to the Hitler Youth, to the youth hostels, to the mother and child fund and to the Red Cross, and to buy posters for Navy Day, for Handicrafts Day and for the *Gau* rally, it is small wonder that people refused and that the order to stop canvassing from July to October was widely welcomed.[70]

This picture, however, should not lead us to ignore three things. First, criticism was limited to certain aspects of the political and social reality and not to the system in principle. Secondly, in the last analysis the disaffection found no practical expression and the regime was not seriously challenged. Thirdly, most of those who manifested dissent appear to have belonged to the 'other Germany'. Vast numbers did identify ideologically with the Nazi regime and consent to its policies. Radical Nazis criticized the government for being too moderate and for not proceeding fast enough with the Nazi revolution. The revolutionary potential of these elements is evident from the contemporary anti-fascist literature, both leftist and conservative; far from disappearing in 1934 with the purges of the SA leadership, which apparently laid to rest the idea of a 'second revolution', they remained a dynamic political force. At the same time, the regime subordinated these elements to its political objectives, when their growing activism endangered the very basis of the social and political order. In the next chapter we turn to this issue and its consequences for policy on the Jewish question.

2

Institutionalization and Radicalization

The gradual loss of revolutionary momentum had direct repercussions on the morale of the Nazi Party. Despite the inner discipline and indoctrination, its members were unable to remain unaffected by the general mood. It is particularly noteworthy that the loss of the fighting spirit can be gleaned from reports from the Protestant north, where the party's potential for a large following was particularly high. A case in point is the Gestapo report from Wesermünde: 'The mood continues to be negative among almost all strata of the population...voluntary participation in party and state affairs has not only failed to rise, but more and more the tendency is toward lack of concern ...these signs are evident also among members of the party and its organizations.'[1]

This state of affairs was presented in more detail by the Wilhelmshaven Gestapo. It stated that, out of 180 people registered with the local party branch, only thirty actually reported for service. The writer added significantly that the reason for this was a total lack of motivation to serve.[2] The same symptoms appeared in Münster too, where thirty out of 200 registered activists reported; and in Hanover, where the response rate was 20 per cent and the observer noted that in one area only thirteen out of 250 registered activists showed up for service.[3]

Within the party, however, unlike in the general public, this tendency was countered and outweighed by a force which strove to revive the movement's *élan*, and whose chief proponents were the radical Nazis of the SA. This organization, which considered itself to be the spearhead of the Nazi revolution, was therefore particularly apprehensive about the political institutionalization and ideological stagnation, and an examination of the conflict in which it was involved sheds light not only on the efforts of the SA to revive the revolutionary spirit, but also on its role in shaping the state's antisemitic policy.

Since Hitler's takeover, the SA had perceived its central function as safeguarding the revolutionary flame from embourgeoisement. As its leader, Ernst Roehm, put it, 'The revolutionary swing of the SA is the guarantee of the revolution in the face of the danger of stagnation and spiritual philistinism.'[4] However, the tactical concessions to various conservative forces in Hitler's dictatorship conflicted with the stormtroopers' demand for a 'second revolution from below'. The disaffection grew particularly noticeable from the second half of 1934 on. The 'night of the long knives', which eliminated Roehm, and further purges within the SA after July 1934 signalled a halt to radical activism in the Reich. As a result of the purges, the SA was given purely symbolic functions and its tasks were restricted to charitable or ceremonial activities, such as collecting donations for the winter aid campaign or marching in parades. In this way it was made totally dependent on the party apparatus. This situation again threw into relief the discrepancy between the SA's aspirations and the political leadership's plans. The latter treated the SA as a propaganda instrument to spread the Nazi doctrine on the streets. State terror naturally continued, for through it the regime sought to realize its claims to rule unchallenged; but the SA's unruly terror was demonstrably quenched in order to demonstrate to all and sundry that the regime was resolute in imposing its will, even at the expense of its veteran fighters.

As early as August 1934, just a year and a half after the Nazis came to power, the Aachen Gestapo reported growing bitterness and discontent in the SA ranks, as a result of uncertainty over the organization's future.[5] This mood cannot be attributed solely to the shock experienced by the SA following the purge of its top leaders on 30 June; nor was it a phenomenon which passed within a few months: rather, it assumed various guises and reached ominous proportions by the eve of the party rally in September 1935. In its reviews of autumn 1934, the Aachen Gestapo again noticed visible signs of a crisis in the SA: stormtroopers were dropping out of current official activities and many of them were joining the rival paramilitary arm of the conservative Right, the Stahlhelm. The commentator again attributed the organization's low morale to its lack of a clear direction.[6] Reporting at around the same time, the president of the Rhine province drew a similar picture: lacking objectives, the SA had lost its inner momentum.[7] This situation explains why so many reports of the time recommend, as a matter of urgency, that the SA should be assigned definite tasks to boost its spirits and morale. The Stettin Gestapo, for example, argues that only by this means can the SA dispel its feelings of being marginalized and regain its strength.[8] In the circumstances, however, it was only natural for the Nazi leadership to take stern measures to keep the SA in check. Thus, hand in hand with waning motivation within the SA, we find repeated purges to ferret out undisciplined elements in its ranks.[9]

Rising unemployment contributed to the deepening crisis within the SA. Dismissed stormtroopers ceased to receive unemployment benefit; sometimes they were fired from jobs and denied a new work permit. Given the occupational profile of the organization, for a good many ejection from the ranks meant immediate loss of any income. Thus, the fear of unemployment, while not the only cause of radicalization, certainly helped stimulate it. Indeed, most commentators realized that the organization's social structure provided a considerable impetus to the process of political radicalization, and linked the threat of unemployment with the SA's potential for violence. The governor of Minden district reported that in his area, 'The purges continue; reports have been received that 1,000 people have been dismissed from the 165th brigade stationed in Bielefeld, and the authorities intend to dismiss 2,000 more.'[10] The Kassel Gestapo noted that the purges not only generated unemployment among the rank and file through the disbandment of units, but also made many SA officers redundant, through the closure of training-camps. The commentator saw the situation as fraught with potential for a radical backlash against the establishment – if, for example, the unemployed officers joined the regime's opponents.[11] The Aachen Gestapo's report for October 1934 supplies further evidence of the close link between unemployment and political ferment: it notes that unemployed stormtroopers were particularly bitter over their lack of political influence.[12] The picture is completed by a report written by an SA officer from Mannheim: 'the mood in the SA must regrettably be characterized as unsteady. The fact that the SA lacks clear tasks has a very negative impact…the consequences are therefore bad economic relations for the greater part of the SA – indeed, unemployment.'[13]

Another factor which contributed to the crisis was the growing resentment in the SA that other party elements enjoyed greater success and advanced more rapidly up the political ladder. The power struggles in Hitler's regime sharpened the antagonism between the SA and the party apparatus, and for the former it became vital to prove that it still had a *raison d'être*, despite its fallen prestige after the purges. The growing strength of the Stahlhelm and its ally, the army, exacerbated the situation: the SA had long deemed these two bodies a stumbling-block in the way of its 'second revolution', and the more rumours there were that the Stahlhelm would renew its activities, the greater the SA's need to prove its zeal for Nazism.

The Stahlhelm had been partly incorporated into the SA in summer 1933, and thus ostensibly strengthened the SA by adding thousands of new members to its ranks. It was nevertheless clear to all sides after the merger that the Stahlhelm continued to serve the interests of the conservative circles, which wanted to establish a dictatorship in Germany with a fascist–corporative hue – that is, a 'national revolution' devoid of all 'socialist' colouring. The stormtroopers suspected that the purpose of the party leaders in creating a semi-independent body within the SA was to counter the organization's 'leftist' elements and neutralize their radical tendencies. The increased political influence of the conservatives in 1934 was reflected in reports that numerous former members of the pre-merger Stahlhelm were leaving the SA and returning to their old allegiance. The Harburg–Wilhelmsburg Gestapo, for instance, reported a considerable increase in Stahlhelm activities and a sharp rise in the number of new members. The reporter added that, because simultaneous membership of both organizations was to be prohibited in the future, many stormtroopers were choosing to leave the SA and join the Stahlhelm.[14] The Cologne Gestapo, echoing the sharp criticism in the SA ranks, went so far as to say that members of the SA were convinced that Hitler's next step would be to dissolve the organization altogether – a measure obviously seen in terms of a further decline in revolutionary idealism through a shift in power to the conservative reactionaries. The tensions between the SA and the Stahlhelm in the run-up to the general reshuffling of forces expected in April 1935 are also to be viewed against this background.[15]

Parenthetically, it is worth mentioning that, even if the SA had been abolished, the Stahlhelm and its supporters would not have exercised a restraining influence on Hitler's antisemitic policy. In keeping with its *völkisch* outlook, the Stahlhelm had demanded measures against the Jews as far back as 1920, and an antisemitic paragraph had been added to its statutes in 1924. Its unbridled agitation against, and boycott of, German Jews, is also well known.[16]

Another major factor which added to the radicals' low morale was the strengthening of the army. In particular, the law of renewed conscription of 16 March 1935 blurred the SA's future even more, and increased the uncertainty about whether it would survive. The same month the Wilhelmshaven Gestapo, for example, spoke of heightened fears in the SA that the growth of the army would reinforce its alliance with the Stahlhelm, to the detriment of the SA.[17] Prior to the Nazi takeover, the SA had been assured that it would serve as the basis of the army in the new regime. Numerous remarks by SA officers bear witness to the high hopes which had been created. But against these expectations stood Hitler's preference for 'legality' – that is, for taking control of the existing army, rather than liquidating it and starting again. For their part, the conservative generals correctly understood that the SA's aspirations endangered the Wehrmacht as currently constituted: the stormtroopers wanted to establish a popular army built on a revolutionary ideology rather than preserve and follow in the tradition of Prussian militarism.

The conflict between the two main trends within the regime – the drive to realize the principles of the Nazi revolution without delay, and a conservative, institutionalizing trend – came to an head in November–December 1934. The old fighter Gottfried Feder was relieved of his position as Secretary of State in the Economics Ministry. Given that Feder was one of the architects of an anti-capitalist economic doctrine, his dismissal clearly denoted the entrenchment of Schacht and his conservative followers. The dismissal of Hellmuth Bruckner, *Gauleiter* of Silesia and local SA commander, and Wilhelm Karpenstein, *Gauleiter* of Pomerania – both known to have 'leftist' inclinations – pointed in a similar direction.[18] The radicals construed these changes as symptomatic of a shift towards the conservatives and away from the objectives of the Nazi programme. Their disappointment increased even more when Hitler made concessions to the churches – a cynical, opportunistic step taken prior to the plebiscite on the Saar, and interpreted by the radicals as an indication of a weak leadership submitting to the demands of its enemies. Small wonder that more now than ever before the SA sought to implement Nazi ideals, in order to prevent, or at least delay, the institutionalization of the Nazi revolution and thereby preserve the activist *élan*. Hence the repeated references, in reports summarizing the SA's mood at the end of 1934, to the organization's need for concrete political assignments. The Sopade reports for this period highlight the antagonism between those who demanded institutionalization and those Nazi fundamentalists who sanctified activism. We come across similar assessments in the Nazi reports. Reviewing developments within the SA, the Düsseldorf Gestapo and reports from Berlin, Bavaria, Pfalz and numerous other regions noted a revival of radicalism, creating an atmosphere similar to that prevailing before 30 June.[19]

It is clear, then, that both the thinning of the ranks and the revived activism derived from the same source: the SA's frustration in face of the progressive institutionalization of the revolution. There is little doubt, therefore, that, contrary to the common view that the SA lost all political importance once Roehm had been liquidated, it still pursued the idea of the 'second revolution' and saw direct and violent activism as the way to justify its independent existence. This militancy is directly relevant to our subject: it explains the outbursts of anti-Jewish violence in the early years of Nazi rule. The violence that the SA directed against German Jews, and its incessant agitation against capitalists and the churches, are to be seen as part of a concerted effort to ensure its own survival; and, while the stormtroopers' radicalism could not itself furnish a coherent political programme, it undoubtedly influenced and pushed ahead the regime's antisemitic policy, as we shall now see.

Towards the end of 1934, with the plebiscite on the Saar impending in January 1935, moderation was the order of the day. The need to clarify the status of German Jews was urgent, in order to unify state and party policy and stop the radical outbursts. The Gestapo and regional government reports repeatedly asked for an official, authoritative decision on how Jews were to be treated, because the lack of clear policy caused undesirable clashes between party activists and state officials. In December 1934 the Wiesbaden district governor's report asked Berlin to define a national policy on the Jews, so as to end the frictions between the party and the Economic Ministry.[20] The district governor of Koblenz made a similar request in his report for the same period. Reviewing the damage to Jewish property, he described the clashes between the party and the local police and, in closing, requested a clear-cut and unequivocal policy.[21] From many places we learn that unendurable difficulties arose from the absence of a uniform antisemitic line: the outbursts could not be checked so long as the party press, in defiance of guidelines laid down by state bodies, incited the population against the Jews.[22]

The SA's expectations reached a high point on the eve of the plebiscite. The political alienation of the SA grew stronger, and with it its revolutionary fervour, giving rise to the hope that harsh measures against internal enemies would become a political norm. Interwoven with reports of bitterness, nervousness and uncertainty in the SA are references to its hopes that the party leadership would fulfil its promises and institute a full-blooded Nazi programme. Clear evidence of these expectations can be found in an internal SA report which states, 'everybody considers that following the return of the Saar, the drive against Jews, political Catholicism and first and foremost the lords of the economy will begin.'[23] Similarly, the district governor in Würzburg noted that the public was rife with rumours about far-reaching changes following the plebiscite – in particular, harsh steps against the conservatives and the Catholic Church, and purges within the party and its organizations.[24] The same mood is echoed in a report from the Rhineland. The governor of the Rhine province wrote in his report for December 1934 and January 1935 on the political ferment in Cologne where local commanders had baldly announced that 'after 13 January we shall deal with the Catholics.'[25] The January report from the local Gestapo clarifies which groups the governor had in mind:

In some small circles of very revolutionary National Socialists, who may be characterized as always unsatisfied, the idea crops up that after 13 January their cherished second revolution will start. What will then happen they call 'Night of the long knives', 'Night of Saint Bartholomew', 'National murder week'. Also in greater SA circles it can be heard that the command to action is imminent.[26]

The poisoned atmosphere did not escape the attention of foreign news correspondents. In its regular column on Germany the *Jewish Chronicle* in

London reported that a harsher antisemitic line could be expected following the plebiscite. The Comintern organ *Inprecor* noted that more and more voices in Germany, particularly the Hitler Youth and the SA, were clamouring for a 'second revolution'.[27] Little wonder, then, that bourgeois sectors which had long feared that Hindenburg's death would remove the last stop on the radicals now felt more insecure.

The high expectations of the radicals are well illustrated by a speech delivered by a Nazi leader at the time. Among other things he said, 'If the Saar struggle gives rise to a fight or even a war, we shall not hesitate to annihilate the whole Jewish society, root and branch.'[28] His words are noteworthy because they highlight the discrepancy between the radicals' aspirations and the politicians' limited possibilities of action. Recognizing the limits that the present configuration of forces set on plans to eliminate the Jews, the radicals saw the outbreak of a military confrontation as the only way of realizing their wishes. This was a typical Nazi way of reasoning. Goering, Heydrich and Hitler also took this line a few years later. All of them made it plain that the opportunities presented by wartime conditions must be exploited. The eradication of the Jews, which could not be carried out in peacetime, would be carried out in wartime. War was the ideal setting for a final solution to the Jewish problem.

It is well known that Hitler scored a remarkable success with the plebiscite. Over 90 per cent voted for the return of the Saar to Germany. What to the general public was an impressive victory was to many radicals a frustrating experience: their hopes of instigating a 'second revolution' were dashed. It is to these circumstances that we must attribute the atmosphere of depression and political weariness which again descended on the SA. And, in stark contrast, voices demanding the realization of Nazi objectives again grew more vociferous. Addressing a large rally in Kiel, the chief of the SA, Viktor Lutze, attempted to instil some hope into the ranks. He emphasized that, although people said that the SA was finished, it would continue to act as the party's evangelists.[29] The Nazi fanatics now channelled their frustration by vigorously concentrating their hatred on those whose very existence manifested the failure of the Nazi revolution – the Catholic Church and the Jews: the Catholic Church because it symbolized the continuation of the traditional, pre-Nazi political culture, which was inimical to Nazism's effort to gain the public's total allegiance; the Jews because Nazi ideology demanded their removal from Germany, yet existing antisemitic legislation and policy had failed to achieve this.

As a result, as soon as the plebiscite on the Saar was over, a new antisemitic campaign was engineered which rapidly assumed gigantic proportions and was then called the 'antisemitic wave'. The terror was throughout accompanied by government orders and directives, prompted by the demand to adopt more extensive and severe legislation. The reorganization of the SA expected by 1 April added impetus to the renewed radicalization. Through acts of violence the party hardliners attempted to encroach on many aspects of the state's authority in order to capture power and gain responsibility. An instructive example is to be found in the Münster Gestapo report for May 1935. After giving the standard information on the attacks against the Jews the report states, 'in broad circles of the movement, in particular in the SA, the view reigns that now the time has arrived to solve the Jewish question ruthlessly; they wish to roll up the Jewish problem and believe that then the government must follow.'[30] These radicals believed that they were fulfilling their duty of 'working towards the Führer's goals', and that Hitler would grant legal sanction to their actions.

What stimulated this upsurge of militant activity, unparalleled since the early months of 1933, is now clear. Behind it were the radicals, particularly the SA, searching for means of survival. Their militancy and rejuvenated radicalism were the result of the need to justify their existence, and their frustration was channelled towards increased violence. This attempt to reintegrate the SA, and the need to reinforce its self-image, were exploited by fanatical antisemites in the leadership who sought an alliance with the SA to mount aggressive antisemitic actions. Central figures in the government such as Goebbels, and regional Nazi leaders such as the *Gauleiter* Jacob Sprenger of Hesse, Josef Grohé of Cologne–Aachen and Julius Streicher of Franconia believed, like the SA, that such actions were an application of the principles of Nazi ideology and would provide the pressure from below that would force the government towards a radical solution of the Jewish problem. The SA's mounting disaffection would thus be channelled into the task of pushing the Jewish question to the top of the agenda. The campaign took various forms: extensive propaganda through antisemitic public meetings; increased incitement in the party press, particularly in *Der Stürmer*, *Der Angriff* and *Der Judenkenner*; and acts of violence initiated from below. Posters advertising *Der Stürmer* appeared in increasing numbers and this notorious organ extended its sales all over Germany, largely through the support of local Nazi organizations. There is no doubt that the radicals interpreted the antisemitic harangues of the *Gauleiter* as the green light to a campaign of physical violence – official backing from high-ranking party leaders for a wave of terror. The Nazi radicals also found particular encouragement for their outrages in Hitler's speeches when he compared the movement to an engine which would continue to run. The SA understood such statements as the Führer's own stamp of approval on their actions.

The effect was immediate. In May all reports record a wide antisemitic drive, which reached its climax in the summer months. The wave of antisemitic vandalism that broke in Berlin on the night of 16 July was unprecedented. Previously the Jewish population in Berlin, by virtue of a relatively efficient system of law and order, had suffered less than the smaller communities in country towns, such as the ones in Franconia or Pomerania. Now this state of affairs changed. In the north and east of Berlin breaking the windows of Jewish shops became common, and other cities were equally hit by anti-semitic agitation. The disturbances in Berlin's Kurfürstendamm were stated by the press to have been instigated by the provocative behaviour of the Jews. At the same time, the Nazi police set in motion a campaign of arrests for racial offences in all areas of the Reich. In many places it was the practice to lead through the streets, under posters describing their 'crime', German women accused of consorting with Jews. The Jews with whom the women were supposed to have associated were in turn arrested for race pollution and put in a concentration camp.[31]

However, the wave of antisemitic terror hardly satisfied the radicals, because it was permanently curbed by the authorities. Actions which blurred the distinction between political struggle, on the one hand, and terror and crime, on the other, exacerbated the tension between the forces of law and order, backed by the conservative elite, and the radical Nazis. On the one hand, the conservatives saw the 'revolution from below' as a challenge to authority, and therefore to be halted. The economic establishment in particular feared that the anti-Jewish terror would spread to include all capitalists, and thus threaten law and order in general. On the other hand, the radicals, heirs of the *Freikorps* tradition, rankled at the legal obstacles placed in their way. The antisemitic campaign raised a fundamental dilemma for the regime: was antisemitism to be managed exclusively by state bodies and subject to 'reasonable' limits; or was it to be allowed to proceed unchallenged, urged on by the violence of the extremists? The conservatives wished the Third Reich to be an authoritarian regime assisted by the Nazi Party in organization and propaganda matters, whereas radical party members, openly disdaining bureaucracy, wished the party to have supremacy over the state. The central authorities sought to contain the violence by prohibiting unauthorized indi-vidual actions – partly because of pragmatic considerations such as foreign relations and international trade connections, but mainly because they insisted that the government alone was authorized to adopt the appropriate measures to change the Jews' status, even if these did not wholly satisfy the party's programme. This stand was most sharply expressed by Hjalmar Schacht in his memoranda to Hitler condemning the riots' disturbing effect on trade. Schacht and those such as Johannes Popitz, who shared his views, agreed that 'the programme of the NSDAP must be implemented' but also vigorously demanded that the policies towards the Jews be carried out 'exclusively on the basis of legal regulations'.[32] Thus, when the government strictly forbade individual actions, the radicals saw only a flagrant betrayal of Nazi principles.

The official curb on antisemitic violence caused unrest and bitterness among the older party members over the failure to follow Nazi principles.

According to the Berlin Gestapo, the party's 'torch-carriers' insisted that the leadership had given way to a political compromise imposed by the conservatives. The SA did not understand why party activists were being punished when in attacking Jews they were merely acting on Nazi ideals.[33] Nor did it grasp why, when rioting erupted in Berlin in July 1935, it was followed by a statement from the local police declaring that the 'natural' anti-semitic demonstration had been misused by irresponsible people to discredit Germany and that in future the party and the state would collaborate to prevent such disruptions of public order. More frustrating still were the explicit directives in August prohibiting individual actions against the Jews. The directives were ordered by Hitler and issued by his deputy, Hess, and the Minister of the Interior, Frick. At the party congress in Thuringia, Frick issued a warning against the '150 per cent National Socialists', condemning them as dangerous saboteurs of the revolution. Moreover, not only Schacht or Frick, but even those party leaders who had formerly stirred up the rioters, now tried to restore calm after having lost control of the extremists. A firm stand against uncontrolled agitation was adopted by one of the inciters to violence, *Gauleiter* Grohé, in his address to local party leaders in Cologne. In a similar manner *Gauleiter* Wagner of Silesia pronounced himself against the individual actions. He issued an order on 31 August stating that undisciplined actions violated the Führer's authority, achieved nothing and harmed Germany's reputation. Thus all anti-Jewish actions were forbidden unless they were on his orders. Even Streicher expressed himself in a similar vein when addressing a demonstration in Hamburg.[34]

The Nazi government had to satisfy the expectations of the party activists but at the same time curb their militancy. There seems little doubt that this atmosphere set the scene for the actions Hitler took against the Stahlhelm at this time. While the official dissolution of the Stahlhelm was not ordered until November 1935, branches in Berlin, Brandenburg and Pomerania were dissolved in early August. The closing of the Berlin headquarters was regarded as the virtual end of the organization.[35] Hitler's initiative lifted the SA's morale by dispelling fears that the Führer had capitulated to conservative pressures, and raising hopes that similar actions would follow against other foes of Nazism. The expectation that the party's annual convention would mark a milestone in official anti-Jewish policy further fanned the stormtroopers' antisemitism.

MASS MOBILIZATION AND ANTISEMITISM

Thus far we have concentrated on the radicals. Let us now consider the effect of the wave of antisemitism on the general public.

A major purpose of the campaign was to mobilize the apathetic public and particularly to raise the morale of its disaffected sectors. The pragmatic value of tackling the Jewish question and manipulating it for purposes of political integration is best exemplified by the words of *Gauleiter* Grohé in his report for February 1935: 'More articulate propaganda against shopping in Jewish stores will not only suit our principles, but also raise the somewhat depressed mood of the lower middle class.'[36] He set an example by calling for the boycott of Jewish stores at Cologne's Spring Fair in March.

An examination of the press in these months shows that this was far more than a local initiative. In the Rhineland Grohé incited attacks upon people buying from Jewish stores; Sprenger urged a renewed fight against the Jews in Frankfurt, and Streicher pushed the antisemitic drive in Nuremberg. Sounding his own praise, Grohé wrote in his March report,

The increase of the party's activities was due to a more harsh and minute treatment of the Jewish question. Apart from being a matter of principle and awakening the racial instinct through its treatment, the topics of the Jewish question, department stores, Jewish shops, etc., restored morale to the resigned lower middle class.[37]

There is a reason why Grohé was so eager to please this segment of the population. The Düsseldorf report for February noted the low morale among shopkeepers owing to the downturn in sales, at a time when price controls had reduced profit margins and a wage freeze had diminished the public's purchasing-power. Small shopkeepers also complained that the party did not actively help them survive by destroying the Jewish owned department stores.[38] The head office of the Gestapo in Saxony likewise noted that this group criticized the government for not having nationalized the department stores as promised and for making the situation even worse through the prices policy of the Reich Food Estate, by allowing the food stamps of the winter aid campaign to be redeemed in department stores. Further, the middle classes claimed that the army was still ordering some of its supplies from Jews, and that, when department stores were taken over by Germans, they were not given to small shopkeepers.[39] It was thus crucial for the leadership to regain the faith of this class, which was one of the Nazis' main pillars.

What about the rest of society, however? It would appear that all gains to national honour in the field of foreign affairs – such as the overwhelming victory in the plebiscite over the Saar, and the renewal of conscription for army service – had only a brief impact on the public, and so did little to advance political socialization and conformity. People were more concerned about their day-to-day problems. Likewise, antisemitic slogans could not distract attention from the deteriorating economic situation, and the violence perpetrated by the extremists, particularly against the churches, simply made matters worse. It failed to galvanize the population for a massive campaign against the Jews, and the breaches of law and order increased rather than diminished disaffection with the regime. It was clear to all that this situation could not remain static. As the Berlin chief of police put it in his report for May and June, people were in a mood to expect harsh measures from the government.[40] The August report from Berlin urges public clarification of the Jewish question, demanded both by the party and by the population at large.[41]

The party's attempts at mass mobilization during July and August 1935 produced a wearied response from the public. On the eve of the party's annual rally in September in Nuremberg, indifference turned into hostility and signs of disappointment with the regime dramatically increased. To a certain extent this happened even in sectors which had strongly supported the Nazi Party. From Berlin, for instance, we learn that the party was being shunned not only by opportunists, but also by 'true believers'. The commentator attributed this to the party's failure to carry out promises made during the struggle for power.[42] The Aachen Gestapo, summarizing events in July, described a similar mood. The workers who had formerly supported the regime were embittered by frustration. In addition to disappointment over the failure to realize economic goals, there was sharp criticism of the radicals' rioting and the absence of a clear policy on the churches and the Jews.[43]

The seriousness of the situation is evident from the stereotyped expressions that the Nazi agents used to describe the public mood: 'bad and unfavourable'; 'continued deterioration of mood'; 'considerably worsened'; 'increasing unhappiness'. In some regions the rift in relations between the regime and the public appears to have been so deep as to constitute a massive withdrawal of support. This was only natural: ordinary Germans wished to know where they stood and what rules they should follow, particularly with regard to the Jews; they did not want their routine suddenly disrupted by arbitrary actions by party activists.[44]

The assessment that 'the mood has reached an all-time low', which we come across in reports from western regions, shows that the situation was especially serious in the Catholic areas. From Cologne and Koblenz we learn of deep disaffection; in Breslau the situation is reported to be at its worst since the Nazi takeover. The Aachen Gestapo commentator warns that it is not just his view that things are bad: observers all over the region had worrying reports.[45] The reason why these attitudes found a firmer footing in Catholic areas is obvious: the population feared a *Kulturkampf* as an extension of the persecution of the Jews. Mounted and motorized SA rode through the towns chanting not only anti-Jewish, but also anti-Catholic, slogans and songs.

The reports also indicate a steady rise in dissent, manifest in various rumours current at the time. This point deserves closer attention, since in a regime of this kind, where the state has a monopoly on information, the analysis of rumours is an important gauge of public mood. The very existence of rumours, despite the barrages of propaganda, shows that the public's senses cannot be completely dulled, and that large parts of the population retain their critical independence despite the risks. In dictatorships, rumours are a token compensation for political impotence. They express anxieties, hopes and expectations which have no other outlet, and act as a valve whereby people release their inner tensions. The intensity of rumours in Nazi Germany at this time points unmistakably to the stress people were under and to their general sense of insecurity, and so provides a fairly reliable indication of their feelings about the regime.[46]

Various sources mention rumours that the regime was to be purged of the radical elements undermining public order, for there was a pressing need to end the state of lawlessness through definitive legislation on the Jewish question. In Dortmund and Magdeburg, for instance, we find rumours about an imminent clearing-away of radicals, patterned on the 'night of the long knives'.[47] The Gestapo and Sopade reports show that the same sort of whispering went on in the Rhineland.[48] This persistent hearsay, reflecting the hopes of the population, is not to be misunderstood as indicating a rise in democratic trends among the German public; on the contrary, there is not the slightest hint that the waning of the Nazi Party's influence produced a desire for democracy. The country's anti-liberal traditions and the fear of political chaos were so firmly rooted that hopes for change were pinned on alternative anti-democratic forces. Many wanted the Nazis to be replaced by a military dictatorship. The Kassel Gestapo registered such a trend when it noted that reactionary circles were speaking of the government falling by winter.[49] In Magdeburg the local Gestapo reported that the population was hoping for an alliance between the army and the Stahlhelm to rout the Nazis and seize power.[50] In the Rhineland, the name of War Minister von Blomberg was being bandied about as that of an alternative leader to Hitler. Similar unsubstantiated rumours mirroring the public's hopes were circulating in Saxony: in Leipzig, for example, people were saying that local party officials, including the chief of police, the *Kreisleiter* and even the *Reichstatthalter* of Saxony, had been arrested and shot.[51]

The Sopade reports for these months give further evidence of this climate, but they do not contain a shred of evidence that people wanted a return to democracy. The socialist observers gained the impression that, in looking for a military takeover, what people really wanted was an end to the rioting and the restoration of law and order. They expected the traditional right-wing and Catholic centre parties to play a crucial role in a new leadership that would quash what was commonly called 'Bolshevism of the Swastika' (*Hakenkreuzbolschewismus*). Many wished a military commissar to be appointed alongside the Minister of the Interior to impose order by clamping down on the SS and the SA.[52] The Koblenz report pointed out the danger inherent in the political polarization: 'Both the Stahlhelm and the SA look forward to a change in the political line and to violent campaigns.'[53]

Finally, the discontent found its most forcible expression in illegal leaflets disseminated by right-wing circles. Rumours circulated that Hitler had become a prisoner of the generals and that a military coup was imminent. The leaflets abound in slogans referring to the coming 'Fourth Reich', such as 'The Stahlhelm fights in the Third Reich and rules in the Fourth', and 'In the Third Reich we march, in the Fourth we rule.'[54] Other agents reported people singing verses such as the following:

> Heil Hitler ist der deutsche Gruß;
> Die Reichswehr steht Gewehr bei Fuß.
> Blomberg wartet auf den grossen Krach,
> Und dann sagen wir wieder 'Guten Tag'.[56]
>
> ('Heil Hitler' is the German greeting;
> The army's poised to give a beating.
> Blomberg's waiting for the mighty fray,
> And then we'll once more say 'Good day'.)

To what extent was Hitler aware of all this? It is hardly conceivable that he remained aloof; on the contrary, his policy-making was deeply affected. Realizing how precarious the situation was and sensing the danger of letting current trends continue, he had no option but to act to defuse the tension. It was no coincidence that the principal speeches delivered at the party congress in September related to internal politics, for the acute unrest caused by antisemitic agitation and violence sharpened the contradictions of the Nazi system. It particularly brought into relief the imbalance between the legal status of the Jews in Germany – and therefore also the practical limitations of the policies against them – and the pervasive hostility towards them. Three issues were at the centre of popular discontent and awaited resolution: Jewish access to German citizenship; the question of 'race defilement'; and the boycott of Jewish enterprises. The need to clarify and define the status of the Jews in Germany was essential if the radical outbursts were to be stopped. It was plain to Hitler that the campaign against the Jews was so far advanced that the only way to control it was to legalize it. This was the reality which preceded the rally of September 1935 and paved the way for the Nuremberg Laws. The racial laws served as a massive tranquillizer. They not only symbolized the exclusion of Jews from German society, but also provided a legitimization of the preceding wave of riots and the arrests of Jews that had accompanied them. At the same time, they stopped the political instability that these riots had created.

THE NUREMBERG LAWS

Two of the laws promulgated in September 1935 served as the legal basis of all subsequent measures excluding the Jews from German life, and of the regime's developing antisemitic policy. Defined as constitutional laws (*Verfassungsgesetze*), they were proclaimed at a special session of the Reichstag summoned to Nuremberg during the annual party rally in that city, and consisted of a citizenship law and a law 'for the Protection of German Blood and Honour'; between November 1935 and July 1943 they were complemented by thirteen implementation ordinances. The citizenship law stated that only Germans or those of related blood could be citizens of the Reich. German Jews lost their political rights and were made *Staatsangehörige* (state subjects), while 'Aryan' Germans were declared *Reichsbürger* (citizens of the Reich). The 'protection' law prohibited marriages and extramarital intercourse between Jews and Germans, the employment of German maids under the age of forty-five in Jewish households, and the hoisting of the German flag by Jews. With the promulgation of these laws the exceptions made for First World War veterans and state officials holding their posts before 1914 were invalidated.[56]

Most historians portray the preparation of these laws as a hasty operation on the eve of the Reichstag convention. Their argument runs as follows. On 12 September, Hitler summoned the Reichstag for an extraordinary session to be held on the evening of Sunday the 15th, to receive a declaration by the government. The last time the Reichstag had been convened was on 21 May, to adopt Hitler's fundamental twelve points of Nazi foreign policy. This time too, it was believed, Hitler meant to deliver an address on Germany's foreign policy, in the solemn presence of the foreign diplomatic staff. However, on the morning of the 13th, because of an unexpected change in Mussolini's course, Hitler decided to evade the foreign-policy issue. To fill the vacuum thus created on the festive day, he decided instead, at the last minute, to drop his intention to deal with external affairs and instead to address the Jewish issue. He ordered the laws to be drafted by Nazi experts on the Jewish question, who were flown to Nuremberg and told to formulate rapidly a law regulating marriages between Jews and Germans. Thereafter, Hitler chose one of four drafts and presented it to the Reichstag for approval.[57]

This account is fundamentally deficient not only because it is based entirely on conjectural circumstances, ignoring the troubled political climate described above, but also because it relies on a dubious source: the testimony given at the Nuremberg trials by Bernhard Lösener, the man in charge of racial affairs at the Reich Ministry of the Interior at the time. We must remember that Lösener's account was part of his defence at the post-war trials. Like other functionaries he justified remaining in his post with the excuse that only thus could he prevent worse things happening. Since he disclaimed any responsibility for the preparation of antisemitic legislation, it was vital for him to invent the legend of Hitler's last-minute improvisation. Lösener's story does not, however, match the facts. These clearly indicate that the laws were not improvised, but the result of meticulous long-term planning, with the party congress providing the appropriate occasion to unveil them.

First, the laws related directly to the party platform and the principles outlined in Hitler's writings. Point 4 of the party programme states, 'None but members of the nation may be citizens of the state. None but those of German blood, whatever their creed, may be members of the nation. No Jew, therefore, may be a member of the nation.' Hitler demanded that the legislators retain this principle.

Second, clear indications of new antisemitic legislation had appeared in government statements long before September. As early as January 1935, at the start of the antisemitic campaign, and as a result of the radicals' political agitation, Minister of the Interior Frick had clearly signalled the Third Reich's intention of revoking the citizenship of German Jews.[58] In fact, since February large groups of Jews had already been deprived of German citizenship, particularly those naturalized after the First World War. Frick repeated the regime's intention in an interview to the press in April, when the tide of antisemitic incitement was again rising. The timing of the statement shows that it was no mere lip-service to the Nazi programme, but an effort to satisfy the radicals and restore calm. His announcement was printed in the local press, both Jewish and German, as well as in the foreign press.[59] Moreover, in May a prominent leader of the Jewish community in Berlin spoke of imminent legislation to revoke the Jews' citizenship: the Königsberg Gestapo reported that Rabbi Dr Prinz, at a meeting called by the Zionist movement, had said that the new citizenship law would make the Jews state subjects (*Staatsangehörige*) instead of citizens.[60] The fact that he used the term actually employed in the legislation suggests that he was drawing on reliable information, rather than indulging in pessimistic guesswork. In August it was expected that Streicher, at a speech in Berlin, would announce new anti-Jewish legislation which would set a limit to indiscriminate violence. Since this did not happen, the matter was expected to crop up at the party congress. Schacht pointed in this direction at the opening of the Twenty-third Eastern Fair at Königsberg on 18 August. Although the part of his speech which dealt with antisemitic violence was censored out of the German News Agency reports, comments on the speech were published by some of the non-Nazi newspapers as well as by the National Bank. In this way its content reached the public in Germany and abroad. Schacht hinted that legislation on the Jewish question was being prepared and that, until it came into effect, the existing law was to be observed. Even foreign correspondents reported on the imminent legislation. In August the *Jewish Chronicle* stated that 'the new citizenship law is to be officially proclaimed at the Nazi party congress to open in Nuremberg on September 10th.' In early September the *New York Times* correspondent reported that Hitler was to proclaim new laws defining the status of the Jews and that the Academy of German Law and the Reich Ministry of Justice were working on the matter. According to him, the new laws would deprive the Jews of citizenship and make them state subjects; forbid intermarriage; extend the areas of activity reserved for 'Aryans'; and confirm business restrictions. Finally, in its rally in the sports palace of Berlin, the SA was ordered to prepare the masses for the introduction of the laws, which were to come as the climax to a series of mass meetings designed to arouse the people to antisemitism.[61] All this evidence makes the allegation that the legislation was hastily improvised untenable.

Furthermore, the individual clauses of the laws were aimed at sanctioning the disabilities already imposed in practice, and the party congress was the appropriate setting for the government to regularize the situation. For example, the clause forbidding Jews to fly the German flag had been preceded in February and April by decrees forbidding Jews to display either of the two national flags.[62] As to the clause forbidding intermarriage, it had been largely pre-empted by local initiatives. In December 1934, Streicher convened a conference of doctors who conveyed a petition to Frick requesting state punishment for 'race defilement'. They demanded that German women consorting with Jews be deprived of citizenship, sent to a concentration camp and sterilized. The Jewish partner was to lose his citizenship, have his property confiscated, and after serving five years in a concentration camp be deported. For months the Nazi press attacked Berlin's marriage-licence office for permitting marriages between Germans and Jews. In other places the SA demonstrated in front of houses of recently married couples in which one of the spouses was Jewish. In May 1935 Streicher referred in his speeches to the forthcoming bar on marriages between Jews and Germans. In early August Goebbels announced that these marriages would be banned, and in the same month the Württemberg Minister of the Interior issued a decree under which applications to license such marriages would be delayed indefinitely.[63]

When the party congress opened, people wondered about Hitler's stand: would he endorse the radicals' violence or the conservatives' denunciations of it? The laws aimed to clarify the situation to all factions. They were presented to the radicals as a move to implement the party's platform and fulfil its original promises; to the conservatives as a measure designed to ensure stability through racial segregation; and to the public, to quote Hitler, as 'a basis which would enable the German people to find some tolerable attitude towards the Jews.'[64] Hitler's own standpoint was made plain in his final speech on 16 September. He warned that the party would be employed wherever the state bureaucracy failed to act on the basis of Nazi ideology. He stated,'I would like to make it clear that...whatever can be solved by the state will be solved through the state, but any problem which the state through its essential character is unable to solve will be solved by means of the movement.'[65] On the Jewish question, Hitler made it clear that the new legislation was not the end of the matter. If bureaucracy or rigid legalism or insufficient enthusiasm hindered state officials in the execution of antisemitic policy, the party, free to act outside the state, would be the appropriate agency to take corrective action.[66]

While internal developments forced the regime to bring in new legislation, external events also had an influence on the timing and nature of the Nuremberg Laws. This was certainly the case with the third of these three laws, the flag law. At the end of July, New York workers tore down the Swastika flag from the German ship *Bremen* and threw it into the Hudson river. As a result, several dock workers were arrested and a serious diplomatic incident clouded relations between Germany and the United States. On 7 September the American magistrate Louis Brodsky ordered five of the six defendants to be released and delivered an attack on Nazism. This turn of events received wide coverage in the German press, and it was held to have so enraged Hitler that he impulsively ordered the Swastika banner to be proclaimed the new German flag. The War Ministry was informed a few hours before the law was due to be passed and voiced the army's protests against having to march beneath a party flag. Finally, however, von Blomberg managed to reach a compromise with Hitler.[67]

The anti-Nazi declarations of the Comintern congress held in Moscow were also presented as an excuse for the antisemitic legislation. A close look at the speeches of Hess and Goebbels, as well as Hitler's address read by Adolf Wagner in Nuremberg, shows that the laws were explained as a response to the Comintern's attack on Nazism. This fitted in neatly with the Nazi theory that Bolshevism and Judaism were synonymous. Hess's opening address on 11 September made this point clear by contrasting Nazism with its antithesis, communism, and by equating the latter with Jewry when referring to the Bolshevist offensive announced at the Comintern congress. In his words, Germany was determined to destroy the influence of Jews who had been open or secret supporters of Bolshevism in Germany. To root out communism was to fight the Jews, and vice versa: 'as national Socialism destroys Jewish influence, Marxism simultaneously collapses', he declared.[68] However, if the speeches justifying the laws were prepared as a response to the Comintern declaration, we must remember that the Comintern congress was held in the first half of August, and closed a month before the Nazi rally in Nuremberg. There was plenty of time for the Nazi civil servants to formulate their laws and for the leaders to prepare their speeches before the Nuremberg rally opened.

Summing up, we have seen that, contrary to the common view, the Nuremberg Laws were not a sudden improvisation having little to do with the actual progress of the Jewish question, but an attempted solution to the internal contradictions and tensions which Hitler perceived as driving the party and country towards political deadlock. With the party convention providing the appropriate occasion, they put into effect a policy which had been in preparation for months, and which enabled Hitler to maintain the precarious equilibrium between the conservatives and the radicals. He preserved the prestige of the party and at the same time prevented it from taking action independently of the government.

3
Internal Crisis and Foreign Policy

We have explored the dynamics of the relationship between developments in the Third Reich and the activation of the public to prevent the loss of revolutionary momentum. In this chapter I shall argue that foreign-policy decisions can also be seen to be intimately bound up with the domestic situation, and that to a considerable extent those domestic conditions triggered the execution of Nazi expansionist plans and accelerated antisemitic policy.

Let us begin by placing this contention in historiographical perspective. The interaction between internal and external policy in the Third Reich has received considerable scholarly treatment and has lately become a highly controversial issue. On the one hand there are historians who claim that the immediate pre-war years were characterized by a profound internal crisis. This crisis both generated and precipitated Germany's aggressive drive for expansion. Martin Broszat advanced the view that Hitler's radical foreign policy was a means to overcome internal emergencies, and he was followed by other functionalist researchers, who similarly attributed the crisis to the decomposition of the 'polycratic' regime in Nazi Germany. In their opinion, the failure of political integration, because of institutional Darwinism, had the inevitable consequence of an outlet in war.[1] For Hans Mommsen, for example, the pressure produced by the never-ending conflicts between the different forces in the Third Reich led inexorably to self-annihilation. Renewed radicalism, the war and even the Final Solution were means employed by the Nazi regime to escape from a state of emergency.[2] This interpretation minimizes the importance of a Nazi programme based on ideological premises, or negates its existence altogether. Hence, while these views recognize the integrative function of the Führer myth, they see Hitler as an insecure dictator, easily influenced by others, and totally dependent on the Nazi polyarchy. If this is the case, the radicalized foreign drive of 1938 and the added mass mobilization were a mere substitute for policy, though in time it became a goal in its own right. Tim Mason, for example, advocated the view that the timing of war was decisively influenced by the need to deflect attention from internal problems, particularly the economic crisis and the growing class conflict. He put this point in unequivocal terms: 'I do not for the moment see a need to modify my own view that the timing, tactics and hence also the strategic confusion of Hitler's war of expansion were decisively influenced by the politic-economic need for plunder, a need which was enhanced by the very wars necessary to satisfy it!'[3]

Intentionalist historians play down the influence of a socio-economic crisis in 1938–9 on the Nazi policy-making process. They maintain that, had there been such a crisis, it would not have had any influence, for terror could have quelled all forces undermining Hitler's authority. Exponents of this view argue that Hitler's popularity persisted in all segments of German society, and hence his decisions derived exclusively from political calculations on when to achieve long-term goals. If this was the case, the timing for Hitler's radical foreign policy depended solely on the existing international situation. To Klaus Hildebrand, one of the leading spokesmen of this school, 'crisis situations never dictated the political direction of the regime.'[4] Otto D. Kulka, although closer to the intentionalist school, accepts the picture portrayed by the SD reports. The Nazi observers considered the intense activation of conservative elements by church circles as endangering the very existence of the Nazi regime. Hence the significance of the year 1938 as a starting-point for Hitler's radicalized policy and the aggressive drive for the realization of his ideological goals in the following years.[5]

It seems that we can, to a certain extent, reconcile the conflicting interpretations of functionalists and intentionalists. There was indeed a crisis in the pre-war years, and its dimensions can for certain be established using a variety of sources from the Reich and abroad. However, what matters is whether or not this crisis influenced Hitler's decisions. In his eyes, the major crisis was not the economic difficulties of 1938–9, but the unprecedented political apathy, coupled with the conservative and clerical oppositionist attitudes towards the Nazi Party, in 1937.

Since the tension between institutionalization and radicalization was a permanent characteristic of relations between the regime and the people in the Third Reich, we should not look at the crisis of 1937 as an isolated phenomenon. It marked a deep trough in the constantly fluctuating relations between the regime and the public. From 1934 on, waves of feverish activism frequently ended in despondency and political fatigue. But the fact that the term 'unprecedented low' keeps cropping up in the reports on public mood of

1937 indicates an accumulated lack of confidence much worse in its scope and scale than in former years. Political weariness and civil lethargy were the source of Nazism's strength as a ruling system. There is no doubt that they became, in time, the pillars which supported the Third Reich, and due to them the Nazis had virtually a free hand to carry out their policy. From Hitler's vantage point, however, the eclipse of popular enthusiasm in 1937 became a sign of Nazism's weakness as a political religion.

That the aggressive foreign policy resulted from the regime's gaining power and stability is beyond dispute, but it is equally true that Hitler's decisions reflect not only the regime's external position but also the domestic order. Strategic goals existed, but the timing changed due to the need to reinforce public support for the regime. Hitler believed that, without an ingenious mobilization of the masses, the very existence of Nazism as a doctrine based on popular acclamation would be seriously endangered and its goals imperilled.

The skilful deflection of political or other tensions onto an external factor whilst waging an aggressive foreign policy is a tactic of which history furnished many examples. But it gained special significance under the Nazi regime, where the possibilities of mass mobilization and manipulation reached supreme refinement. Here, foreign policy was utilized to the maximum degree as an integrative factor for purposes of political socialization and system consolidation.

Hitler's resolute decision to quit the League of Nations in 1933 can be attributed, at least partially, to considerations of political integration. If we are to believe Hermann Rauschning, Hitler tickled the patriotic vanity of the Germans through this move. He said, 'I had to do it.... Perhaps the difficulties increased temporarily, but opposite these difficulties weighs the trust I gained from the German people.'[6] At a meeting with the military senior command in 1944, he gave similar reasons when he explained his motives for going to war. To other factors

The psychological aspects must be added: the mobilization of German national power. It is impossible to keep enthusiasm and readiness for sacrifice placed in a jar and preserved. Enthusiasm and readiness for sacrifice appear once in the context of revolution, and then they wither. Grey day-to-day routine, comfort, cause the magic to fade and turn the people back into satiated bourgeoisie.[7]

Both quotations point not to the opportunistic nature of Hitler's foreign policy but to something far more significant. Parallel to his success in consolidating his power base and winning the support of the German public, the whirling escalation in foreign policy and the tremendous impulse to reach immediate objectives were aimed at preventing internal ideological and political paralysis. The radicalization to reinforce consensus and recapture revolutionary momentum was by no means a substitute for ideological motives; in fact, the opposite is true: it served as a means to reach these objectives, in both internal and foreign affairs.

THE REMILITARIZATION OF THE RHINELAND

The remilitarization of the Rhineland shows that, even when the strategic objectives were firmly anchored in Nazi doctrine, the actual timing of measures was dependent on, and derived from, the internal situation in the Reich.

Hitler saw the appropriate time for this step in the spring of 1937. This becomes apparent in a memo from Ulrich von Hassell, then German ambassador in Rome, as well as in the words of Hitler himself in an address delivered in April 1937.[8] Strategic considerations and an assessment of the international balance of power undoubtedly helped determine Hitler's move. He assumed that the international alignment of forces would facilitate a more aggressive foreign policy: Britain would do no more than impose economic sanctions; Italy, busy with its campaign of conquest in Ethiopia, was cut off from the Western powers; and he could count on quiet on the Polish border. The remilitarization did not take place as originally envisaged, however, but more than a year earlier. What changed Hitler's schedule? On the basis of our sources we can argue that the tense climate in the Reich called for measures of some kind and most likely precipitated the remilitarization.

In February 1936, von Hassell marked in his diary, 'It is interesting to note from a conversation with von Neurath that in his view, Hitler's chief motive in foreign affairs is internal policy: Hitler senses the waning of public backing for the regime and is looking for a national motto which will revive the enthusiasm of the masses.'[9] The opinion voiced by the German Foreign Minister was well founded. The attentive examination of the reports on the mood in Germany at the end of 1935 and the start of 1936 suggests that the Winter Olympics, and the excitement surrounding the preparations for the summer games in Berlin, were not a sufficient substitute for a comprehensive solution to the acute internal problems, particularly the economic ones.

There is abundant evidence that at the end of 1935 the overall picture showed growing dissent. The deteriorating economic situation, the diminishing foreign-currency reserves and the added hardships of importing raw materials continued to affect the daily life of all sectors of the population. Sopade's November report on Rhineland-Westphalia says that in all social classes disquiet was reaching a critical stage. Socialist informers attributed the restlessness to the severe shortage of raw materials.[10] The Bavarian report from the same source observes that the Nazi Party had instituted a systematic propaganda campaign to boost public morale in light of the prevailing discontent.[11] In December another socialist reporter concluded, without mincing his words, 'There is a general confidence crisis in the regime at the moment.'[12] This emphatic assessment should not be dismissed as the wishful thinking of an active anti-Nazi, for it is confirmed by the reports of the German security services themselves. In January the Berlin Gestapo detected a further deterioration in the public mood, and pessimism that grew from week to week. It stated that, even if there were no blatant denunciations of Nazi principles, there was no mistaking the enveloping apathy and utter political weariness, accompanied by complaints and criticism. The public sensed that there was no hope of the situation improving. The Gestapo commentator believed that the voices of dissent were reaching dangerous proportions because the public was not prepared to turn a blind eye to trivial problems, but tended to place them within a broader context of overall negative criticism.[13] The message of this report was clear: so long as there were spectacular victories, the Germans were prepared, despite their grumbling, to put up with personal inconveniences. Without such victories in the near future, criticism would mount.

A considerable amount of material has been preserved on the mood of the workers. From Dortmund, for instance, we learn that workers' opinions on political issues were significantly influenced by whether they expected party promises to be fulfilled. The facts that millions remained unemployed and that real earnings continued to be eroded were seen as underlining the regime's failure to close the social gap.[14] The Aachen Gestapo gave a concrete illustration of the public mood in this area, pointing to the poor participation in the festivities of 30 January, the anniversary of the Nazi Party's accession to power. The commentator warned of the political consequences of this atmosphere, and predicted that in the elections to the workers' councils, scheduled for April, a considerable number of workers would give expression to their negative attitude to the party by rejecting its candidates.[15] In Berlin pessimism coupled with political weariness was vented in similar forms of non-conformist behaviour: by demonstrative abstentions from displaying the German salute, by deriding and discrediting the news reported on the radio and in the press, and by criticizing the activities of the SA and the Hitler Youth.[16]

It could be argued that local factors in industrial districts brought about this crisis of confidence, but these do not seem to have been particularly significant. The displays of non-conformity among peasants in agricultural regions seem to have been much like those of workers in urban areas. This we learn from surveys from Kiel, Koblenz, Münster, Dortmund and Frankfurt. The report from Frankfurt noted that especially in Catholic districts the farmers were utterly uninterested in mass politics, and this was expressed in their refusal to contribute to the winter aid campaign and to participate in party rallies.[17] Even coming to rallies hardly indicated commitment. The Cologne Gestapo was particularly perceptive when it pointed out that attendance at meetings could not be taken as an indicator of real mood.[18]

The mounting tension in the relations between the regime and the population, evident in the reports from November 1935 to January 1936, grew even sharper in February, the month in which the decision for remilitarization was taken. A report from Berlin throws light on this low in relations:

Whereas three months ago the public still stood behind the Third Reich's foreign policy, its position has since then changed. The signing of the Franco-Russian agreement, which the press had considered unlikely, and Great Britain's cautious attitude towards Germany have increased the sense of international isolation. In addition, the military agreement between Czechoslovakia and the Soviet Union has only reinforced the public feeling that Germany is under siege. Internally, matters have deteriorated even further: numerous groups are expressing dissatisfaction, and concern over the future has invaded the ranks of even Hitler's faithful followers. While it is true that these attitudes are not easily discerned on the surface, because of the policy of surveillance, they are nevertheless voiced openly in restricted circles. The public is increasingly beginning to feel that matters cannot continue this way, and change must come.[19]

The vast amount of available material also reveals what people complained about. They criticized political favouritism, widespread nepotism and the corruption of functionaries, especially the luxurious life styles of party leaders in a time of general shortages. The guidelines issued to industrialists to reward local party leaders in order to gain their good will were also well known and criticized. And it was equally no secret that newspapers were instructed on what to report and what to hide. The reports even mentioned oppositionist trends reminiscent of the crisis of the summer of 1935: the possibility of a takeover by the army and the establishment of a right-wing dictatorship by means of a 'second 30 June 1934' seemed real. The Gestapo warned against underestimating the reports, or misinterpreting them: these were not common grumblings about the shortage of consumer goods, but indications of a widespread basic lack of faith in the regime.[20] A similar assessment of the situation led the Düsseldorf Gestapo to conclude that temporary tactics to distract the population would not be effective.[21]

Indeed, all indications are that the success of the Winter Olympics may have momentarily distracted the public, but that apathy soon returned and stayed, despite attempts to restore confidence in Nazism. Sizable sections of the urban population, who had facilitated the party's successes, betrayed visible signs of weariness and lack of faith. The farmers became even more apathetic than in previous months. The Münster Gestapo again reported that the peasants were staying away from political meetings.[22] In Wesermünde, they and the 'better circles' also refused to wave flags and openly rejected party symbols.[23] The general climate was aptly summed up by the Frankfurt Gestapo, which categorically affirmed that 'the public mood has reached its lowest ebb since [the party] came to power.'[24]

As the analysis of previous years has shown, the party did not remain immune to this atmosphere. It is evident from both regional and national reports that pessimism filtered into its ranks. The Bad Kreuznach county, for example, reported that political enthusiasm had waned everywhere, to be replaced by gloom, apathy and fatalistic resignation. The fighting spirit had vanished even in the party itself, and its members felt that the Nazi movement was experiencing a worse crisis than the one it had undergone before gaining power.[25] Summarizing the situation for the entire district, the Koblenz Gestapo complained that, while party members might not voice the same sort of criticism as was heard from the general public, it was nevertheless exceedingly difficult to mobilize them for action.[26] Again, this was not just a local problem. The Gestapo in Schleswig-Holstein reported that the general opinion among party members was that there was no longer any point in campaigning on behalf of the Nazi world view.[27]

It is clear that, despite Hitler's popularity, the Nazi Party was losing ground in its attempt to mobilize a devoted racial community. It had largely succeeded in obtaining conformity, but was failing to mobilize the masses. Hence the artificial, outward homogeneity was rightly regarded by the leadership as fragile and in need of permanent reinforcement. From this we may reasonably conclude that the need for a propaganda coup precisely at this time, in February–March 1936, was symptomatic of the Nazi regime's insecurity rather than its strength. A system based on mass politics could hardly afford public apathy, let alone mounting criticism. A propaganda coup appealing to nationalist instincts could return momentum to the party, and annul the growing feeling that slogans had no guiding influence on the public. Thus we can hypothesize that Hitler found in the remilitarization of the Rhineland a way to overcome basic difficulties and prevent the diffusion of pessimism.

It is striking that this time there was no attempt to mobilize the masses through aggressive antisemitic policy, as had been the case in previous years. On the contrary, in the period following the proclamation of the Nuremberg Laws the Jewish question died down, for two major reasons. First, in giving top priority to Germany's rearmament, Hitler had to take into account Schacht's warnings that antisemitism damaged Germany's efforts to acquire raw materials. Second, and equally vital, there was the need to consider Germany's image during the Olympic Games. As is evident from the reports, local antisemitic activity was still a significant factor, but the policy of restraint and the enforcement of public order designed to protect the festive atmosphere surrounding the Winter Olympics in Garmisch and even more so the summer games in Berlin, gradually made themselves felt. Eminently illustrative of this policy were the orders curbing all independent actions following the killing in February 1936 of Wilhelm Gustloff, the party leader in Switzerland, by a Jewish student. Hitler himself repulsed spontaneous requests for retaliation on German Jewry, fearing that Jewish pressure might induce the United States to withdraw its team and thus do irreparable propaganda damage.[28]

The remilitarization of the Rhineland could not solve all the problems, but it could temporarily dull public senses and restore faith in the party. However, like all the other propaganda coups, this one hardly changed the general atmosphere and did not succeed in converting apathy and fatalism into enthusiasm. The summer of 1936 was therefore again marked by a significant worsening of the public mood. This assertion is not based on the Gestapo or local-government reports, since they were stopped that April, but on other surveys compiled by various party organizations. And, if the party reports, which on the whole tend to present a rosier picture of reality, say that the public were in a despondent mood, there can be no doubt that they were.

The picture conveyed by the party surveys strongly resembles the one in the Sopade material for the same period. A glance at the reports of the Nazi Women's Union immediately reveals the growing alienation between the public and the party. We repeatedly read that the variegated propaganda campaigns were widely and disdainfully spurned. Thus, the party official in charge of canvassing in Krefeld was definite in her assessment: 'The statements of the collectors on the mood of Krefeld's population are shattering.'[29] In reading the documents for this period it is impossible not to notice the mounting feelings of frustration among the party's activists. The Sopade report for July 1936 refers to the sense of disappointment among party veterans, particularly in the SA.[30] Once more, in the absence of real activity to sustain momentum, processes of dissolution gradually set in and the already familiar situation returned. The sense of strength and confidence from Nazism's achievements was mixed with apprehensions of political stagnation. Small wonder, then, that the reports from all parts of the Reich point to the resurgent conflict of tendencies we encountered in 1934 and 1935: on the one hand waning discipline and the dissolution of entire units in the SA, and on the other the radicals again clamouring for the fulfilment of the Nazi platform and the preservation of its vital spirit. It must be borne in mind that the SA, which was supposed to preserve the revolutionary *élan*, in fact busied itself with competitions, parades and selling party symbols on the streets –

activities which could hardly enhance its members' sense of advancing the revolution.[31]

Given this situation the Nazi leadership again sought a way to rouse the public from its apathy and find some objectives for the radicals, so that the party would not appear to be failing in its tasks. Integrative propaganda campaigns consequently intensified. The pre-eminence given to the campaign to combat waste, for example, was to have practical political results – to foster among the public the illusion of common responsibility for the success of national programmes. It seems, however, that the regime was unsuccessful in restoring faith to the apathetic masses. The Sopade report on Westphalia encapsulates the general climate in the Reich: on the whole the population was not enthusiastic about the Nazi order.[32]

Despite the propaganda efforts no change occurred, for the vicious circle detected in previous years repeated itself. The fatalistic mood that took root, coupled now with the beginnings of war psychosis, nullified any oppositionist force. Depoliticization produced a political paralysis which assured the stability of the regime but at the same time was contrary to Nazi objectives, since it entailed a lack of readiness to act on behalf of any ideal, including those fostered by party propaganda.

Underlying Hitler's speech at the party rally in September 1936 was the reality we have described from which he wished to 'escape forward'. By raising the party's prestige and creating a renewed radicalization, he hoped to prevent a loss of revolutionary momentum after the Olympics. Among other things he reminded the party of its duty to overcome the public's defeatist attitudes:

The party must first of all be the carrier of our optimism which characterizes us as National Socialists. Any vice must be subdued and this is easier to do than to remove pessimism and its consequences.... The party must penetrate in the hearts of the masses for it is our best and strongest belief-carrier.[33]

FROM CRISIS TO WAR

In 1937 the Nazi Party enormously expanded its organization, seizing total control of all spheres of life in Germany. In many areas, especially in small towns and villages, the party functioned as a substitute for traditional and even religious institutions, becoming the focus of social and cultural life. Thus the process of imposing totalitarianism apparently reached its zenith. On the face of it, the extent to which Nazism took root was indicated by the millions of Germans who joined the party in this year. In sharp contrast to the outward image of political dynamism and inner cohesion, however, the reports on the public mood indicate the exact opposite: political decline and ritualization, public apathy and ideological stagnation – processes which ran contrary to the Nazi ideal of mass mobilization.

The increased membership of the party cannot serve as an indicator of active popular support, since a wide range of motives, ranging from sincere identification to unscrupulous opportunism, drive people to join the ruling party in a political system such as Nazism. The relations between the regime and the people in fact seem to have reached their lowest level in this year, and numerous signs clearly point in this direction. The public enthusiasm that had greeted the Nazis when they came to power had diminished. It seems that one of the underlying motives for the campaign in 1937 to expand party membership was – in addition to the wish to raise money from membership fees to finance the growing bureaucracy – the desire to increase the numbers who could be brought to rallies, so as to create an image of internal strength. However, despite the end of unemployment and despite Germany's foreign-policy gains, these rallies could no longer ensure the political dynamism of the people and convince them to become involved in the fight for Nazi goals.

As research has shown, economic factors continued to erode public morale; price increases and shortages of raw materials played a prominent role in creating a climate of social unrest. Added to this, the frequent call-up exercises and the stepped-up military training fuelled the fear of an approaching war – a mood which appeared in 1936, and reached new heights in 1937. Particularly influential on the public mood were the developments in the international arena: Germany's involvement on the Spanish front; the Japanese offensive in China and fears of Russian intervention there, which could bring about German actions against the Soviet Union. A socialist commentator monitoring the mood in Berlin said that

According to the assessment of different observers, unconnected to each other, there is a mood change in the Berlin population of dimensions not previously seen. Whoever wishes to gain a picture of the attitude of the population to the regime has to draw the conclusion that there are almost no followers of National Socialism any more.[34]

Even if this report was exaggerated, there is no doubt that it pointed in the correct direction. Other sources furnish a more judicious evaluation of the state of affairs: for instance, a British diplomat in Berlin reported his impression that 'At no time since 1933 has there been so little genuine enthusiasm for the regime.'[35]

Different sectors voiced their own particular criticisms. Nationalists and representatives of 'big business' condemned the way in which the country was governed. They complained that Hitler stood aloof from current affairs, and expressed their bitterness over the incompetence and failure of the Nazi administration. The better-educated Germans were deeply disappointed by the brutal nature of the Third Reich. In their eyes National Socialism was merely National Bolshevism. One of the reports, for example, recorded the mood of intellectuals who had never been close to the Left, yet were now inclined to adopt anti-Nazi attitudes. They were seeking a new political orientation and, in contrast to the general apathy, held lively political discussions.[36] A report from north-western Germany tells of the utter contempt in which the vulgarity and philistinism of the regime were held. Compulsion to attend propaganda meetings at which uneducated party activists preached the Nazi doctrine was found particularly annoying by the educated classes.[37] However, as in other sectors of the population, criticism was not translated into the active opposition that could lead to political upheaval. All hopes for overthrowing the system were centred on a right-wing dictatorship under the armed forces.

The general atmosphere did not escape the attention of foreign diplomats. The British ambassador was impressed by the negative mood in Berlin and reported examples of what he had heard from Nazi circles. A Nazi official in Berlin had stated that the contributions in his district to Hitler's birthday present were very bad. 'Of over 4,000 potential subscribers, only half had contributed anything; of course the remainder would be forced to pay up, but the fact that they had not done so voluntarily revealed a bad spirit.'[38] The Italian ambassador went so far as to claim that Hitler had little genuine popularity in Berlin, a judgement which seemed to be confirmed by the lukewarm crowds at Hitler's birthday celebrations.[39] This public mood expressed itself in reluctance to take part in party ceremonies and parades, even in the party conference celebrations, which were naturally of a political nature. Whereas in the early years of Nazi rule the participants in party celebrations were received with applause when marching through the streets, in 1937 the enthusiasm virtually disappeared. People claimed that the ceremonies were boring and the speeches too familiar; the party was no longer seen as a redeeming force. It proved difficult to recruit people to travel to the Nuremberg rally. The only ones whose faith was still strengthened by these rallies were the fanatics.[40]

The picture drawn by socialist exiles and foreign observers is supported by internal Nazi documents. We find concrete evidence of a growing crisis of confidence even in party surveys which attempt to prettify reality. Reports by the Nazi Women's Union often contain assessments of worsening public attitudes to the Nazi Party. Even the growth of party membership failed to improve the situation. The apathy continued to manifest itself and weakened the self-confidence of party members themselves. Thus, for example, a party

leader from Berlin vented his bitterness saying, 'the public is entirely uninterested. We run four times a week to party meetings and who comes? Always
the same people.'[41]

Nazism, as a system of mass politics based on charismatic leadership,
needed permanent acclamation; it could not complacently acquiesce in a
reality which called into question its very nature. It is hardly surprising that it
tried to stop the public from descending into lassitude. Consider the huge
propaganda campaign which began in 1937. In one month 320 political
meetings were reported from the Rhineland, Westphalia and Silesia. In
Saxony alone, 1,350 meetings and rallies were held in the space of two weeks.[42]
It seems, however, that these national campaigns, like their predecessors,
failed to achieve the desired results. In most cases they merely added to
people's feelings of having had enough and so deepened their apathy and
alienated them still further. When examining the reports for the months
following the propaganda campaigns, we once again notice the limits of
indoctrination. From Bavaria, for example, we hear that the public had
become so apathetic that never since the Nazis came to power had participation in political events been so poor.[43]

In reading about the 1937 campaign we again confront the paradoxical
situation of previous years. The system managed to break social and cultural
frameworks and achieve a certain atomization of society. It succeeded in
isolating individuals but failed to harness them to Nazi ideals, whether
through compulsory organization or indoctrination. This resigned apathy, and
the ensuing depoliticization of large segments of the population, dulled their
receptivity to any political message, the Nazi one included.

It is noteworthy, however, that there was a distinct limit to apathy. In
earlier years, particularly in the summer of 1935, it was provided by the
breach of law and order through antisemitic violence; now it was the attack on
the Catholic Church and Christian values that prompted the public to rise
from its lethargy. When the conflict between the Nazi state and the Catholic
Church worsened, following the Pope's proclamation of the encyclical 'With
Burning Concern', the Catholic public became openly hostile. Encouraged by
the enthusiasm of the flock and by the reluctance of the Nazis to react
sharply, the Catholic clergy adopted an aggressive attitude.

Reports from Catholic areas convey the mood of the church-going
Catholics at the time. Goebbels' suppression from the newspapers of any
reference to the encyclical on Germany was to no avail. The Pope's words
reached the Catholic population through the Church's own channels and
triggered a barrage of criticism. From Easter onwards, the bishops sent out
pastoral letters in which they called on their flock to protest in writing against
the restrictions on Catholic education. The Bishop of Trier even suspended a
priest who expressed approval of the undenominational schools. Against this

background a Nazi woman observer from the Catholic south commented, 'It seems that during the previous month there has again been a worsening of the public mood. Almost all local party cells have received reports that the public opposes the party and anything connected to it.'[44] A report from Westphalia corroborated this point: 'We are informed by Catholic circles that the state of affairs is worse than it was before the rise to power',[45] and a commentator from a neighbouring area summed up, 'the dissatisfaction in the public is greater than even before.'[46] As in 1935, there were again widespread rumours of a general realignment of forces in the Reich; and, although wild rumours and political jokes cannot convey exactly what was happening, they do, as before, provide a kaleidoscopic reflection of the public's expectations, tensions, anxieties and wishes. From Upper Bavaria we hear of a rumour that the army had set up a secret unit to wipe out the SA and the SS.[47] Similarly, rumours circulating in Munich and in Silesia referred to a coming clash between the army and the party.[48]

The significance of these developments extended far beyond their impact on the mood of the general public. It looks as though Nazi leaders feared that these waves of dissatisfaction would spread to the party itself. In the contagious atmosphere of articulated discontent, with the conservative circles increasing in strength, a new dimension of disappointment developed among party activists. And, indeed, in 1937 as in previous years, the processes that produced demoralization also generated renewed radicalism. The familiar picture of 1934, 1935 and 1936 returned. On the one hand, frustrated expectations in the party organizations brought a relaxation of discipline. A report from Saxony for July 1937 said that the local SS and SA had little taste for action.[49] A similar survey from Silesia noted that the fighting spirit had entirely disappeared from the party organizations.[50] On the other hand, the disappointment of many radicals stimulated them to fresh outbursts of radicalism. Some of them allegedly went so far as to accuse Hitler of treachery.[51] Reports from all corners of the Reich – Bavaria, Berlin, Silesia and Pfalz – tell of a rejuvenated revolutionary mood among Nazi veterans and SA men, who claimed that Hitler had betrayed the revolution and that Goering had sold out to the reactionaries.[52]

At this point we must ask whether a majority of the population were disaffected with the regime, and, if so, whether the consensus underpinning the Nazi system was really endangered. One must be constantly wary of unwarranted conclusions. We have always to bear in mind that the reports never speak of dissent mounting to active opposition. The various manifestations of non-conformity remained isolated and thus without political importance. We do not find during this period, or later, the crystallization of trends in an organizational framework which could be of practical, operative significance. And, though we can point to deep dissonance between large segments of the population and the party, there is no doubt that this tension was decisively mitigated by Hitler. There is not the least hint that the bulk of the public lost its religious faith in Hitler and his charismatic leadership. We constantly meet the claim that the Führer was surrounded by a wall of corrupt functionaries who prevented him from knowing the true situation in the country. Beyond the adoration of Hitler, another major reason for the consent granted to the system, despite the criticism of specific issues, was the fear that chaos would reign once Nazism, and what remained of state order, was routed.

For Hitler this was not enough, however. In *his understanding of reality*, the party's loss of power in shaping public opinion, along with the mounting unrest among workers and Catholics, and the dissent among conservatives, was endangering the system's ability to mobilize the *entire* German population, create a monolithic *Volksgemeinschaft* (racial community) and realize Nazi ideals.

An SD report from January 1938 is an eloquent example of the leadership's perception of the significance of the crisis in the Reich. It alludes to the unparalleled impact of the two chief opponents to the Nazi world view and the Nazi state:

During the latest developments, two main opponents to the National Socialist world view and state have crystallized: the political churches and the reactionaries.... The results are felt in all areas of public life and in the ideological strengthening of all opposition groups.... In addition, the higher church leadership – both Catholic and Evangelical – intends to change the believers' resignation into dissatisfaction, urging them to display their opposition to the state. Cardinal Archbishop Faulhaber of Munich has been especially active in this direction. It is said that he has excellent relations with the rest of the ideological opposition in the Reich, who are undoubtedly most pleased with these church tactics. At the same time, the forces of the reactionaries have initiated unprecedented activity. This activity is intended to marshal all their power to remove all influence from the party and its organizations, especially the SS – even to exclude it completely from political life, transferring its authority to the army and giving the task of ideological and spiritual education to the churches.[53]

This alarming assessment also included the SD's views on the effect of these processes on the Jewish question: it claimed that increasing apathy, declining confidence in the regime, and growing oppositionist trends were preventing the active, antisemitic public pressure necessary to reverse the assimilation of Jewish society and rid Germany of the Jews. This danger had been pointed out in a SD document of January 1937, and was now repeated more emphatically.[54]

It is clear, then, that towards the end of 1937 and early in 1938 the struggle between the conservatives, the Catholic Church and the army, on the one hand, and the party, on the other, reached an open clash, and the delicate balance of power-sharing in the Third Reich was upset. The conservative supporters of the authoritarian state became too dangerous for Hitler and his radicals. It can be hypothesized that these developments were a major determining factor in Hitler's decisions from the end of 1937 and throughout 1938 to adopt a more aggressive policy. This was particularly so because Hitler, given his obsessive concern with ideological principles, granted these developments not only political but also ideological meaning: the increased strength of the conservatives and the Catholic Church could, according to Hitler, lead to ideological decay, stabilization of the state on the fascist model, and eventually the removal of Hitler himself. This contention can be based on an analysis of both his public and private statements.

First he had to regain the confidence of the radicals. An attempt to deal with their criticism of his 'moderate' political line was marked, for example, in the speech delivered before the party leadership at the end of April 1937. In his address, he presented at length the guidelines of the new regime in Germany, while making it clear that only the leader was entitled to decide when to implement this or that policy. In order to calm those who feared that revolutionary momentum had been lost, Hitler referred to the issue of Germany's foreign policy:

There are subjects which need not be mentioned…you already know what I mean. If we organize certain things in Germany, need we explain the why and wherefore? We know that, if the army is being rebuilt, we say that this is done only in order to ensure the peace; if we carry out the Four Year Plan, it is for the sake of economic survival. Only 'thus' should these subjects be mentioned. Every one of us knows this. There are thoughts which should not be translated into words.… This iron rule must be strictly kept. Each one may look into the eyes of the other, and see there that both are thinking the same way.[55]

Hitler likewise reassured party radicals who were pressing for antisemitic policies to be stepped up. In reaction to a newspaper article demanding that Jewish shops be marked he commented, 'As a matter of principle, in the party there are no demands.… Of whom does he [the journalist] make the demand? Who can decide on this question? I alone.… The question of marking has been studied for some years, and it is clear that one day it will be decided on; the final aim of our policy is entirely clear to every one of us.'[56]

In his speech at Augsburg on 21 November 1937, marking the fifteenth anniversary of the party's foundation in that city, he repeated his call on party members not to become unduly impatient and to retain full confidence in the leadership. He reminded his audience that in the Nazi system only those who gave orders, and not their subordinates, could criticize. To reassure his followers, he deliberately took this opportunity to hint again at his plans for the future: in foreign policy, an expansion of *Lebensraum*; at home, a return to the sources of Nazism, while enlisting mass support for the leadership.[57]

Furthermore, what was insinuated in his speeches was declared openly in a secret meeting at the end of 1937. The Hossbach protocol, one of the key documents for the history of the Third Reich, further proves the link between conditions prevailing in Germany and decision-making in foreign policy. Hitler's obsession with ideological principles is striking, as is the extent to which they dominated his decisions. It appears that he thought Germany to be thoroughly devitalized, and a renewal of revolutionary momentum the only escape from political sterility. In this case he sought to rejuvenate the system by means of an aggressive foreign policy, which was to begin with the annexation of Austria in March 1938, and continue with the Sudeten crisis in September 1938, the invasion of Czechoslovakia in March 1939, and the staging of the crisis which led to the attack on Poland in September 1939. Seen in this wider context, the memorandum is not just a plan for territorial expansion and for revision of the Versailles Treaty, but reveals how seriously foreign policy was affected by the internal situation in Germany.

The link between Hitler's racial ideology and his policy is clearly illustrated by his line of reasoning in the Hossbach memorandum:

To arrest the decline of Germanism in Austria and Czechoslovakia was as little possible as to maintain the present level in Germany itself. Instead of increase, sterility was setting in, and in its train disorders of a social character must arise in course of time, since political and ideological ideas remain effective only so long as they furnish the basis for the realization of the essential vital demands of a people.[58]

The ruthless suppression of conservative tendencies in Germany during this period is another aspect of the leap forward to overcome stagnation. The organizational and personnel changes at the upper levels of the Economics, Foreign and War ministries resulted from Hitler's resolve to bring forward the expansion of the Third Reich and realize his aspirations at any price, including war. The conservative Right was promptly driven out of all positions of influence. On 26 November, Goering was appointed to the post of deputy to the Minister of Economics, and thus received powers of enormous importance. With this appointment, the dismissal of Schacht and the amalgamation of the Economics Ministry with the Four Year Plan, a new era opened in the economy of rearmament. In the military field, the commanders of the armed forces, von Blomberg and Fritsch, were forced to resign, bringing to a dramatic end the relative independence of the General Staff. Party interference in army matters also increased, notably with the appointment of

Goering as Field Marshal, and the abolition of the War Ministry when the Supreme Command of the Wehrmacht was established. The systematic elimination of the conservatives from power was completed with the attack on their citadel, the diplomatic service: von Neurath was removed, and Ribbentrop appointed Foreign Minister. Along with these developments came the dismissal of ambassadors of the old school: of von Hassell in Rome, Dirksen in Tokyo, and von Papen in Vienna.[59]

The radicalized policy towards the Jews in 1938 should also be understood in this context. In order to comprehend fully what triggered the harsh anti-semitic measures of 1938, we must consider Hitler's unidimensional pattern of thought based on his paranoid antisemitism. When we examine the inner logic of Hitler's thinking – if the term 'logic' can be used at all – we realize that he interpreted political developments, whether in Germany or abroad, as a historic confrontation with Judaism and what it stood for. Judaism was always aiming at overthrowing the rule of the racial elite, thus disturbing the hierarchy established by nature. Antisemitic measures were a means to fight the biological root of Judaism, the physical Jews, but this had to be com-plemented by combat with the 'Judaized' tendencies which in Hitler's eyes were draining the racial life will.

In his mind, the decline of the revolutionary spirit, the loss of ideological tension and the upsurge in reactionary activity were all interrelated and directly attributable to the advance of 'Judaism'. The objective reality was obviously different: the conservative and clerical opposition had no obvious relation to the Jewish question, and actually approved of the removal of the Jews through state antisemitism. Even the Papal encyclical of March 1937 touched on the Jewish question only indirectly, through the reservations it expressed about race hatred, racial rites as a new form of idolatry, and the war against the Old Testament and Jewish components of Christianity. However, it hardly makes any difference whether or not this was the objective reality. What matters is Hitler's subjective perception of it – what he *thought* was happening and what meaning he assigned to this reality. In his thinking, conservative and clerical opposition to Nazism was aimed at undermining the natural political order and therefore necessarily stemmed from an adoption of Jewish modes of thinking. Thus fighting this opposition was not only a prag-matic political move, but part of his permanent confrontation with 'Judaism'.

When we consider Hitler's propensity for thinking in biological categories, we manage to penetrate into this sordid and vulgar version of Social Dar-winism. The backbone of his ideological assumptions was constant struggle as the fate of humanity and the will of what he calls 'providence'. Nature created the Jews to serve as a ferment of decomposition which arouses the nations from their tendency to decline. Combating the Jewish presence brings the nation to a state of permanent vitality by activating its defence mechanisms.

Any loss of the instinct to fight, which ultimately would destroy the human race, was necessarily symptomatic of the Jews' ascendancy, either physically through racial contamination, or through ideologies which incarnated Judaism: Christianity, liberalism, democracy, capitalism and Bolshevism. This awkward naturalistic pattern of thinking explains Hitler's otherwise paradoxical statement in one of his table talks:

Probably many Jews are not aware of the destructive power they represent. Now he who destroys life is himself risking death; that's the secret of what is happening to the Jews.... This destructive role of the Jews has in a way a providential explanation. If nature wanted the Jews to be the ferment that causes people to decay, thus providing these peoples with an opportunity for a healthy reaction, in that case people such as St Paul and Trotsky are, from our point of view, the most valuable. By the fact of their presence they provoke the defensive reaction of the attacked organism.[60]

In 1937, it was again St Paul (now dressed in the garb of the churches and the conservatives) who was provoking the defensive reaction of the German nation. Added to this imagery of a healthy German body attacked by a Judaic disease was Hitler's sense of the urgency of fighting the Jews here and now. In his address to German officers ten days before the war started, he again reminded his audience that in the future no man would have the authority that he enjoyed. Germany needed the conflict now in case someone proposed a peace project which would harm it. Only war would prevent the decline of the nation and strengthen it against Jewish aggression.[61]

In Hitler's eyes the prevailing reality in 1937 was a manifestation of a 'Jewish' spirit; if so, he could not remain aloof from a Jewish mentality making headway and subverting the will to struggle of Germany's racial organism. Without an immediate breakthrough, the Jews would defeat the Aryan race in this historic confrontation. Hitler's stepped-up policy during this period should thus be seen as a way out of what he considered a threatening internal crisis. His embarkation on war and his choice of targets were obviously not a direct result of this crisis, but the consistent realization of political and racial objectives through Germany's expansion. Only the schedule of his plans was pushed forward by the internal crisis of 1937.

The same racialist ethos – indeed, the same Hitlerian terminology regarding the need to overcome sterility through an onslaught on the Jews and 'Judaized' trends – is echoed explicitly in the Foreign Ministry circular of January 1939. That antisemitic policy was the foundation of Germany's foreign policy is made clear at the start:

It is not by chance that the fateful year 1938 has not only brought about the realization of the idea of a Greater Germany, but at the same time has brought nearer the solution to the Jewish question. *The policy towards the Jews was both cause and consequence of the events of 1938.* The increased Jewish corrupting influence and Jewish mentality in politics, the economy and cultural life had once again paralysed the strength and will of the German people to revive.... Recovery from this disease was, therefore, one of the preconditions for the energetic effort made in 1938 to ensure the unity of the Great German Reich against the will of the entire world.[62]

This interpretation was not confined to the Foreign Ministry. The SS assessment is further proof that the developments in German society were interpreted in the same manner and with the same emphasis by Hitler's faithful followers. The significance of the internal crisis generated by growing oppositionist activity was clearly expressed in the SD's first monthly report of 1938. Reporting on state policy it voiced its concern that 'liberal tendencies' were gaining ground in the press. And, of all measures to counteract the crisis, the SS emphasized antisemitic ones as being the most crucial.[63] The annual report of the SD for 1938 made this point plain: 'the most influential factor in internal policy was the steps taken against Jewry.'[64] This evidence demonstrates the centrality of antisemitism not only to the Nazi world view, but also to Nazi policy in 1938. Viewed in this context, the aggressive antisemitic onslaught of 1938 was a prerequisite of Hitler's attempts to rejuvenate the system. The way the Nazis tackled the Jewish issue is to be seen not as another outburst of antisemitic rage, but in the overall context of the repression of right-wing and church opposition perceived as Judaizing tendencies.

The antisemitic policy proceeded on all planes: on the legislative and administrative levels came increasing pressure for Aryanization and a deluge of new antisemitic directives, ordinances and laws. In typical Nazi fashion, the torrent of legislation was issued to make it appear that everything was being done on a strictly legal basis. Most measures which aimed to eject the Jews totally from the German economy were clearly signalled in the final months of 1937, when the whole radical drive began. The severe economic restrictions that accompanied accelerating Aryanization; the registration of Jewish property in April; the registration of Jewish businesses and the wave of arrests and physical violence in June: all these paved the way for the awesome events of *Kristallnacht*.

The first sweeping change in the situation of the Jews of Germany came in January, with the law demanding that all Jews take the additional name of 'Sarah' or 'Israel'. In March the law was passed annulling the legal status of the Jewish communities in public law. Concomitant with these developments was the imposition of stringent economic regulations designed to intensify administrative terror and the pressure for emigration. Of particular importance was the decree in April which required the registration of all Jewish property over RM 5,000. The decree applied to all Jews owning property in

Germany, whether or not they were German subjects. The provisions of the executive order restricted the contractual liberty of Jews and the opening of new concerns or branches of concerns. The object of the decree was to ensure the orderly transfer of Jewish business to German hands and to prevent unregulated independent actions; it represented a preparatory step to further economic measures. It also empowered Goering, the head of the Four Year Plan, to use this declared wealth in accordance with the needs of the German economy; the ordinance to prevent the transfer of Jewish property to German hands and the law of June defining Jewish businesses and requiring their entry in a special register enabled these enterprises to be marked. The fixing of time limits forced the liquidation of Jewish businesses for a ridiculously small proportion of their real value.[65]

Added to these provisions were laws by which dozens of occupations were forbidden to Jews. For example, Jews were no longer permitted to practise as lawyers and doctors, except among fellow Jews. In addition, special identity cards for Jews were introduced, and the passports of Jews had to be stamped with the letter 'J'. Finally, the annexation of Austria heralded a new stage, because, with the establishment of the Authority for Jewish Emigration, the SD for the first time had exclusive charge of the solution of the Jewish question.

4

Public Responses to Antisemitism, 1933–1938

The initial months of Hitler's rule, and especially the week that followed the victory at the polls on 5 March, were marked by a wave of violence: arrests, maltreatment, kidnappings of people singled out for political reasons, assassinations of politicians and of those suspected of Marxist tendencies were daily affairs. The assaults on Jews were part of the ruthless eradication of the regime's opponents, a direct continuation of the antisemitic attacks which preceded Hitler's rise to power, and an outgrowth of the euphoria that came after the seizure of power. Prominent examples of this situation were the large-scale outrages that members of the Nazi Party and its affiliated organizations provoked: harassment, murder, vandalizing of synagogues, desecration of Jewish graveyards, and destruction of property. During this period a large number of Jews were removed or suspended from all positions of prominence, subjected to arrest and stripped of their jobs at various public institutions. Jewish lawyers, doctors and teachers were dismissed throughout the Reich. Many had to flee for their lives, and others were incarcerated in prisons and camps. About the middle of March the physical attacks diminished in intensity, chiefly due to Hitler's appeal to his followers to adhere to 'blind discipline'. However, the unrest did not cease: there was a growing demand for measures against German Jews because they had allegedly instigated the reports of outrages which had appeared in the foreign press.

The antisemitic atmosphere reached a climax with the nationwide anti-Jewish boycott staged by the Nazi Party on 1 April 1933, which also signalled the beginning of a new phase. Although the party apparatus formally planned, organized and carried it out, the boycott was *de facto* a state act and, as such, its impact on the Jews of Germany went far beyond the material damage involved. The boycott itself was officially stopped after one day, but from this point on antisemitic policy also took the form of state legislation.

The very first law passed by the new regime, the Law for the Restoration of the Professional Civil Service (7 April 1933), established race as a condition of employment and led to the removal of thousands of officials. Overriding the Constitution, it removed 'non-Aryans' from the civil service with the allegation that the Weimar Republic had filled the bureaucracy with incompetent functionaries, although in reality the Nazis wished to purge it of Jews and politically unreliable officials. This law was a milestone in Nazi antisemitic legislation because it furnished a new and important definition of a 'non-Aryan': i.e. anyone who had a 'non-Aryan' parent or grandparent. Besides, given that Jews in cultural, artistic and media occupations were being fired, academics discharged and teachers forced to relinquish their jobs, the law merely regulated existing practice by granting retroactive legality. The antisemitic legislation also prohibited Jewish conscription into the army when, at the end of February 1934, the law of 7 April 1933 was made applicable to the armed forces. This was not entirely new: already in December 1933 the army, on its own initiative, had proposed to observe the Aryan clause when dealing with appointments of officer cadets. Further measures included the dismissal of Jews from state, municipal and public services; a prohibition against employing Jewish judges and magistrates; harsh restrictions on Jews studying at schools and universities and the adoption of a law to annul the citizenship of Jews who immigrated to Germany after the First World War. Jewish rights were henceforth restricted by the ordinances and directives issued by the local and provincial authorities, as well as by professional organizations which implemented the principles of the new law.

How did the German public react to this reality? It is impossible to determine from the reports what the population felt about the antisemitic drive. Few surveys exist on 1933, and from the crumbs of evidence it appears that the Jewish question was of marginal concern. If the reports provide scanty evidence on public reactions, there is little difficulty in finding other sources: diplomatic dispatches, eyewitness accounts and recollections allow tentative conclusions. From the impressions of a variety of observers representing a wide range of viewpoints, it looks as though the public identification with Nazi antisemitic policy was not clear-cut. Although in general the public recognized the necessity for some solution to the Jewish problem, large sectors found the form of persecution abhorrent. The impression these accounts give is that the boycott failed to achieve its objective and that there were misgivings about the brutal methods employed. These sources further suggest that a good many disapproved of the barbarity, which they feared would have disastrous economic consequences at a time when the country could ill afford them. Not only did sizable parts of the population severely condemn the persecution, but even Nazi sympathizers did not fully endorse it. Sometimes there were animated discussions in front of Jewish shops and fighting broke out between the public and party men. Even generals wearing medals came to stores owned by Jews in Berlin to demonstrate their disapproval of the Nazi policy. The educated bourgeoisie seized the occasion of the rioting to take a stand and vent expressions of censure and protest. This sector in particular did not subscribe to the boycott, showing indignation and disgust that Germany should resort to such medieval methods.[1]

Aside from the criticism of violence, the campaigns conducted against the Bible caused heavy resentment in the church-going population. Yet the churches scarcely voiced these reservations officially, although they were still relatively independent. The churchmen who levelled public criticism, such as Cardinal Michael Faulhaber in his sermons in December 1933, were exceptional. None the less, foreign observers rightly perceived that, while all these acts indicated opposition to the Nazis and their methods, they did not necessarily imply feelings *in favour of the Jews*.[2] In the short run most of those who felt embarrassed learned to turn a blind eye and retreat into non-political privacy. It was much easier to conform than to swim against the stream.

Where dismissals of Jews are concerned, the picture changes. In contrast to the criticism aroused by boycotts and violence, there seems to have been little public objection to the sacking of Jews, for a number of reasons. First, there was almost no disruption of bureaucratic activities, because the purge was limited to avoid any disastrous consequences. In Prussia it affected only 12.5–15.5 per cent of the administration, in other states even less: between 4.5 and 5 per cent.[3] Second, all purges are a source of upward mobility: the extensive dismissals opened jobs for the unemployed and allowed young people to advance their careers. The expulsion of Jews and leftists from the universities and public service opened up posts and created opportunities for promotion, thus contributing to complacency and conformism in the academic and intellectual public. Third, and far more important, the absence of negative reactions in the existing sources – mainly recollections – seems to suggest that the removal of Jews from influential positions was consonant with the wishes of the great majority of the public. Just how far these wishes permeated German society is shown by the fact that even anti-Nazis subscribed to the measure. Following the removal of Jewish civil servants Thomas Mann wrote in his diary, 'It is no great misfortune after all that…the Jewish presence in the judiciary has been ended',[4] and later on he added, 'I could to some extent go along with the rebellion against the Jewish element.'[5]

Further evidence of such attitudes among people who opposed the regime is provided by a report for February 1937 which cites the outlook of a

Catholic teacher from southern Germany who definitely disliked the Third Reich. The reporter says, however, that 'The Jews are for her another world. It is true that she finds barbarian their persecution and economic extermination. But she would think reasonable the introduction of a numerus clausus and certain limitations on candidacy for the civil service.'[6]

Similarly, the application of the Aryan principle in the army elicited no public reaction, for it also left the military structure unharmed and only seventy officers were affected. We should not attach any importance to the few voices of protest which were heard from army circles. They objected to the army's subordination to a party's ideology, not to the Aryan principle itself.[7]

For subsequent years, the broader documentary base allows more precise analysis. As shown earlier, the most striking development from 1934 on was the sobering of the spirit of 'national renewal' and the growing apathy towards indoctrination. If in this context we measure the results of the propaganda by its success in moulding attitudes and integrating the uncommitted public in the antisemitic drive, we can safely conclude that in most cases it failed. Whereas antisemitism played an integrative role for the party and its followers, it did not have the same function in spurring the general population to action. Abundant evidence of this appears in the responses to the renewed antisemitic wave in the autumn of 1934.

Reporting on public attitudes, the Gestapo station at Potsdam commented in September of that year, 'Undoubtedly the Jewish question is not the main problem of the German public.... Utterances on the Jewish peril are diminished and those engaged in enlightening the population are to a certain extent depicted as fools.'[8] Reports from different regions show that this state of affairs was fairly widespread: the public was not galvanized by antisemitic propaganda, and Nazi observers realized that there was a gulf between the ideal of a society mobilized to fight the Jews and the reality that they encountered. Even if those who launched raids on the Jews cannot always be identified from the reports, it can certainly be assumed from endless testimonies that these were mostly members of Nazi organizations. Hence antisemitic terror ought to be attributed mainly to the Hitler Youth, the SA and other party formations; the bulk of the public remained passive on the sidelines. Many were amused, but many were also deeply troubled by what they witnessed.

These attitudes were not confined to periods of relative calm, but featured prominently in the summer months of 1935, when the antisemitic thrust reached unprecedented heights and swept the Reich. Even during these turbulent months the propaganda scarcely motivated the public to respond positively to Nazi agitation. The harangues did not crack the wall of indifference: most of the population did not join in. One of many examples of this is to be found in the report of the Kiel Gestapo for July 1935: 'It is noteworthy that, whenever there are actions against the Jews, these emanate chiefly from members of the party and its affiliated organizations, whereas the majority of the population shows little participation in the Jewish question.'[9] Furthermore, if this report, from an area in the Protestant north noted for its vast support for the Nazis, shows that antisemitic campaigns did not bear fruit, then the response in other regions was even less favourable. In surveys of the public mood in Catholic regions, such as the Rhineland, with more liberal traditions, we find flat rejection of the incitement. Large sections of the population were repelled by the *Stürmer* methods and refused to comply with demands to take action against the Jews.

We should also bear in mind that certain elements exploited antisemitic incitement in order to settle personal accounts, especially by damaging Jewish business competitors. In a number of reports we find the public suspicious that the true motives behind the boycott were not ideological but a matter of personal interest. If this was the case, there was no point in taking part in the antisemitic campaign and fighting other people's wars. The fact that the reports' authors themselves mention the harmful role of the Nazi Craft and Commerce Organization (NS-HAGO) on the antisemitic front is significant as an indicator of the Gestapo's sensitivity on the matter. When the NS-HAGO set the boycott in motion, the district governor in Würzburg noted that the general opinion about this organization was that it was only out for itself and did not care at all about the wider population.[10] These claims seem to have been fairly common, for they crop up in many surveys, such as those from Königsberg, Dortmund and Harburg–Wilhelmsburg.[11] The last-mentioned station significantly observes that local people saw no ideological motives behind the antisemitic campaign, because the NS-HAGO was heading the boycott. Everybody regarded the campaign as an attempt to destroy business competition and not as an expression of racialist policy.

Gestapo stations repeatedly said that the amount of verbal, or even physical, violence engendered could not serve as an indicator of the success of propaganda in convincing people of the need for antisemitism. This was precisely the point made by the Kassel station with regard to the campaign of incitement in that area: 'It is easier to invite attacks on the Jews, than to persuade the public of antisemitism.'[12] The station repeated its assessment in September, concluding that incitement against Jews in meetings and rallies did not contribute to the desired goals. It did bring about rioting, but was of little help in winning over the apathetic public to the antisemitic cause.[13]

The fact that most people took little part in the antisemitic movement has a simple explanation. It is easier to arouse hooligans and the young to attack some concrete target than to win general adherence to an idea. Agitation against the Jews struck a chord first and foremost in the Hitler Youth and the

SA, whereas the ordinary Germans remained passive onlookers. This point can be elaborated by exploring a number of representative cases.

The concentration on the Jewish question in the late winter months of 1935 was part of a nationwide propaganda campaign to activate the lower middle classes and restore their faith in Nazism. In September 1934, the Koblenz Gestapo had reported that retailers were still waiting for the fulfilment of promises made by the Nazis before they came to power. The traders demanded the immediate liquidation of the agencies, consumer co-operatives, department stores and other companies owned by Jews. The commentator also expressed his personal opinion that the lack of real policy in this field was depressing the morale of the lower middle class, generating negative attitudes towards the state and the party.[14] From the Aachen Gestapo report for March 1935 we gain much information on the methods employed in connection with the new antisemitic drive to lift the spirits of small shopkeepers. The local party organ, the *Westdeutscher Beobachter*, brought out a special supplement devoted entirely to the Jewish question; and antisemitic propaganda, which multiplied throughout the country, foreshadowed physical attacks on Jews and their property. The walls of Jewish homes and shops were smeared with faeces and red paint; *Stürmer* stickers were plastered on the walls; shots were fired into Jewish houses and so forth.[15] This hostile climate set the stage for the Cologne–Aachen *Gauleiter*, Grohé, who boasted that this drive had revived the morale of the lower middle class.[16]

As for the population in general, however, did this campaign win it over and bring it into line with Nazi policy? To answer this question let us look at the region in Grohé's charge, for there, fully supported by a fanatical Nazi, the antisemitic drive was whipped up to an exceptional degree.

It is particularly striking that even the surveys from Grohé's jurisdiction point to the limited effects of propaganda on the behaviour of the general public. A report for March from Cologne indicates that workers failed to respond to the call for a boycott and continued shopping in department stores. Workers' wives, the commentators noted, said they couldn't care less whether the store was owned by a Jew or a German.[17] Further proof of the failure of indoctrination to penetrate the public consciousness is furnished by the report for April. The Gestapo agent concluded unequivocally that the public in general understood very little about antisemitic propaganda and the boycott.[18]

The same gap between the avalanche of propaganda and the public response to it emerges from surveys of the Trier area. Summing up the anti-semitic activities during April and May 1935, the Nazi agent proudly declared the party's achievements: notices were posted demanding a boycott of Jewish shops, windows were smashed and Jews were beaten up in the streets. He also mentioned the role played by children in this campaign. Yet he admitted that the majority of the population refused to comply with the demands of the party and continued shopping at Jewish stores. In one shop during the Easter sales there were so many customers that the Jewish shopkeeper was forced to close several times, in order to serve all of them properly.[19]

It should not be assumed that such behaviour was typical only of working-class opposition to the Nazis. Businessmen also did not react favourably to the party's appeals, though not out of ethical considerations. They complained that antisemitic activities damaged Germany's economic interests, showing that they merely feared the anti-Jewish boycott would hamper their ties with traders abroad.[20] What worried those involved in the tourist industry is illustrated by the Bielefeld Gestapo, which commented, 'For ten years the Dutch consul spent his holidays in Bad Oeynhausen, and now he will not return because of the scenes of hooliganism he witnessed.'[21] Added to these worries was concern for Germany's image, especially if such actions were observed by foreigners and could be used for anti-German propaganda abroad. For similar reasons brutal attacks alienated the educated bourgeoisie in Potsdam and Königsberg.[22] For a good many inhabitants of Cologne the question was merely a practical one: who would pay the bill for the damage caused by the rioting? They were troubled by the cost of antisemitic outrages. In the course of a fortnight rioters smashed plate glass to the value of RM 20,000, a loss which would be met by German insurance companies and so would, in the final account, have to be paid by people such as themselves.[23]

It seems, therefore, that at this stage of Hitler's rule people did not co-operate willingly with the party organizations in enforcing antisemitic boycotts. On the contrary, they mostly continued shopping in stores owned by Jews despite the heavy pressures exerted by the SA to frighten off customers. We should not conclude, however, that refraining from participation in the antisemitic campaign originated in, or was identical with, principled opposition to persecution of Jews. We rarely find rejection of Nazi antisemitism on ethical principles, or indignation based on humanitarian values. Moreover, expressions of solidarity with the persecuted Jews are quite exceptional. The real motives behind the refusal to accept the party's calls are usually stated in the reports themselves: very rarely did they exceed utilitarianism or self-interest.

A comprehensive examination of the violent disturbances which erupted in the summer of 1935 contradicts two widespread images: the one of a terrorized German population whose silence enabled the Nazis to pursue antisemitic persecution; the other of a brainwashed society mobilized to endorse unconditionally any sort of Nazi policy. In stark contrast to these popular images, it is clear that the public was neither silent nor brainwashed. The prosecution of anti-Jewish policy depended, to a large extent, on the public's reaction. There is conclusive evidence that on the whole the population consented to attacks on Jews as long as these neither damaged non-Jews nor harmed the interests of the country, particularly its reputation abroad. As a passing comment in a report from northern Germany puts it, far from being passive, the population demonstrated opposition when it feared that its own interests were being endangered.[24]

Occasionally the Gestapo illustrates its surveys with concrete instances of public, non-conformist behaviour in the face of antisemitic policy. A report from Magdeburg, for example, records an unusual form of opposition to the boycott: buyers stood demonstratively in front of the camera placed by the party at the entrance to a Jewish shop and bade defiance to the Nazis.[25] It is impossible to know what lay behind the courageous stand in this place. There seems little doubt, however, that in most cases the fate of the Jews was not important enough to elicit criticism. The Jewish theme was instrumental for some discontented sectors in expressing their dissatisfaction with the Nazi system. The Gestapo stations in Münster and Dortmund correctly captured the reality when they stated that the public went to Jewish shops not as a demonstration of solidarity with the persecuted, but as a way of expressing disillusionment with the regime.[26] Furthermore, people could support the Nazis and yet disapprove of measures against the Jews. A striking example of rejecting Jewish persecution from an antisemitic stand is provided by a report from Harburg–Wilhelmsburg. The local Gestapo admitted that the public did not just fail to understand the attacks on the Jews, but actually condemned them. The reason for this attitude was given by the commentator himself: people felt that maltreatment of Jews was counterproductive, since it turned them into martyrs; the party thus achieved the opposite of its original objective.[27]

Criticism of the political wisdom of persecuting Jews reappears in a later report from the same station. This time what upset the public was not the tragic image Jews presented to their neighbours, but anxiety over Germany's reputation: in the face of the rioting many went on saying that it ought to be stopped because it harmed Germany's image abroad. The Gestapo noted further that, even when most people firmly adhered to a tough policy on the Jewish issue, they nevertheless objected to its implementation through violence. The population, explained the reporter, argued that such excesses only added fuel to the atrocity propaganda spread against the Third Reich.[28] The Gestapo in Kiel likewise noted the negative reaction of people who worried that the Jewish question had cost too much from the point of view of foreign policy.[29] This case is worth noting because intertwined in the utilitarian argument over Germany's image we find a rare humanitarian motive: the belief that Jews should be left in peace because they also are human beings.

All signs point to the conclusion that, even in a Catholic region with considerable anti-Nazi feelings, it was not the fact that Jews were being victimized that upset the public but the brutal and vulgar nature of the persecution. The Cologne Gestapo throws light on this matter: 'The following factors must be considered for the prevailing bad mood: (1) the unclear situation in foreign policy; (2) the struggle against the Church; and (3) *the form* of the anti-Jewish struggle.'[30] The report from Magdeburg for July bears witness to the fact that it was not antisemitism as such, but its extent and degree, that aroused public criticism. There was a point at which the bourgeoisie felt that the violence, and the antisemitic campaign that had produced it, might have gone too far.[31] The Königsberg Gestapo summed up public reaction in almost the same terms.[32]

If the population criticized the antisemitic policy because it feared retaliation in the form of an anti-German boycott organized by Jews abroad, or because it was anxious about the possible damage to Germany's prestige, it was all the more alarmed when antisemitism harmed it directly. An array of reports mention people who approved antisemitism in principle but, afraid of its consequences for themselves, criticized its application. A case in point is a Gestapo report from Kösslin. The writer had his finger on the pulse of the public mood when he wrote that the local population was indeed antisemitic but did not want to be harmed by anti-Jewish policy.[33] Many of those objecting had good reasons to worry. They were alarmed that the violence initiated by party activists would spread to those Germans depicted as targets in the surging tide of propaganda. This included the Catholic Church as well as anyone who maintained social or economic contact with Jews or was suspected of such. The feelings of insecurity generated by unbridled denunciations became especially intense towards the summer. Small wonder, then, that those Germans who feared that they might be casualties of the antisemitic drive asked party leaders to retard the implementation of anti-Jewish policy. How far practical interests outweighed loyalty to Nazi doctrine can be clearly seen in a report from Koblenz for August and September 1935. A town in the district requested a reduction in the pressure on the Jews. The reason cited was that antisemitism did not pay: the inhabitants made their living from a medical institution owned by Jews, and its closure would deprive many family heads of an income.[34]

What effect did these attitudes have on the Nazi authorities? There is no doubt that they were taken very seriously. Some commentators mention local decisions to discontinue violent anti-Jewish methods because they had antagonized the public. The Bielefeld Gestapo, for example, realized that the antisemitic campaign had become counterproductive when outrages made the victims into martyrs, and Germans, instead of keeping away from Jews, felt sorry for them. In view of this, it decided to set a limit to antisemitic outbursts.[35] It seems, then, that the exile periodical *Weltbühne* was not far from the truth when it stated that the attacks on the Jews lessened at the end of May to diminish political disaffection.[36]

With this background in mind, we can analyse the reactions of the German public to the Nuremberg Laws.

REACTIONS TO THE NUREMBERG LAWS

There can be no doubt that the desire of the public for an end to the internal contradictions of the regime's Jewish policy, and the widespread confusion and fear generated by the wave of violent antisemitism, provided an added incentive to push through the Nuremberg Laws. These included two laws that crucially affected the status of German Jews – the Reich Citizenship Law and the Law for the Protection of German Blood and Honour – and the law establishing the Swastika banner as the new German flag. This new flag law provides a useful point of reference for our analysis, since the reports convey responses to all three laws. We can thus compare public reactions to the anti-semitic legislation, on the one hand, and to the law bringing about a break with Germany's imperial heritage, on the other. In both issues the legislation simply legalized what was already the case: the flag law regularized the fact that the Swastika banner was far more in evidence than the imperial flag; the antisemitic laws created a legal framework that curbed the violence against Jews and Jewish property which was undermining public order.

Sometimes the Nazi agents do not go into great detail on the responses to the legislation. The report from the Harburg–Wilhelmsburg Gestapo only states that, in relation to the citizenship law and the 'protection' law, there was no reaction, while the public talked a great deal about the flag law.[37] The actual content of the conversations becomes apparent from reports from other parts of the country. The political police in Munich distinguished sharply between the laws in reporting people's reactions to them. Whereas the popu-lation did not express any opinion on the citizenship law, the 'protection' law produced a positive response. The flag law, however, was openly criticized by officers and war veterans.[38] This was also the assessment of foreign observers. The British consul in Munich noted that the new flag law 'was beyond doubt universally unpopular in Bavaria, where the Swastika is known as the circus flag.'[39] From Koblenz we hear of a wider range of public responses: the party congress excited great interest, and the 'protection' law was received with much approval – because, people thought, it would help prevent disturbances and isolate the Jews – but the flag law met severe criticism from the older generation.[40]

The different reactions elicited by the three laws show that for the bulk of the German population an assault on a historical symbol such as the black–white–red imperial flag was far more serious than ostracizing Jewish fellow citizens. The law annulling Jewish citizenship was not much discussed: it was accepted as an obvious and absolutely natural measure. There was no point in reacting to a law that just rubber-stamped an existing reality. On the other hand, the abolition of the old flag was a matter of public interest and consequently elicited criticism, at least from the older generation.

Let us consider the different reactions to the two laws dealing with the Jews. As to the revocation of Jewish citizenship, the Sopade reporter from Saxony missed the point when he observed that there were no reactions to the law because the German population had other things to worry about.[41] The absence of comment was not a result of indifference to the Jewish question or of simple acceptance that the law, whatever its moral basis, had been enacted by the state and was therefore binding ('legal positivism'); it was a silence of tacit consent to the Nazi solution, based on a deep identification with the spirit of the law, which institutionalized the principles of racial separatism by isolating and removing Jews from the *Volksgemeinschaft*. The Potsdam Gestapo fully captured these feelings. It stated that all believed that with the stabilization of the regime the time was ripe to realize this item on the party's agenda. At the same time, the commentator added, the public hoped that other points of the Nazi programme would be acted upon, especially those related to social issues.[42] In Kiel, too, there was approval of the antisemitic laws, and people expected the status of the churches to be resolved in an equally satisfactory way.[43]

The Law for the Protection of German Blood and Honour was especially applauded because it checked antisemitic violence by confining it to the framework of law and order. This law expressed the desire of most Germans to remove the annoyances caused by uncontrolled terror, establishing a legal basis for the policies towards German Jews. The public assumed that the legislation would restore calm to the streets and put an end to behaviour that was besmirching Germany's image as a civilized country. The situation in various districts before and after the laws were adopted fully proves this point.

In August, according to the Bielefeld Gestapo, there was widespread public unrest over cases of *Rassenschande* (race defilement), leading to popular demands for steps to be taken against it.[44] In its report for September, after the law had been adopted, the same station described the public as content. Everybody hoped that from this point on the Jewish problem would be solved within the framework of the new law and therefore without acts of terror.[45] We hear the same from Berlin. As early as March the Gestapo had noted that the population expected the matter to be settled, and in the summer it indicated that what really disturbed the public was the lack of a clear line towards the Jews. In the Gestapo's view, given the abundance of denunciations of race defilement, common police methods were inadequate to prevent the renewal of anti-Jewish riots.[46] These circumstances clarify the reactions to the laws in Berlin. They aroused great enthusiasm everywhere because it was believed that they finally defined the relation between Jews and Germans: 'Jewry is converted into a national minority and gets through state protection the possibility to develop its own cultural and national life.'[47] Similarly in Merseburg the Gestapo station observed that the legislation had won public approval; people expected the restoration of law and order, and, particularly, the scrapping of *Der Stürmer*.[48] It was only natural for the public to deem *Der Stürmer* obsolete after the enactment of the 'protection' law: Streicher's pornographic newspaper, among others, had deliberately provoked antisemitic rioting by spreading libels about race defilement; but, now that discriminatory practices had been legalized and a legal definition of race defilement provided, the excuse for radicals to take the law into their own hands had been removed.

Thus far we have considered the reactions of the population in general. How did the party radicals respond? As discussed above, the reports for July and August touched on the clashes between radicals and the various agencies charged with keeping public order. The extremists' acts of violence did not stop even after Hess and Frick issued restraining directives, which in Berlin and Trier, for example, produced protests from the radicals.[49] The Nuremberg Laws, in their turn, were received by party activists with mixed feelings. The flag law was greeted with jubilation, for it symbolized the victory of party over government. The antisemitic laws were also seen as rekindling the revolutionary flame and thwarting the conservatives. Many saw in their promulgation a ceremonial declaration of antisemitic principles and, as such, a victory for Nazism in realizing the party platform. Thus, for example, the report from Kassel recorded the fervent enthusiasm of radical circles: 'The state is still revolutionary. The party platform has not been forgotten.'[50]

Many, however, thought the new laws too 'moderate', too 'mild'. Only a few justified this as a political manoeuvre to camouflage antisemitic terror from the outside world.[51] The Dortmund Nazis were more typical, considering the provision allowing the Jews to use their own symbols too great a concession. The author of the Dortmund survey added his opinion that this was liable to bring renewed troubles.[52] Similarly, the Potsdam Gestapo stated that party men deemed the laws too mild. They drew solace from their hopes that the reactions of world Jewry would raise the topic again and consequently sharpen antisemitic policy.[53] The Koblenz district governor reported activists' demand that the clause forbidding the employment by Jews of German maids under the age of forty-five should be extended. In Bielefeld the local Nazis wished that the law had specified no age limit.[54] The criticism of this clause seems to have been quite widespread. Some considered it should also have included a ban on the employment of German maids by mixed couples, or by a single Jewish woman.[55]

The reports recorded a few pockets of dissent to the new laws. Some Gestapo agents furnished interesting information on the response of the communist underground to the riots and antisemitic laws. The Dortmund Gestapo, for instance, reported that communist youth had disseminated underground leaflets in Bochum warning of the dangers inherent in the demagogic use of antisemitism among the masses, and calling for a common front between communist, Protestant and Catholic youth. Alongside an appeal for the release of political prisoners, the leaflets asked for tolerance towards the Jews.[56] The sharpest reaction seems to have come from a communist cell in Berlin. The local Gestapo's report for September informs us that the propaganda against antisemitism occupied a prominent place in underground material. Some of the slogans printed by clandestine communists in pamphlets and on stickers are also quoted in the report.[57] It is worth noting, however, that, even though the communists responded vigorously to antisemitic legislation, their basic conceptions of the nature of Nazi antisemitism remained unchanged. As underground publications from this period show, the communists resorted to stereotypical and dogmatic assertions: some stated that only poor workers were arrested for race defilement, while rich Jews were not touched by the Nazis.[58] Others maintained that there were no racial principles behind the ban on keeping maids under forty-five years of age; rather, the clause was simply an excuse for firing thousands of women from their jobs.[59]

The churches had more than once been forced to react to incitement against the Jews, although they actually preferred to avoid this thorny issue altogether. The reports cite a few instances of aversion in church circles to racialist rituals and agitation, and even of protests regarding them; we learn from the Aachen Gestapo that such attitudes were especially prevalent among Catholic priests in the Rhineland.[60] In addition, some Protestant priests reacted against the regime's racial laws: a report from Speyer tells us that sermons hostile to them were distributed among the public by Evangelical pastors.[61] It is not impossible, however, that the motives here were not so much concern for the Jews as anxiety over the status of converts of Jewish origin.

Some misgivings and criticism by the liberal intelligentsia are also recorded. A few opposed the laws on principle; others on pragmatic grounds, mainly out of fear of economic reprisals against Germany. In Potsdam, for example, the better-educated worried about an international boycott that would punish Germany for its racial policy.[62]

Finally, some individuals employed by Jews made their feelings known since they feared for their income. Bielefeld Gestapo echoed the apprehensions of German clerks working for Jewish firms: they had reservations about the laws because they were afraid of losing their jobs. The same reaction was heard in Munich: commercial circles believed that Jews abroad would use the laws as an excuse to step up the anti-German boycott.[63]

The clause forbidding employment of German women under the age of forty-five upset those directly affected by it. Maids in Koblenz and Hildesheim criticized it as a threat to their livelihood and therefore asked for its revocation or for exemptions in order to retain their work, arguing that otherwise they would become a burden to the public.[64] It is clear that in most of these cases, too, the objections stemmed from self-interest rather than from opposition to discrimination.

To sum up, the vast majority of the population approved of the Nuremberg Laws because they identified with the racialist policy and because a permanent framework of discrimination had been created that would end the reign of terror and set precise limits to antisemitic activities.

THE YEARS 1936–7

During 1936 and 1937, the whole country experienced a period of relative calm and there was no essential change in public reactions to antisemitic policy. The first half of 1936, when Germany was in the limelight owing to the Olympic Games, was particularly quiet: in order to avoid international controversy, almost no attacks were directed against the Jews in that period, even after the killing of Wilhelm Gustloff, head of the Nazi organization in Switzerland.[65] Immediately after the games were over, however, the antisemitic agitation started up again, both among local activists and at the party's headquarters. In November 1936, Munich University held a festive opening of the Department for Research into the Jewish Question in the National Institute for the History of the New Germany; *Der Stürmer* published *Der Weltverschwörer*, a special edition prepared for the party congress, which reprinted passages from the Protocols of the Elders of Zion, and *Stürmer* showcases appeared again all over the country.[66] In addition to the renewal of antisemitic propaganda, various governmental agencies issued new regulations and guidelines to increase pressure on the Jews, to force their removal from Germany. The Ministry of Education forbade non-Aryans to teach in private schools and recommended *Der Stürmer* for religious instruction; Jewish doctors and assistants were restricted to working in Jewish hospitals; and the number of arrests for alleged currency offences or race defilement again multiplied.

Were there any changes in the reactions of the population in this period of relative calm? A thorough examination of reports for these years shows that people's moral insensibility to the fate of the Jews became more profound and widespread. This was not necessarily a result of Nazi indoctrination: on the contrary, propaganda continued to bore people, and antisemitic indoctrination evenings were still considered dull and tedious. A socialist observer from Schleswig perceptively noticed the lack of correspondence between responses to antisemitic propaganda and antisemitic attitudes. Although the public had no interest in indoctrination evenings on 'National Socialist historiography', 'The race question', 'Judaism and Freemasonry', and so on, the regime did succeed in driving a wedge between Jews and Germans.[67] This is hardly surprising, for, as we have seen, the bulk of the public did not need Nazi propaganda in order to ostracize Jews. The growing urge to avoid them stemmed from deep-seated anti-Jewish prejudices, and the resulting wide-spread approval of segregation. It is true that the *Stürmer* methods and the violence met with the same disapproval as in the past and remarks condemn-ing the *Stürmer* showcases appeared in almost every report. Nevertheless, the picture of what the public thought of the Jewish question is totally uniform: the general opinion was that the race laws should be carried out and the Jews removed from posts in administration, science and the arts.[68]

It is against this background that the attitudes of educated Germans to the Nazis' antisemitic policy are best viewed. Their criticism of the regime had been aroused by the earlier riots and boycott campaigns, but, once the Nuremberg Laws had been introduced and the violence dampened down, total indifference to the fate of the Jews became dominant. The January 1936 Sopade report from Berlin, which examined the influence of antisemitism on the population, asserted that the race question as an ideological issue had not penetrated the consciousness of the educated classes. The incitement of *Der Stürmer* was seen as a national disgrace and elicited occasional manifestations of pro-Jewish feelings, but otherwise they were not interested in the issue and did not find antisemitism deserving of concern.[69]

Still, even when the Jews were socially segregated, commercial relations with them continued as long as it made economic sense and German customers went to Jewish shops. The peasants in particular were slow to give in. As long as it was possible to deal with Jewish cattle-dealers, peasants traded with them.[70] Again, it has to be emphasized that this fact should not lead to conclusions of sympathy for the Jews. Since most Germans were not 'fanatically' antisemitic, practical interest outweighed 'common' anti-Jewish sentiments.

THE YEAR 1938

From the end of 1937 the Jewish question was again central to a massive onslaught which resulted in reckless maltreatment and terror. The new campaign was sharply differentiated from previous ones by the fact that the state was active in arbitrary persecution; hitherto the party had been the main perpetrator. The Aryanization process was abruptly stepped up; new regulations on relations with Jews were published; antisemitic legislation and extensive administrative measures rapidly encompassed all areas of life. The state's initiative did not mean that the party lagged behind: it unleashed a barrage of propaganda to escalate the pressure to expel the Jews. In the space of two weeks in Saxony alone, 1,350 antisemitic meetings were held under the slogan 'A nation breaks its chains.'[71] As usual, agitative propaganda preceded terror: vandalizing of Jewish institutions, businesses and private homes; abuse and torment of individuals, and arbitrary arrests. Whenever the foreign press gave prominence to these events, wholesale arrests followed. The Nazis hoped that as a result the Jews would restrain foreign observers from recording abuses.

The euphoria which followed the annexation of Austria in March led to such outrages that Austrian *Gauleiter* Bürckel had to arrest members of the Austrian Legion.[72] At the end of April a boycott was started in Frankfurt and a month later pogroms broke out in Berlin. The terror was undoubtedly also fed by concrete 'show' examples such as the demolition of the Munich synagogue after Hitler's referendum in May. These initiatives from above always served as a signal for a tide of abuse against German Jews. The mayor of Bad Kissingen, for example, was one who understood this green light: Jewish visitors to the town's spa were issued special yellow tickets, prohibited from frequenting the concert hall and reading-rooms, and restricted to properly designated baths and garden benches.[73]

In the summer this policy assumed even more serious dimensions. The most embracing act of state terror was the *Juniaktion* (June Action). In Berlin, as well as in other cities, there were systematic house-to-house searches and arrests; cafés were raided and even cinemas were emptied of Jews. Those who had a police record of any kind, even for parking a car on the wrong side of the road, were treated as criminals and transported to concentration camps. The fact that release was made conditional on leaving Germany clearly demonstrated that the main purpose of the operation was to force emigration.

Again the party sought to show its zeal by outdoing the state in persecuting Jews. Police arrests were matched by revived party brutality. From 10 June antisemitic furore masterminded by the Berlin *Gauleitung* and perpetrated by party organizations erupted: Jewish stores were defaced with signs; clinics and lawyers' offices were marked. In several cases businesses were smashed and gutted, and in the coming weeks the storm extended to south-western Germany. That these attacks were engineered and carried out by the party is clear from internal SD material. The initiative came from the local party chiefs and not from the Jewish section of the SD or a government agency.[74]

An atmosphere fuelled by fears of impending war at the time of the Sudeten crisis found expression in the antisemitic mood of party elements and in the recourse to violence. During the month of October there were a number of outbreaks in Vienna and provincial towns, staged mainly by the SA and the Hitler Youth, which discharged accumulated passions. Bands of SA men who had been demobilized after being called up for service raided Jewish houses in Vienna in search of means to punish Jews for their 'unpatriotic' attitude during the Munich crisis. The most virulent outbreak was a large-scale pogrom lasting from the 14th to the 21st. Hundreds of Jewish houses, schools, synagogues and businesses were raided, wrecked and looted. In Krems the Jews were compelled to turn over the synagogue to the local Nazi Party. As a consequence of these events suicides multiplied.[75]

The persecution reached a climax in the mass expulsion of Jews of Polish origin, whose tragic fate sent ripples throughout the world. Some 15,000 of them were rounded up, bundled into trains and unloaded at the Polish frontier. That this was not the first expulsion of Jews is often overlooked. In April the Nazis planned to expel all Jews from the Burgenland province for 'strategic reasons', and prohibit any Jew from residing within 50 kilometres of the border. In fact, some 400 were ordered to leave twelve towns in the Burgenland and sent over the frontiers into Hungary and Czechoslovakia. Since many were refused permission to enter Czechoslovak territory, they remained interned in barracks on the border.[76] All these measures made it clear to everyone that, unlike in previous years, this time antisemitic policy would be pursued regardless of its effect on Germany's image.

After two years of relative calm on the Jewish question, how did the population respond to these developments? The dimensions and character of the wave of anti-Jewish terror prior to *Kristallnacht* received particular mention in the SD's national report of 1 November 1938. In its view, the public attitude toward the Jewish question was expressed in the proliferation of rioting, and on the whole enjoyed the support of the local party organizations.[77] This generalization by the SD requires closer scrutiny.

The events of 1938 brought no significant change in the pattern of public reactions established in previous years. The overwhelming majority approved social segregation and economic destruction of the Jews but not outbursts of brute force. Notwithstanding the fact that traditional anti-Jewish attitudes not only persisted but even grew in this period, practical interests had priority over loyalty to the official doctrine. The Berlin observer of the Sopade rightly noticed that, although antisemitism was gradually taking root in the population, it was not Jew-hatred in the Nazi sense. The public did not feel sympathy for the Jews, but this fact did not lead them to abstain from shopping in Jewish stores, and many workers frequented them without encountering difficulties.[78]

In Cologne a pattern of non-conformist conduct we are already familiar with appears again: some continued to shop in Jewish stores, but as a way of expressing their opposition to Nazism and not necessarily out of sympathy for the victims.[79] As in previous years, economic measures against the Jews were universally welcomed. Thus the decree which provided for the registration of all Jewish property over RM 5,000 received general acclaim and the public hardly regretted the state taking possession of wealth which they believed Jews had stolen from the German people.[80] Yet the Sopade reporter in Schleswig asserted that many did not understand the point of reviving the antisemitic drive after the Jews had already been marginalized economically.[81] Similarly, another report states that even those who endorsed the expulsion of the Jews from the economy and public life rejected the brutal methods employed.[82] As previously, those condemning the disturbances did so out of opposition to the form of antisemitism and not to the policy itself. An observer in Berlin noticed that as a result of the constant incitement many had become antisemites. However, the report adds, more than a few voices had been raised against the hooligans: 'the general public witnessed these ongoings with morbid interest, and the outrages were regarded by many as being inconsistent with modern civilization.'[83] As in the summer of 1935, people thought that the authorities had gone too far in their crusade against the Jews.

The reports on rural areas reflect the specific reality of small communities. The dominant pattern of behaviour was identification with antisemitic policy so long as it was not applied too close to home. Hence absolute indifference to the victimization of unknown Jews was compatible with manifestations of sympathy towards local Jews. Despite the propaganda, the peasants did not cease to distinguish between 'their Jew', who should stay in the village, and the rest of German Jews, who should be expelled so that the Jewish question in general could be solved. A report from Saxony in a region with a small Jewish population exemplifies these attitudes: people endorsed the antisemitic measures they read about in the newspapers, but when a Jew trading there was harmed by this same policy they regretted it.[84] A Sopade contact from south-western Germany got the same impression: in villages where Jews had lived for generations and were part of the social landscape, even though there were no more social contacts between Jews and Germans, people felt sorry that the local Jews were leaving.[85]

It is true that we could explain this absence of interest in what was happening to the Jews by the fact that the German public had its own troubles which concerned them more than the Jewish question. Indeed, one commentator emphasized that 'The population fears a coming war. In this mood the whole Jewish question arouses little interest. People have better things to worry about than the Jews.'[86] To be sure, the mood of the population in 1938 was characterized by an almost universal fear of war. Hitler's foreign-policy successes generated more relief than rejoicing. In domestic affairs, economic hardships caused mounting discontent and tension. However, to attribute people's lack of interest in the Jews to the effect of these competing factors would be too simplistic. The attitudes in previous years explain the reactions in this period. On the basis of the reactions from 1933 on, it can safely be concluded that the attitudes from the early months of Hitler's rule became a normative pattern of behaviour.

REACTIONS TO *KRISTALLNACHT*

The comprehensive SD report for 1938 merely sketched the contours of the population's reaction to the *Kristallnacht*: generally speaking, in the south (except Austria) and in the west (mainly Catholic, more populous and urban) criticism was stronger than in the north (Protestant, rural and less populous). Economic circles protested against the damage, and the bourgeoisie feared the possible consequences abroad.[87] This picture, although basically correct, deserves further elaboration.

The nationwide pogrom of *Kristallnacht* – while initiated, organized and executed throughout Germany by state and party agencies – belonged to the renewed anti-Jewish wave of terror. Hence the reactions of the public cannot be detached from the responses throughout 1938, particularly to the turbulence of the summer and autumn months.

It must be borne in mind that behind the widespread distrust of the regime's policies as well as discontent over internal conditions were the waning of the optimism which the Munich agreement had aroused, the shattering of hopes for international appeasement, and the feelings that another eleventh-hour conference could not be conjured up to prevent war. The pogrom was just the straw that broke the camel's back; overall criticism ensued. And, while a critical tone is apparent in all the reports, the dominant motif is not condemnation on moral grounds. Shame at the act, shock at its extent, and regret for the property destroyed converged to create a negative reaction. Nevertheless, the responses to *Kristallnacht* far outstripped public reactions to any other antisemitic outrage.

For the first time, *all* Germans were personally confronted with antisemitic violence. For this reason there is no trace of indifference. All sections of the population reacted with deep shock. The public was polarized on the handling of the Jewish question: party circles and their periphery gave full support, while the large majority condemned it.

For the first time, there were large displays of shame. People felt humiliated that Germany's *Kultur* was disgraced in the eyes of the world. According to eyewitnesses, people in the streets of Berlin who saw Jewish camp inmates returning home looked as though they were ashamed, and numerous stories went round of Germans who tried to compensate Jews for what the regime did.[88]

For the first time, non-Jews sensed a *real* danger of being the next victim of Nazi terror. Many who had hitherto profited from Aryanization felt they were not secure because they stood to lose from revived radicalism. They feared that the confiscation of Jewish property could be a precedent for plundering other well-off sections of the public. For example, Carl Goerdeler, the leader of the 20 July 1944 plot, forecast further persecution of capitalists and Christians.[89] Hence it was only natural that the most vehement condemnation of the pogrom came from those sectors who suspected they were next in line for such treatment; these apprehensions were especially noticeable among the Catholic public. The fact that in certain places the pogrom was accompanied by attacks against the Catholic Church, when SA men who did not have Jews to attack deflected their fury onto Catholic churches, destroying crosses and effigies, aroused a fear that the government was losing its grip.

It was not coincidental that the communist underground directed its propaganda at the Catholics. It knew very well that they were particularly sensitive about the violence against the 'foes of Nazism', and that they feared that once terror had been unleashed the churches and religious leaders would be the next victims. In this light it is no surprise that the communists tried to win over the Catholic population by drawing parallels between the fate of the Jews and the fate of the churches. Again and again they said that the pogrom was the beginning of a process which would eventually destroy Christianity. A communist underground leaflet disseminated in the Rhine region is an eloquent example of this line of reasoning: 'Catholics were horrified to see that the burning of synagogues was frighteningly similar to the attacks of the Hitler gangs against the bishops' manses in Rothenburg, Vienna, and Munich.'[90]

Added to the underground responses to the pogrom, the Berlin Gestapo report for November tells us that the Jewish question was of central interest to communist activity throughout the Reich. The reporter stressed that the communist underground's call for solidarity with the Jews fell on sympathetic ears among the upper class and Catholics, and even among certain sectors of the public who supported antisemitic policies but rejected vandalism. The Gestapo stations of Schwerin and Cologne also recorded lively debates in factories which had previously been under communist influence.[91] It is particularly noteworthy that the underground reaction did not necessarily mirror the attitudes of all workers. Even a Sopade report had to admit that condemnation was by no means unanimous.[92]

Even though the communist underground spoke out strongly against the pogrom, its chief complaint was the waste of public property – contrary to the objectives of the Four Year Plan. In this respect there was no essential difference between the reaction of the communists and the responses of other groups in Germany. Condemnation of material damage and regret at the loss of property came before the immorality of abusing defenceless civilians. This is evident in one of the underground circulars issued at the time:

No one in Germany believes that the burning of synagogues and Jewish homes, the destruction, plunder and burning of Jewish shops, warehouses and factories, the bestial maltreatment, the murder, the mass concentration of Jews in camps, is due to the 'rage of the German people'. Workers are calculating the number of extra hours they will need to work to repair the damage done to German national property. Workers' wives who manage to buy something for their homes only after much work and hardship watched the waste of much property with bitterness, and numerous housing-candidates watched with repressed rage as Nazis burned houses, villas and synagogues.[93]

The treatment of the Jews aroused disapproval among many who had hitherto endorsed 'moderate' antisemitic measures. For example, only *Kristallnacht* shook the educated bourgeoisie out of their apathy. Up to this moment many of them felt the utmost contempt for the regime's vulgarity and lack of culture. Up to this moment they were ready to tolerate this because the Nazis were seen as the saviours who could prevent Germany's collapse into Bolshevism. But the pogrom was too much, disappointing and politically alienating the bourgeoisie. A Sopade report from Saxony for January 1939 told of scientists, intellectuals and army officers who were deeply affected by the acts of vandalism. They vigorously condemned the action, especially the foolish destruction of property. The reporter added that the few who had supported Nazism in these circles had begun to detach themselves from the system, voicing hostile criticism against this sort of 'National Bolshevism'. Following the pogrom, the bourgeoisie no longer considered it *bon ton* to invite party members to tea parties and concerts.[94] Some were so deeply troubled that they wrote to the British Embassy in Berlin to express their shame. One monarchist asked for help to liberate Germany from the gang of terrorists ruling it. He called for retaliation against the Germans in the United States, Britain and France, and efforts to enable German Jews to find refuge in former German colonies.[95] Even party circles condemned the way the pogrom was carried out. Their reasons were obviously different: they argued that the arson contradicted the goals of the Four Year Plan, and that it was politically unwise to arouse sympathy for the Jews.

5

Workers, Peasants and Businessmen

A systematic analysis of the attitudes to antisemitism of all social classes, churches and ideological groups in the Third Reich would be an enormous task, far beyond the scope of this study. I have instead chosen to examine three segments of the German population for which our sources provide sufficient evidence to reach tenable conclusions: the workers, the peasants and the moneyed class.

THE WORKERS

Historical literature dealing with the German Left, the Jews and antisemitism has centred mainly on the attitudes of prominent socialist figures in the Second Reich and the Weimar Republic. Obviously the views of the heads of the workers' movement cannot be considered representative of the beliefs of the rank and file. It is equally obvious that from statements of individual anti-fascists, no matter how prominent, we should not infer the attitudes of the entire working class to the Jewish question during the Third Reich. Declarations of the exiled leadership of the socialist parties do not necessarily reflect the views of the working class within Germany. The clandestine publications smuggled into the Reich and containing declarations opposing antisemitism served only to convey the opinions of the leaders abroad.[1]

The reaction of workers to the antisemitic policy of the Nazis thus remains a complex matter which has not yet been sufficiently clarified. One of the reasons for this is the paucity of primary sources related specifically to the workers, such as reports from factory informers or chambers of commerce.

Documents which could have served as an adequate basis for research, such as the reports of the officials responsible for labour relations (*Reichstreuhander der Arbeit*), have mostly been destroyed. In the little that remains, relating to 1937–9, virtually no relevant information is to be found. Nor can we gather data pertinent to this subject from reports composed by Nazi workers' organizations such as the German Labour Front (Deutsche Arbeitsfront, DAF) or the Nazi Factory Cells Organization (Nationalsozialistische Betriebszellen-organisation, NSBO). Nevertheless, we can reach certain tentative conclusions on the basis of available sources.[2]

Research on the Wilhelmine and Weimar era has demonstrated that many workers commonly identified Jews with the bourgeoisie, and thus anti-capitalist resentment was in many cases instrumental in developing antisemitic feelings. These attitudes were not directed solely towards German Jews, but extended to Jews in general, even towards fellow party comrades. The hostility of German workers towards Jews was especially noticeable where the Jews were East European immigrants. In this light, the *Weltbühne* warned that 'It ought to be clear to us, that the German proletarians do not welcome the Jews of their class with open arms. Atavistic feelings rooted in them cannot be extirpated by means of Marxism or information campaigns. Anti-semitism is more ancient than internationalism.'[3] Therefore, when antisemitic propaganda succeeded in penetrating the German working class, it did not create anti-Jewish attitudes, but rather created a bridge between existing resentment of the Jews and the Nazi doctrine which promised to reform society by removing them.

Dislike of Jews was by no means a marginal phenomenon among workers. In the account given by a former senior leader of the republican paramilitary organization Reichsbanner, we read not only of the shift from Left to Right but also of the antisemitic character of many members of left-wing organizations. The writer emphasized that not only the masses but also the leaders had gone over to the Nazis, and as early as 1932 antisemitism was voiced in internal arguments among deputies in the Landtag (provincial assembly) and among workers' representatives. He estimated that in February 1932 80 per cent of his former friends in the Reichsbanner had adopted a Nazi outlook. Although given by a senior member of the Reichsbanner, this testimony is definitely exaggerated, but it none the less contains a measure of truth.[4]

Let us begin our analysis with the attitudes of workers active in underground cells during Hitler's rule. Some of the communists' publications, especially those disseminated in the early years of the Nazi dictatorship, were clearly tainted with antisemitism. In Halle, for instance, a communist stencil was circulated bearing the heading 'Organize the mass struggle against the fascist dictatorship.' It pointed to the hypocrisy of the Nazi regime: 'The real face of the capitalist dictatorship has been unmasked. Contrary to past declarations on Jewish capital and department stores...it is now patently clear that the regime is actually protecting Jewish capital.'[5] Equally revealing is a Gestapo report for March 1934, apparently from the Hamburg area, according to which a favourite topic in communist propaganda was the Jewish question. The communist underground tried to discredit Nazism by stressing that Hitler had not succeeded in removing the Jews and their financial activities.[6] These attempts to fight Nazism by striking an antisemitic chord were not new, the note having been sounded several times during the Weimar Republic. Only in the summer of 1935, with the United Front policy and a clearer perception of antisemitic dynamics, was this approach dropped. By then the communists understood that inciting antisemitism was a highly effective means of blurring class consciousness and diverting opinion from domestic troubles; and this, along with the sheer scale of the antisemitic outrages, forced them to redefine their stand on the Jewish issue. The Potsdam and Bielefeld Gestapo stations registered this shift in their reports for August, mentioning that the communists were disseminating clandestine propaganda sharply criticizing the pogroms.[7]

The publications of the communist underground complete the picture painted by these reports. The familiar interpretation of antisemitism was used in a pamphlet entitled *Wir kämpfen – Organ der KPD, August 1935*. Among other things it says that through the use of pogroms the Nazis sought 'not only to satisfy the SA's activism but also to please those who have anticapitalist instincts.'[8] Another pamphlet, intended as a manual on how to refute Nazi propaganda slogans, dealt incidentally with the Jewish question. It shows that, although the communists realized how vital it was to combat antisemitic policy, they still failed to understand its nature. In their view, racialism was purely functional, serving twin objectives: in internal policy, it glorified capitalist exploitation by asserting that the Nordic masters were born to rule capital; in foreign policy, it provided a first-class means of predisposing people to war. Thus racial doctrine concealed Germany's longstanding imperialistic aspirations to world rule. The 'leadership principle' was also explained as a mere stratagem for setting up a capitalist system. Nazi doctrine, the communists argued, also allowed Jewish capitalists to become integrated in the leadership echelons. In explaining the nature of antisemitism, the pamphlet draws on a common communist thesis: the boycott and the terror instituted against the Jews in the summer riots were a result of Hitler's inability to satisfy the demands of the workers, and the Nazi candidates' failure in the elections to the workers' councils.[9]

In stark contrast to the communists, socialist workers in Germany produced hardly any clandestine material condemning Nazi antisemitism. With exiles it was different: in their publications antisemitism is seen as an outlet for the anger of sectors threatened by the processes of modernization, and thus as an issue manipulated by the Nazis for their own ends – as a diversionary tactic to achieve political aims and as a means of oppression. This understanding of antisemitism – as inextricably connected with the economic interests of the bourgeoisie, who made demagogic use of anti-Jewish feelings – diminished or dismissed the uniqueness of the Jewish ordeal. The Jews were seen as suffering what the workers had suffered through long years of hardship and oppression. Thus socialists in exile customarily insisted that the Jews should not emphasize their sufferings in Nazi Germany.[10] Why was it, though, that socialists *in Germany* produced virtually no clandestine material on the Jewish question? It is true that they had problems of their own, but so had the communists, who did not ignore the matter. Perhaps their naïve belief in the workers' ability to combat the forces of darkness, including antisemitism, simply consigned it to the margins. We should not exclude the possibility, however, that the socialist underground preferred not to address the Jewish issue on pragmatic grounds. They probably believed that, since Jews were commonly identified with capitalism, an overt pro-Jewish stand could be misinterpreted by workers as a pro-bourgeois attitude. Their belief was not unfounded. As we shall see below, it was not uncommon for former members of the Socialist Party to voice the view that the Jews who had led the party were of bourgeois extraction and had only an idle ostentatious interest in socialism. These Jewish *Salonsozialisten*, they claimed, were responsible for the party's failure.[11]

Nor should we overlook the fact that leftists were not intrinsically immune to racial theories. The syndicalist Rote Kämpfer (Red Fighters) are a striking example of how deeply racial thinking penetrated some sectors of the Left. Headed by Karl Schröder, Alexander Schwab and Arthur Goldstein, this group opposed parliamentary tactics and for that reason split from the Socialist Party towards the end of the Weimar Republic. It was active after 1933 until discovered by the German security services. During his interrogation by the Gestapo, Schwab referred to his organization's stand on the race question:

We do not deny the existence of a racial problem. Care for new blood [racial quality] has always been a concern of the workers' movement. The Jewish question was underestimated by social democracy, i.e. negated under the influence of old middle-class liberalism. We, however, do not believe that all calamities stem from the Jews.[12]

Thus far we have looked at the negligible minority of workers organized in clandestine networks. Let us now examine the majority, who were not active anti-Nazis.

Whereas the Nazi surveys furnish only fragmentary evidence on the attitude of workers to antisemitic policy, the Sopade reports supply information from all German provinces. This material is particularly useful because it considers the structural and regional variables, and the fluctuations in employment conditions and wages, as well as comparing responses to anti-semitism in industrial urban centres with those in rural districts.

If we bear in mind that other social groups reacted negatively to antisemitic policy when it conflicted with their material interests, we will better under-stand the reports on workers' reactions. They too displayed hostility towards antisemitic measures in the economic sphere, particularly the boycott, and in some cases they opposed the boycott in order to demonstrate opposition to the Nazis. A report from Saxony, for example, indicates that workers' readi-ness to patronize Jewish shops did not lessen, though not as an expression of solidarity with the persecuted: rather, they used this means to indicate disappointment with Nazi social policies.[13] In other cases opposition was grounded not on political issues but on self-interest. There is ample evidence that, whenever a conflict emerged between the demands of the party and the material interests of the workers, the latter always triumphed. For example, the Gestapo stations in Cologne and Düsseldorf observed, 'When the worker is asked why doesn't he support small German enterprises, he answers that he goes wherever things are sold cheap.'[14]

Another instructive example of the primacy of self-interest is given in a report from Sigmaringen. The author describes the disturbances caused by the Hitler Youth at a Jewish assembly as part of an antisemitic demon-stration organized by the DAF. He adds that the local workers severely condemned this outrage, and as a result a breach opened between them and the DAF. However, it is clear that it was not the antisemitic character of the incident which upset the workers but its possible consequences for them. They instinctively feared that, if the local Jewish businessmen were forced to leave town, the employment situation would worsen.[15] Such a reaction is essentially no different from the one manifested by people in the Cologne area, who objected that because of the boycott a local Jewish department store had been forced to close, making its 100 employees a charge on the public.[16] A significant example of opposition to Aryanization, again not for principled but for pragmatic reasons, appears in a DAF review from Bamberg dated June 1938. This mentions the resentment of the expropriation policy in an area in which Jewish-owned textile plants employed some 4,000 workers, and no German buyers for the enterprises could be found. As a result the owners stopped production and closed down.[17]

When antisemitic policy collided with the reign of law and order it failed to gain the approval of the workers as of other social groups. Yet when such a clash did not occur they were well satisfied with the exclusion of Jews and scarcely objected to their persecution. Many in fact approved it. A Sopade observer reported that, even when the workers did not espouse Streicher's methods and condemned pogroms, they lived in such an antisemitic atmosphere that they still believed that the Jews' power should be broken, and their rights forfeited.[18]

It is small wonder that workers reacted to antisemitic measures in the same way as other sectors of German society. More surprising is what also emerges from this last report, as well as from other Sopade surveys: that the Nazi regime did succeed in getting significant portions of the working class to identify with Jew-hatred and even to endorse antisemitic policy.

There were several reasons for this success. First, it should be remembered that the working class was neither uniform nor homogeneous. Workers affiliated to the Christian trade unions, such as the Christliche Gewerk-schaftler, never rejected unconditionally a right-wing autocracy as a solution for Germany's social problems. They contemptuously repelled liberal and individualistic ideas, looking for a romantic collective experience which would bring about social reforms. The Nazis successfully exploited this yearning for anti-capitalist reforms and the workers' fascination with slogans of a socialist *Volksgemeinschaft*. In these groups there was an extreme antisemitic climate prior to Hitler's rise to power.[19]

Second, the conspicuous success of the Nazis among the former supporters of socialism and communism was one of the consequences of the belief that democracy was unworkable and the Left not a viable alternative. Incessant incitement in the media and at indoctrination meetings awakened and reactivated the anti-Jewish feelings dormant in many members of the German working class. It is not therefore too surprising to find a socialist observer reporting that the workers in the north-west approved of the Nuremberg Laws. He added that in private conversations the workers expressed the view that the Jews deserved punishment for their arrogance during the Weimar Republic, and because they had always pushed to the top.[20] Similarly, a Sopade report from Saxony for January 1936 noted that a significant number of workers had accepted the racial doctrine and that one of the Socialist Party's strongest sympathizers had responded to a speech of Goebbels by saying that it had indeed been a mistake to hand over the leadership of the party to the Jews during the Weimar era.[21] Another socialist informer, reporting for November 1937, had to admit that, while many of the bourgeoisie were highly reticent about antisemitism, all but a few strong-minded workers had succumbed to the official racialist doctrine. Even those who had never seen a Jew in their life attributed all their afflictions to Jewish influence.[22]

It is clear that many who did not become Nazis advanced anti-Jewish views and endorsed antisemitic policy. In Bavaria, for example, many who did not consider themselves Nazis nevertheless agreed with the drastic curtailment of Jews' rights and their separation from the German nation. Even a good many socialists who disapproved of the Third Reich's brutal methods believed that 'it is not so terrible to treat the Jews in this manner.'[23] Furthermore, criticism of the Nazis did not necessarily indicate a rejection of antisemitic policy. A report from Berlin for February 1936, in one of the periods when relations between the workers and the Nazi regime were difficult, details how workers contemptuously rejected the party's activities, refusing to attend political meetings and expressing their enmity to the system. At the same time, however, former members of the Socialist Party blamed the Jews for the party's failure, claiming that the Jewish party leaders had family ties with capitalists and therefore only pretended an interest in socialism.[24] A report from south-western Germany, based on impressions of a journey through the Reich, eloquently demonstrates that workers' support for nationalist chauvinism did not entail complete identification with Nazism, just as hostility to the Nazi Party did not entail opposition to antisemitism. That report asserts that, even when workers criticized the regime's policies, they excluded two subjects: the restoration of national honour through returning the army to its former size, and the solution to the Jewish question.[25]

From these reports it looks as though the Nazis' success in awakening resentment against the Jews stemmed from the party's ability to connect its own peculiar brand of antisemitism with the stereotypes of Jewish intellectualism and Jewish capitalism already imprinted on the minds of many in the working class. Furthermore, this situation, which the socialist leaders themselves portrayed in their periodic reports, and the fact that, unlike the communists, socialists in Germany did not produce clandestine literature opposing antisemitism, reflects the total failure of socialist activists at home and abroad to come to grips with and counter their followers' ideological erosion on the Jewish question.

THE PEASANTS

Nazi doctrine raised the peasants to the level of a kind of biological aristocrat, the nucleus of the mythical Nordic race. Shortly after the party's assumption of power, however, its inability to create an agrarian utopia became apparent. Investment in urbanization and industrialization occurred to the detriment of rural development and increased the flow of country people to urban centres. If, till the end of 1936, the farmers benefited from the state extended protectionist policy, with the implementation of the Four Year Plan and the acceleration of the rearmament economy the stream of peasants entering industry in search of improved pay and conditions grew steadily. In addition, agricultural prices were subjected to stricter control in order to check criticism. Detailed regional studies show that this policy kept the rural population and the regime at odds, deepening the gulf opened by the regime's pressure for the Jews to be excluded from the rural economy.[26]

Throughout the Reich, the policy of forcing the Jews out of the country-side frequently aggravated relations between the peasants and the Nazi Party. The reports on the Rhineland state, *inter alia*, that farmers objected to plans for agricultural co-operatives within the Reich Food Estate,[27] the aim being to supplant Jewish stock-dealers. The farmers demanded that the Jews remain, maintaining that they were gifted capital-owners who paid higher prices than German dealers and were more skilled at trading in stock. This sort of reaction was typical of countrymen who were actively engaged in commercial transactions with Jews and expressed no serious interest in breaking off those ties. Another report from Rhineland-Westphalia shows that local adherence to ancient customs and to traditional ties played a major role in determining the nature of relations with the Jewish traders. Here again, despite the Nazi propaganda, the peasants claimed that Jews knew how to deal in stock better than anyone else.[28] It is clear, however, that the will to continue trading had nothing to do with sympathies for the Jews themselves but with objections to the interference with peasant traditions. The compulsion to operate agriculture within the Reich Food Estate bureaucratized peasants' work, set rigid price regulations, and limited production and marketing. It therefore was bound to alienate the peasants.

Even party reports which tend to paint a rosy picture reflect the tense relations between the regime and the peasants over the Jewish issue. The official in charge of propaganda in a Bavarian district reported in March 1935, at the time of the tempestuous antisemitic drive, 'The Jewish question was tackled impressively this month. In some places schoolchildren were included in the campaign; nevertheless, the rural population is not cutting itself off from the Jews; and we still need to continue with the information campaign.'[29] Several months later, the campaign had still not succeeded:

There is not a place without a *Stürmer* showcase, or other posters; every child learns about the Jewish menace; antisemitic propaganda is delivered in lectures everywhere; at every meeting, the party raises the Jewish question – and despite all this, the campaigns have not the slightest success. Whether because of money debts or opposition in principle, the peasants do not wish to sever their ties with Jews.[30]

Another graphic example, showing how antisemitic policy acted as a source of clashes and friction with the regime, is found in a report from Pfalz. Given the policy of restricting expansion in order to maintain high prices, farmers were naturally anxious about the future of the autumn grape harvest. Although the party employed all means available to forbid sales of grapes to Jewish wine merchants, the peasants resisted the pressure. They complained that the party did not provide any suitable alternative to these traders, since the German traders were few in number and lacked sufficient capital.[31]

In all these cases we do not find peasants criticizing Nazi policy from opposition to antisemitic principles. What they disliked was anything that interfered with their own interests, and this was the reason for their unwillingness to support the party boycott. This also explains why, after the riots of November 1938, their reactions were much like most other people's: regret at the property destroyed. This theme is repeated over and over again in, for example, the surveys prepared by the National Socialist Teachers' Association, and reports by the district governors of Munich and Würzburg.[32]

THE MONEYED CLASSES

The attitude of industrialists and big business to Nazism is still a matter that arouses acrimonious historical controversy. This longstanding dispute is usually accompanied by vehement polemic, influenced by *a priori* ideological assumptions. The present discussion, however, is not concerned with the relationship between big business and the Third Reich, but will concentrate on the reactions of industrial and commercial circles to antisemitic policy, as revealed in our sources.[33]

To begin with, it must be borne in mind that the attitudes of the moneyed classes to Nazism was ambivalent. They sympathized with and approved of the destruction of socialist and communist organizations and the regimentation of the working class. Yet Hitler's order was not their cup of tea. It is true that the economic elite endorsed the efforts to stabilize and consolidate the regime as an authoritarian–totalitarian–racialist government. It certainly welcomed the purge of the SA's top echelon in June 1934, for one of its consequences was a strengthening of the conservative forces. Nevertheless, there still were factors creating discord between big business and the Nazi regime. One was increased government intervention and bureaucratic control in the sphere of private enterprise. Capitalists would have preferred a fascist type of corporatism to ensure their autonomy, but eventually they compromised and accepted the Nazis' state control of business organizations.

Industrialists were annoyed by the NSBO, the Factory Cells Organization, which, run by radical Nazis, tended to interfere with factory management, demanding concessions from the employers. Especially after the beginning of the Four Year Plan, the party penetration palpably grew, destroying Schacht's powerful influence and granting wide prerogatives to party officials. Industrialists felt production disturbed by a noticeable shortage of raw materials, a situation attributed to Hitler's over-aggressive foreign policy. A concrete example of these attitudes is found in a report from Rhineland–Westphalia. It states that factory-owners who had previously been connected with parties of the Right, and later gave their support to Nazism, had significantly changed their attitude to the regime. They now claimed that Hitler and his foreign policy were hindering the development of the German economy, placing the country under economic siege.[34] Although the commentator does not specify, it seems likely that these were the firms in the Reich Association of German Industry which opposed Hitler's plans to achieve autarky and policies of deficit spending. Commercial sectors also had some reasons to complain. They were the first to be hit by financial difficulties resulting from the serious depletion of foreign-currency reserves. Hugenberg's protectionist economic policy brought Germany a foreign-trade deficit, which in turn prevented the import of certain raw materials.

What was the attitude of these sectors of society to the party's antisemitism? It is clear from our sources that the economy, and not antisemitism, was their chief concern. They did not approve of, and indeed feared, the outbursts of the radical elements, since these extended their attacks beyond Jewish targets and were out to eliminate the churches and capitalists as well. Given that anti-capitalist motifs played a significant part in SA propaganda, big business could not be sure that terror would be restricted to the Jews. On the other hand, and for the same reason, antisemitic legislation was approved: antisemitic laws not only allowed the ideology and policy of discrimination to be expressed, but also were a means to restrain terror and stabilize the status of the Jews in the Nazi state. Franz von Papen made this point clear in his memoirs, claiming that even the rich Jews concurred with him.[35]

Especially active against the boycott were representatives of the conservative factions of the coalition: Schmitt, Popitz, Schacht, Hugenburg, who saw a need to improve both the state's economic position and Germany's image in the community of nations. In March 1933 von Winterfeld, the acting chairman of the Nationalist Party, appealed to Hitler to suppress the radicals and force them to observe the law. Von Hindenburg, von Papen, Schacht, and von Neurath were all genuinely worried about possible repercussions of the boycott. They knew Hitler had to co-operate with them in order to achieve economic growth. And, indeed, their assessment gained Hitler's backing in July 1933, when he affirmed (for the time being) the need to control unrestrained revolutionary fervour by rerouting it into evolutionary channels and institutionalizing it within the system. Similarly, on the first anniversary of the boycott of 1 April 1933, the party planned to orchestrate a new one. Again, the arguments of von Neurath, Schacht and Schmitt convinced Hitler to call it off.[36]

Many reports suggest that industrialists criticized antisemitic policies because they thought that a continued boycott would harm their interests, particularly a steady supply of raw materials and export markets. Beyond this, they were apprehensive over the negative effects of the campaigns against modern marketing agencies such as the Jewish-owned department stores. In a survey from Hesse, for example, we learn that, when a sign with the slogan 'Jews are not wanted here' was erected by the local community, the owner of a local factory asked for it to be removed. He did so after agents of foreign firms threatened that they would cancel orders if the sign remained.[37] In another location, a Gestapo observer recording reactions to the unrestrained agitation against department stores in the spring of 1935 noted, 'The actions against Jewry again took harsh forms. That this occurs now is seen as unpleasant by industrialists because exports are damaged as a result of it.'[38] Similarly, the Münster Gestapo stated that a number of major industrialists engaged in the export trade expressed deep anxiety that harming the Jews would damage German foreign trade.[39] A Bielefeld Gestapo agent reported on the prevailing mood in commercial circles. They had received threatening letters from Holland warning that, as long as the boycott of Jewish shops and antisemitic riots continued, economic ties with Germany would be limited or even broken.[40] And the Aachen Gestapo mentioned that shop-owners objected to the rioting since it drove customers away to quieter areas.[41]

Another concern was that the boycott organized abroad in retaliation to actions against German Jews would produce unemployment. The district governor in Ansbach noted that the foreign boycott was affecting factories producing metal goods and stationery, and that a cotton factory's orders had been reduced by 90 per cent. He further exemplified these worries by echoing the feelings of a factory-owner in the neighbourhood of Erlangen who employed over 100 workers.[42] There is little doubt that even Hitler took these worries seriously. German banks granted support to the Jewish-owned Tietz concern, which employed 14,000 workers. The Economics Minister's inter-cession with Hitler made possible a credit of over RM 14 million to this chain of department stores.[43] The bulk of complaints from industry probably came from those branches of it adversely affected by the attempt to shift from trade to autarky, or from firms involved in commerce and consumer-goods manu-facture. Those involved in the armament programme, which enjoyed a boom, or those whom Aryanization relieved of Jewish competition were not heard to complain. Whereas their silence suggests consent to and approval of anti-semitic policy, the objections of others again indicates that criticism arose under specific conditions or as a result of particular policies but was not directed against antisemitism itself.

The promulgation of the Nuremberg Laws renewed the criticism of those circles who feared the repercussions on the German economy. Their reactions should be seen against the background of the economic crisis in the second half of 1935, which was worse than the depletion of foreign currency in 1934 and explains the fears of the moneyed elite about the damage to German economy. Munich's political police gave concrete evidence of such reactions. The Nuremberg Laws, they reported, 'Unleashed the fear in commercial circles that the Jews abroad will exploit the legislation as an excuse for a boycott of the German economy.'[44] Others also shared this view. The Kassel Gestapo noted that, even if the public's understanding of the need for anti-semitic policy had improved, the bourgeoisie deemed the policy too drastic. Some thought that its relaxation would improve foreign-currency reserves.[45] Estate-owners in the Munich area had similar notions. Their criticism focused on the economic damage done, but they did not censure the policy itself.[46] Businessmen also would have liked to subordinate antisemitism to profits. In Augsburg people were worried about the effects of the laws on employment and commercial orders; and in Harburg–Wilhelmsburg they complained loudly that because of the laws orders had been cancelled and many foreign companies had withdrawn from trade fairs. Industrialists in Hanover similarly deemed antisemitism bad for business. They attributed the considerable decline in foreign trade in recent months to the attitude towards the Jews; others asked that posters be removed because foreign Jews did not come shopping to Germany.[47] These circles' anxiety between September and the publication of the ordinances in November is reflected in declining trade on the Stock Exchange because of rumours that Jewish investments in Germany were to be liquidated. Many feared that the Jews would take their investments out of the country. The ordinances were a relief, as they did not affect economic issues and business was not harmed.[48]

Only after the pogroms of November 1938 did a new motif, not wholly confined to self-interest, emerge. The Sopade survey of reactions to *Kristall-nacht* indicates that businessmen not only criticized the removal of Schacht and the intensification of government involvement in the economy, but also sharply condemned the violence and renewed terror.[49] It can hardly be assumed, however, that this report indicates condemnation of antisemitism in principle. Once again, it was the primitive expressions of hatred rather than the policy itself that drew protests.

6
Awareness of the Holocaust

Let us re-examine the much-discussed question of the German population's knowledge of the Nazi extermination policy. What did the German public know about the Holocaust? To what extent was it aware of the mass shootings in the east, the gassing and the extermination centres?

The most significant sources scholars have used for this topic are the *Meldungen aus dem Reich*. These confidential periodic surveys of the public mood were compiled by the German security services, particularly the SD.[1] Yet evaluating the German public's knowledge on the basis of these reports is fraught with difficulty. When one compares the small number of existing reports from gendarmerie or local SD stations with the relevant national summary, for instance, it becomes evident that certain information furnished by the local stations was deliberately deleted and suppressed, while the writer of the national digest specially stressed other aspects. The bias of the reports is thus manifest, revealing how the information-gathering process was conditioned by the perceptions and predilections of the reporters at various levels. Distortions and omissions crept in when the reporter disregarded details peripheral to his main theme. In addition, we can see how generalizations and exaggerations of local events were made to fit the Nazi world view and its own evaluation of public mood.

Some issues were also partially or entirely omitted in the national summaries, probably because their compilers were instructed to omit them. For example, these reports give no indication of the massive opposition to the euthanasia programme. The same problems arise in examining the Jewish question. Selectivity or emphasis stemmed both from subjective factors – the reporter's personal views – and from objective considerations: the need to summarize and generalize. Moreover, the conclusions of the SD summaries cannot be verified by different sources of information from the same area or other areas during the same period. These obstacles make it imperative, then, to compare these sources with other records, such as diaries, eyewitness accounts and Allied intelligence reports.[2]

A view commonly found among the general public, but also in many scholarly works, is that very little was generally known about the extermination at the time, and that only unsubstantiated rumours about the Jews' fate circulated in Germany.[3] This allegation rests mainly on various testimonies. A case in point is a letter of March 1943 written by one of the leaders of the plot of 20 July 1944, Helmuth von Moltke, in which he asserts that the German people did not know that the Nazis had killed hundreds of thousands of Jews. In his words, 'They went on believing that Jews had just been segregated and led an existence in the east pretty much like the one they had in Germany.'[4] Von Moltke's contention is further endorsed by some of the memoirs of Jewish survivors written after the war. Hans Rosenthal, for example, said that he had not known about the extermination camps.[5] Another survivor, Bruno Weil, who held a key position in the Jewish community and therefore may have had better access to information, states that only towards the end of the war, when he was an inmate in Theresienstadt, did he become aware of the transports' destinations.[6] Even Leo Baeck, the leader of German Jewry, whom we would expect to have known more about what happened to the deported Jews, maintained after the war that only in Theresienstadt did he learn about the gassing in Auschwitz.[7]

While there is difficulty in proving or disproving the accuracy of Rosenthal and Weil's statements, at least in Baeck's case we are able to reveal the weaknesses of post-war testimonies as reliable sources for the reconstruction of a historical reality. Perhaps he might not have known about Auschwitz, but what was happening to the deportees could have been no secret to him. Baeck himself recalls that a Gentile woman, who voluntarily accompanied her deported husband to Poland in the summer of 1941, gave him the first indication of what was taking place in the east. We also know that Jacob Jacobson, a top-ranking official in the Jewish community, personally introduced him to a German officer who wished to inform him about the massacres. So, notwithstanding Baeck's affirmation, it is hard to believe that he learned about the killings only later on.[8] This is more than another instance of how misleading memory can be. Here we are probably confronting a typical example of recollections which were shaped by selective memory and post-war values and knowledge. Much care is therefore needed when dealing with such sources. We cannot rely on them unless they match the evidence drawn from other material. It is very possible that Baeck, like many others, was unaware of the existence of specific extermination centres. The journalist Lili Hahn, for example, merely knew, as she noted in her diary in May 1943, that Birkenau was the railway station for the Auschwitz concentration camp.[9] It is also true that a psychological defence mechanism of repression may often have affected the recipient of the appalling news. This seems to have been the case with a member of the anti-Nazi underground, Ursula von Kardorff, who, after writing in her diary that a girl had poisoned her Jewish mother out of love to spare her from being deported, added, 'If only one knew what is happening to the Jews who have been deported.'[10] She wrote this in spite of the fact that six months earlier she had been told by somebody who came from the east that Jews were shot down in front of mass graves.[11]

Nevertheless, the vast number of testimonies given during and after the war by both Germans and Jews, as well as contemporaries' diaries, lead to the conclusion that large sections of the German population, both Jews and non-Jews, either knew or suspected what was happening in Poland and Russia. A few testimonies illustrate this contention. One survivor commented that in December 1942 he did not know about the gassing but suspected that death was awaiting the Jewish deportees.[12] A woman who worked in the Jewish hospital in Berlin testified that rumours about the camps seeped through what they called the *Jüdische Mundfunk* (Jewish mouth radio), and the rate of suicides always increased sharply two or three days before a transport was due to leave.[13] Her words are confirmed and illustrated by the report of Edwin van D'Elden, former representative of the American chamber of commerce in Frankfurt, who was in that city till May 1942. He commented that, when soldiers came back from Poland and told about mass shootings, dozens of Jews who had received deportation orders in May 1942 committed suicide.[14] Another German Jew, who survived clandestinely, asserted that, on visiting theatres and bars and talking to civilians who did not know he was Jewish, he heard about the mass shootings, which made him decide to go underground.[15] We learn the same from a socialist Jewess who had heard rumours about the fate of the transports prior to 1943.[16] If these recollections seem untrustworthy as historical records, it must be added that stories about evacuated people being shot in the east also occur in contemporary letters and diaries. In his diary Ludwig Haydn noted that Viennese Jews were openly mentioning that deportation meant starvation or being shot in front of a grave they would dig themselves.[17] Such bleak prospects also appear in a letter of Hermann Samter, an official in the Jewish community of Berlin, as early as January 1942.[18]

The fact that the SD reports say very little about the fate of the deported Jews may give the false impression that what befell them was unknown to the public. However, the paucity of SD reports on this topic by no means indicates that little or nothing was known in Germany. If we followed such an erroneous line of reasoning on the question of the euthanasia killings, we would have to conclude, incorrectly, that because this topic is hardly mentioned in the SD reports very few knew anything about the murder of the mentally ill. Yet Marlis Steinert convincingly argues that the SD summaries deliberately suppressed information on public discussion of this issue; rumours concerning the killings are almost wholly confined to local party and jurists' reports. In sharp contrast to the silence of the SD surveys on this issue, there is massive and conclusive evidence that it was widely discussed and that the information the population obtained was accurate: in the autumn of 1941, people were talking about 70,000–80,000 murdered in the euthanasia centres.[19] Similar remarks appear in contemporary testimonies and diaries of ordinary German citizens. Lisa de Boor, for example, noted in her diary that people were talking about the euthanasia programme in which '80,000 were to be murdered on Hitler's orders.'[20] After the programme was officially halted, in August 1941, the public still linked the extermination of the Jews with that of the mentally ill. Thus, it was reported that the following phrase was going the rounds in the city of Leipzig in 1943: 'After the Jews, the sick and the helpless.'[21]

Having clarified these methodological points, let us return to our main topic and examine in depth the question of how much and what was known about the extermination process.

Very few SD national summaries mention the information on the murder of the Jews that circulated among the German public. By reading the local reports before they were summarized in Berlin, however, we may assess with greater precision what the German population actually knew. Such an inspection confirms that people heard of the slaughter of civilian Poles and Jews from the very onset of hostilities. Thus as early as November 1939 a party report from north-western Westphalia states that soldiers in a train had openly recounted the SS atrocities committed in Poland. According to them, Jews were pushed into ditches and killed with hand grenades; some of the Jews had committed suicide in order to escape the agony of dying at the hands of the SS.[22] This sort of information recurs at the end of April 1940, when a local SD station reported that soldiers on leave were talking about the mass killings of Jews and Poles.[23] In view of such sensational disclosures, it is hardly surprising that the events in Poland definitely interested the public, and we thus understand why people in Weimar, Dresden, Breslau and Kiel were so curious to know more about the solution to the Jewish question.[24]

More detailed and frightening accounts again circulated at the start of the Barbarossa campaign. Soldiers on leave often spread stories of widespread hunger and the death of the population in the Soviet Union. They made no secret of how Russian prisoners of war were murdered and of the fate awaiting the Jews deported to the east.[25] In sharp contrast to the misleading silence of the national SD summaries, the accuracy of the information in local reports is sometimes highly instructive. Such is the case with the informer from the town of Steiger who heard people discussing the shootings of Jews who had previously dug their own graves, and the nervous breakdowns of some of their executioners.[26] Another local SD survey referred to public speculation on the possible activities of the top secret unit Sonderkommando 1005. As is known, this unit, under the command of SS Colonel Paul Blobel, was established in June 1942 to obliterate the tracks of the SS murder squads and burn the corpses of those murdered in the *Aktionen* in the eastern territories. A local Bavarian SD reporter noted,

A rumour was going the rounds in Münnerstadt that the Allies had posed a question to Hitler, via the Red Cross, on the whereabouts of the Jews who were in the Reich. The Führer ordered the exhumation of the buried Jews and the burning of their corpses so that in the event of a retreat on the Eastern Front the Soviets would not gain possession of propaganda material such as that on Katyn.[27]

This widespread discussion of the murder was aptly summarized in unambiguous terms in a party report dated 9 October 1942:

In the course of the work on the final solution of the Jewish question, the population in various parts of Germany has recently begun to discuss the 'very harsh measures' against the Jews, especially in the eastern territories. Inquiries have revealed that these discussions – often distortions and exaggerations – stem from stories told by soldiers on leave from units fighting in the east, who themselves had been able to witness such measures.[28]

When Germany began to suffer reverses in the war, talk of the mass murder seems to have gradually increased; now facing the bitter end, people began to have fears of retaliation. This particularly occurred when the anxious population began to seek some sort of spiritual comfort after learning of their relatives' fate on the Russian Front. In response to such apprehensions, some clergy preached that the Stalingrad disaster was God's punishment on the Germans for their treatment of Russians, Jews and Poles.[29] Nazi propaganda also excited discussion of the killings, as when in the spring and summer of 1943, in response to propaganda on the Katyn and Winneza massacres of Polish officers, intellectuals, churchmen and others criticized Goebbels' hypocrisy, claiming that hundreds of thousands of Serbs, Poles, Russians and Jews were treated no better by the Germans. Informers also reported that peasants commented with reference to the mass graves of Poles and Jews, 'Neither did we treat our enemies better, especially the Jews, who were eliminated ruthlessly.' After the release of the news of the Katyn graves, there were some who expressed concern that the enemy might find graves of Jews killed systematically by German soldiers.[30] Some of the public made it clear that they understood that these were the rules of the total war proclaimed by Goebbels. In this type of war the British and American bombers were wreaking havoc on German cities, and the Germans were pursuing their extermination campaign against the Jews.[31]

People commonly try not to dwell on what is too upsetting. It seems therefore that, in the Germans' efforts to maintain a 'normal life' at any price, the annihilation policy was a sort of taboo topic to be mentioned only in family circles or among close friends. However, the Jewish theme came up in public discussion when it had implications for the life of the population or when people reacted to certain political stimuli. These implications were sensed especially when fear of defeat began to emerge after Stalingrad, or when the propaganda on the Katyn affair acted as a stimulus to comment on other killings in the east.

The next question is: was there a specific awareness of what became known as the Holocaust? In other words, did the public perceive the killings of Jews as so many individual acts of murder, as 'normal' war brutality against the civilian population, or, more than that, as some new phenomenon of monstrous dimensions? Since the SD reports provide no satisfactory answer to this question, we are obliged to turn to other sources – hitherto not used by researchers dealing with the topic – which attest to the information that circulated among the German public.

British intelligence material allows us to sense how the German public felt about the war against Russia. By reading letters written by German civilians to their relatives and friends abroad, the British censors obtained the following picture: on the one hand, the anxiety and grief caused by the losses at the front, combined with war-weariness and depression; on the other, the firm belief of many that the war against the Soviet Union was a crusade for the benefit of mankind. The Germans saw themselves as conducting a historical war of liberation, and in such a context the term 'extermination of the enemy' was more than just a metaphor.[32] This perception of the true nature and far-reaching implications of the Russian campaign also comes to light in other sources. Most revealing is a British diplomatic despatch which included a memorandum of a conversation with the Swedish banker Jacob Wallenberg. He returned from Berlin in 1941, where he had met mainly businessmen and officials in the economic departments. Reading the memorandum, one is struck by the cold-blooded manner in which Germans talked about *millions* of human beings who would perish. Wallenberg noted that 'There was much talk in Germany about the starvation which would ensue in Russia as a result of the scorched earth policy and that it was estimated that between *ten and twenty million* Russians might die of hunger during the winter. *Two and a half million* would starve in Leningrad' (emphasis added). In this context he casually voiced his opinion: 'Many Germans were disgusted at the way in which Jews were deported from German cities to ghettoes in Poland. Several begged him to put a word in with the Swedish government to get visas for Sweden for some of their acquaintances who otherwise would be sent to Poland to a lingering death.'[33]

Bearing in mind both the SD material and the confidential Allied reports on conditions in Germany, the German people appear to have grasped the meaning and significance of the unprecedented war with the Soviet Union. Therefore the news of the massacres of Jews was not internalized in a mental and emotional vacuum. The Germans were fully aware that what was happening in Russia was not the sort of thing that ordinarily happened in war, and this awareness was articulated in everyday conversation. They were cognizant of the horrible consequences of this campaign and understood that it was costing the lives of millions, who were dying in a variety of ways. We could, therefore, hypothesize that they were psychologically conditioned to comprehend the news of the extermination of Jews. However, awareness of the magnitude of the atrocities against Poles and Russians created a psychological framework in which the public submerged the specific annihilation of the Jews. The killings of the *Einsatzgruppen* were fitted into it and were not necessarily perceived in their own right.

The German population furthermore sensed what this war entailed, but many had no need to imagine what was taking place since they had themselves witnessed the atrocities. At the end of 1942 and beginning of 1943 the population of the village of Wohlau assembled on the shore of the Vistula to watch hundreds being undressed and killed. German soldiers and civilians talked about the gas van used in exterminating the Jews of the Semlin camp in Yugoslavia.[34] In inner Germany, too, it was no secret that more than 'ordinary' war atrocities were being perpetrated in the east. The famous resistance group led by the Scholl brothers realized this when they stated in their manifesto that since the defeat of Poland 300,000 Jews had been killed in the most brutal fashion, in what they called 'the most horrible crime against the dignity of man, for which there is no parallel in the whole of human history.'[35] This was also the reaction of another opponent of Nazism, Paul Freiherr von Schoenaich, who wrote in his diary that the Jews were being murdered in hundreds of thousands. He too regarded this as 'the greatest shame of mankind of all times', and he added, 'If God's justice does exist, there must be a punishment for it', and he hoped to live to see it.[36]

It is unnecessary to repeat here the findings of historians such as Wilhelm, Krausnick, Streit and Förster on the massive involvement of the Wehrmacht in the extermination process. Ordinary soldiers serving in the vicinity of the extermination centres certainly knew the purpose of these places. When French POWs at the Rawa Ruska camp near Bełżec asked their guards where all the trains packed with Jews were going, they received an unequivocal answer, 'To heaven.'[37] It is obvious that the main sources of information on the liquidation process were those who returned from the front and told their acquaintances about it. Ludwig Haydn learned of the mass shootings when a friend of his, an army major, told him how an SS man had invited him to join a 'dove-shooting' (*Taubenschiessen*), a euphemism for the slaughter of Jews.[38] So widespread was the information on the killings that even foreigners knew about the hideous work of the murder squads. One who did was Edwin van D'Elden:

Of the five convoys leaving Frankfurt prior to his departure, he learned from incontestable sources that only one reached Łódź and that three never reached destination. The Jews of these three [convoys] were compelled to leave the train in Poland, were stripped of their clothing and then were summarily executed by Nazi firing squads who mowed the victims by machine-gun fire. He learned of these events from friends who secured the information from soldiers who actually participated in the executions in Poland and who subsequently returned to Frankfurt on leave.[39]

If foreigners managed to obtain this sort of information, we must assume that ordinary Germans also possessed it. A common citizen such as Karl Dürkefälden knew about the atrocities against Russians as early as August 1941, and a letter from his brother-in-law merely confirmed that no Jews remained in Kiev.[40] When the brother-in-law came on leave in October 1942 he supplied the missing details: no Jews remained in Kiev because they had all been exterminated.[41] He learned of the killing by gas from a soldier who had come from Vilna; from the same source he heard about the gassing of Jews from France. In the summer of 1942 Dürkefälden again noted down what he had heard from soldiers about the fate of the Jews in Russia, and the BBC broadcasts on the extermination confirmed their stories.[42] Ludwig Haydn reacted in the same manner: 'With regard to the mass murder of Jews, the broadcast merely confirms what we know here anyhow.'[43]

Soldiers not only confided their knowledge while on leave: in their letters too, they mentioned the massacres, despite the censorship and the terror. Germans thus became familiar with the war experience, including the fate of the victims of Nazi occupation and stories about the extermination.[44]

In Haydn's view the soldiers' reactions to the killings ranged from utter incredulity to approval.[45] In their letters some condemned the murders, while others commended them. Some merely provided cynical hints, in phrases such as 'Jews will not harm anybody anymore.' Others expressly wrote about the shooting of tens of thousands of Jews.[46] That shortly after the beginning of the massacres many in Germany knew about them and passed on what they had learned to their friends is not surprising. Obviously individuals located where information on the killings was readily available had greater and more accurate knowledge. The diary of Ulrich von Hassell aptly illustrates this point. From October 1939 he began to obtain news of the SS atrocities in Poland. This information was confirmed by a memorandum that General Ludwig Beck, who in turn had received it from a third party, read to him. Hassell was likewise informed about the actions of the *Einsatzgruppen* in the Soviet Union by Hans von Dohnanyi and General Georg Thomas, and Johannes Popitz told what he had learned from Erich Gritzbach, Goering's aide-de-camp. By May 1943 his reaction to the propaganda on Katyn was similar to that mentioned above: he recalled that 100,000 Jews had been poisoned in gas chambers.[47] Similar channels were probably available to the virtuous Margaret Sommer, who gathered information on the murders. She was thus able to inform Cardinal Bertram about the massacre of Kovno Jews three months after the event.[48]

Apart from the German soldiers who spoke openly about the extermination during their furloughs or mentioned it in their letters home, another source was the foreign slave workers in various German camps and enterprises in the east. Many who either witnessed the murders themselves or heard of them carried information when they were put to work in Germany. We should not rule out the possibility that they confided their experiences to Germans whom they trusted and who wanted to know what the SS was doing in the east. If they were lucky enough to escape, their accounts reached the Allied intelligence services, as seen in the following two examples.

In July 1942 the SS, aided by the Wehrmacht and the Ukrainian militia, began the systematic liquidation of Jewish communities in eastern Galicia. Their victims included the communities of Jezierno, Trembowla and Tarnopol. Some of the young Jews were taken to work; the rest joined the aged, women and children on their last journey to Bełżec. During these events, French POWs were dismantling the Jewish cemetery of Trembowla in order to build roads with the gravestones. Several months later the POW camp was closed and its inmates sent to Germany.[49] One of them, who had worked in Tarnopol and witnessed the mass murder of Jews, revealed what he had seen to a German trade unionist.[50] Two others managed to escape; they left Stettin on a Finnish cargo boat and arrived in Malmö, in Sweden, on 4 February 1943. Recounting their experiences in the Polish province of Lublin, they testified that in August 1942 the French prisoners working in Jezierno and Trembowla had seen a train of cattle trucks on its way to Tarnopol:

In every carriage, the Germans had piled up 200 old men, women and children although there was at the most room for 50–60 persons. A few days later the trains came back, empty; the walls and doors of the trucks were staved in, many Jews having tried to escape during the journey. Jews who came back later told that all these 10,000 Jews had been massacred at Tarnopol, and Jews had to bury them. Some said they had been electrocuted *en masse*.[51]

Our second example concerns two Belgians at Rawa Ruska who witnessed the mass killings and later recounted their experiences. The Rawa Ruska penal camp was located 18 kilometres from Bełżec and among its inmates were French and Belgian POWs who had arrived there in April 1942. Since almost all transports from outside Poland, West Poland and Galicia had to stop at Rawa Ruska, the POWs saw hundreds of wagons piled with Jews going to Bełżec and returning empty. The bodies of Jews who died during the journey or were shot while trying to escape were thrown on the tracks.[52] These two Belgian prisoners of war, who escaped from Germany at the end of April 1943 and arrived in Sweden a week later, gave an account of what they had witnessed at Rawa Ruska and in Stettin. In the words of the British agent who spoke with them,

What made the most impression on them was the extermination of the Jews. They had both witnessed atrocities. One of the Belgians saw truck loads of Jews carried off into a wood and the trucks returning a few hours later – empty. Bodies of Jewish children and women were left lying in ditches and along the railways. The Germans themselves, they added, boasted that they had constructed gas chambers where Jews were systematically killed and buried.[53]

Now let us inquire what was known in Germany about specific extermination centres and the use of gas as a method of killing. In his study of Bavaria, Kershaw noted two cases of people sentenced to imprisonment for having spoken openly about the gassing of Jews and for having made denigratory comments about Hitler. The absence of SD reports conveying public comments on gassing brought him to conclude that, although rumours might have circulated, the gassing was not widely known in Germany,[54] but he judiciously admitted that these particular cases might merely be the tip of an iceberg for which documentary evidence was lacking. Similarly, Stokes conceded that some reports on the extermination centres did reach Germany, but argued that rumours about them were probably not believed. Therefore the operation of extermination camps was, in his opinion, generally unknown.[55] Here again we see the limitations of the SD abstracts as a basis for assessing what sort of information went the rounds in Germany. They prove particularly inadequate with regard to what was known about the use of poison gas. This deficiency can only be corrected by broadening our documentary base. Once we do this we realize that talk of the gassing of enemies of the Reich could be heard as early as the end of 1941 amidst rumours about the euthanasia programme. This comes to light in, for example, the report of an American newspaper correspondent repatriated from Germany following the entry of the United States into the war. He learned that Jews and hundreds of Russian prisoners had been either shot or gassed, and added that, 'when typhus had broken out in one camp in Poland, it was checked by herding Russian prisoners into rooms by scores and gassing them on the pretext of de-lousing their clothes and bodies.'[56]

The data on euthanasia gathered by British intelligence in Basle and Geneva also included information from a German railway guard that trains with wounded soldiers entered a tunnel in which they were gassed.[57] The story of a gassing-tunnel seems to have spread rapidly, for we find it mentioned on various occasions by people who were totally unconnected. Thus Lili Hahn, while living in Hesse, was informed in November 1941 that the last two transports of Frankfurt Jews were gassed in a tunnel near Minsk.[58] Likewise, at the end of 1942 Ludwig Haydn in Vienna heard this rumour about how Jews were murdered in the east: they were forced to undress, then were loaded on trains whose heating-pipes injected gas instead of steam. These examples show that, though the details were clearly distorted and blurred, rumours about gassing were more widespread than the SD reports would suggest.[59] Moreover, on the basis of the available evidence we may venture to say that by 1943 the use of gas as a killing-method was fairly widely discussed, though obvious inaccuracies and distortions gave rise to misconceptions of how such murders were carried out.

Even foreigners such as the Spanish counsellor Fermín Lopez Robertz, who was in Berlin in March 1943, heard of a gassing-tunnel. According to his account, when Jews from Berlin were deported to an unknown destination, it was, in his words, '*generally* believed to be a certain tunnel outside the city, where they were to be gassed.'[60] A similar report was offered by Salazar Soriano, a Bolivian who had been studying engineering in Frankfurt, and who after leaving early in March 1943 was interviewed in Lisbon by the British. He stated that in general people disliked the Jews, but the majority opposed the severe treatment meted out to them. In June 1942, he said, 4,000 Jews were driven out of Frankfurt during the night, packed into a closed and sealed goods train and taken into the country. There gas was pumped into the wagons, and those who survived were machine-gunned.[61]

If these foreigners heard about the use of poison gas, we must assume that local Germans had. A member of the Berlin Philharmonic Orchestra, when questioned in Lisbon, gave general details regarding the persecution of the Jews. Although he was certainly distant from the extermination process, his reply was much more accurate: 'Deportations to Poland and Russia were equivalent to a death sentence, for Jews were being gassed there.'[62] Ruth Andreas Friedrich wrote on 22 December 1942 about the ghastly rumours concerning the evacuees: Jews digging their own graves and undressing before being shot, or death by starvation and gassing. On 10 August 1943 she again refers to the use of gas in the annihilation of the Jews.[63] The fact that people talked about the gassing of deportees on the outskirts of Berlin or Frankfurt clearly indicates how nebulous and distorted their information was. But it also reveals that rumours about the gassing of Jews were current, however people filled them out from their imaginations.

What the general public knew about specific gassing-centres is much more difficult to establish, as sources referring to them are very rare. Nevertheless, the camps were not hermetically sealed and, despite all precautions, some information about them filtered into Germany. Those living close to Auschwitz obviously knew that it served as an extermination centre. We learn this from a report of the *Gauleitung* of Upper Silesia for May 1943, sent to the Nazi Party Chancellery. In reaction to the propaganda on the Katyn affair, the mass killing of Polish officers by the Soviets was equated with the murders perpetrated in Auschwitz.[64] According to the testimony of SS *Rottenführer* Pery Broad, the German and Polish civilians who built four crematoria at the end of 1942 were not the only ones who knew about the extermination centres. In January 1944 SS officers posted photographs showing the construction of crematoria and ovens with corpses. They were seen by railway personnel, many civilian employees of building-companies, and women working in telephone and telegraph services. From the end of 1943, as Broad noted during his duty trips to Germany, rumours about gassing in concentration camps were circulating in the large German cities. People travelling on trains which passed Auschwitz stood up to get a better view. Civilians and police were wont to comment, 'It's being fried nicely in Auschwitz.'[65] Those who sought facts, though vague and distorted, obtained them. Thus in March 1943 Adam von Trott mentioned the construction of a large concentration camp in Upper Silesia for 40,000–50,000 inmates, of whom 3,000–4,000 were to be killed monthly.[66]

News of the extermination centres reached the public in Germany through various channels. Despite the fact that the Final Solution was supposed to be a closely guarded secret, some of those involved in it, or who knew about it, publicly divulged information. Some openly boasted about the liquidation of the Jews, as we learned from the testimony of the Belgian POWs who escaped to Sweden. Likewise, Ruth Andreas Friedrich mentions an SD man who vaingloriously declared in a suburban train that 2,000 Jews were being murdered every week in Auschwitz.[67] This sort of information, like that about the mass shootings, was divulged by army personnel in casual conversation. Lili Hahn recorded in her diary her conversation with an army officer who spoke of the death camps.[68] Those who still wavered after having heard about the existence of the inconceivable death factories could corroborate their impressions by listening to Allied broadcasts.

As a source of information on the extermination, the Allied radio broadcasts should be neither dismissed nor underestimated. We know from various sources – including the SD reports – that they were widely listened to and discussed.[69] A German journalist from Berlin stated when in Sweden that the BBC had an extensive audience and that people knew a great deal about what was happening.[70] Underground organizations such as the Hamburg group Kampf dem Faschismus (Fight Fascism), disseminated the content of these broadcasts to influence the population.[71] Allied stations conveyed extremely accurate information on the fate of the Jews. Transmitting in German, they gave coverage in 1943 to the deportation of French Jews to Poland and to the uprising of the Warsaw ghetto. They stated that between 2 and 3 million Jews had been exterminated in Poland. On 16 July 1944 the Allies broadcast the urgent appeal by the Swiss Evangelical Church Union to the Swiss Bundesrat (Federal Assembly) and the International Red Cross to do whatever was possible to rescue the Jews still alive in Hungary.

The BBC launched a massive broadcast campaign on the extermination of the Jews at the end of 1942. It provided information on the unparalleled murder and the numerous suicides of Jews who did not want to be transported to the east; it cited the Archbishop of York's call for a crusade to save the Jews. Several times a day for a whole week, starting 16 December 1942, the BBC repeated the official statement of the Inter-Allies Information Committee on the annihilation of the Jews, as well as the declaration of the Polish National Council in London. These statements were echoed by the Russian station transmitting in German from Kuibychev.[72]

It is hard to believe that these announcements had no impact on the listeners. Others must have reacted in the same way as Karl Dürkefälden or Ludwig Haydn, because these broadcasts merely corroborated what they had already learned from other sources.[73] Some Jews, indeed, managed to save their lives because they took these broadcasts to heart. Käte Cohn, who left Berlin for Switzerland in February 1942, told of a Jewish workers' group of some sixty persons who met daily in front of the factory where they were employed and who received there from a group of women workers the gist of the previous evening's BBC news.[74] 'ML' decided to go underground when he received information on the fate of the deported Jews from people who listened to the BBC.[75]

The Allied radio also provided information on gassing-methods. With extreme accuracy it told the tragic story of the Czech Jews sent to Auschwitz in December 1943 and gassed there on 7 March 1944. There were similar broadcasts from the Soviet Union about the mass gassings in Auschwitz, and the president of the British railway union appealed to his Hungarian opposite number to rescue Hungarian Jews from murder. The Americans, for their part, reported that since April 1942, 4 million Jews had been murdered in gas chambers, hanged or killed with lethal injections in two camps in Silesia. They also broadcast the declaration of Anthony Eden that Hungarian Jews were being moved to Poland to be gassed, and the appeals of the Pope and the King of Sweden to rescue Hungarian Jewry from murder.[76]

The leaflets dropped by Allied planes over Germany also relayed this information. Some of them included data on the annihilation policy, warning the population about the future consequences of these atrocities, and, as we know from the SD reports and other sources, people read and discussed the contents of the Allied leaflets. Between January and March 1943 the Royal Air Force dropped leaflets dealing with the murder of Poles under German occupation, cautioning that whoever participated in these acts would be held responsible. The extermination of Poles and Jews was expressly mentioned in other leaflets distributed in February and March 1943. The pamphlet *Die andere Seite* ('The Other Side'), dropped by the RAF between December 1943 and March 1944, contained an article by Thomas Mann and the Scholl brothers' manifesto, which mentioned the mass shootings of Jews. Between 15 and 19 April the US Air Force scattered over Schweinfurt, Oranienburg, Wittenberg, Kassel and Eschwege 9 million copies of a printed warning from President Roosevelt to the German people. It called attention to the atrocities perpetrated by Nazis and Japanese upon civilian populations, referred specifically to the massive and systematic murder of European Jewry as one of the most terrifying crimes recorded in history, and warned that a similar fate was awaiting the Jews of the Balkans and Hungary. Various leaflets gave concrete details of the extermination centres. *Das Sternbanner*, scattered over Germany on 27 August 1944, provided information on Majdanek. In the three quarters of a million copies of *Die Luftpost*, dropped between 15 and 24 September 1944 over Kiel and Dortmund, the British war correspondent on the Russian Front, Paul Winterton, described in detail the gas chambers and crematoria where 2,000 Jews had been murdered daily.[77]

What were the reactions to these disclosures? It seems that such information activated complex psychological processes of denial and repression in those who heard the broadcasts or read the leaflets. A typical example was the incredulity of Ursula von Kardorff when in December 1944 she read a copy of the *Journal de Génève* containing the account of Vrba and Wetzler, the two Slovak Jews who had escaped from Auschwitz and reported that the Jews were being gassed there. Although she herself had previously referred to the horrible fate of the Jews, on reading this she commented, 'Is one to believe such a ghastly story? It simply cannot be true. Surely even the most brutal fanatics could not be so absolutely bestial.'[78] Manfred Fackenheim also noted that prior to his deportation in May 1943 he had heard on the BBC that Jews were being gassed in Auschwitz, but believed that this was no more than anti-German propaganda.[79] Clearly there was no scarcity of information, but some people could not or would not take it in. There is no doubt that those who wished to know had the means at their disposal to acquire such knowledge. Those who did not or could not believe reacted so because they did not want to believe. In one sentence: they knew enough to know that it was better not to know more.

Admittedly the material on which this chapter is based is unquantifiable and impressionistic, which precludes definitive conclusions. Nevertheless, some tentative conclusions can be suggested. Much information on the extermination of the Jews circulated in Germany. We must be careful to distinguish between various levels of knowledge, however. Soldiers who were eyewitnesses gave clear and vivid accounts in conversations and letters of what was happening in the east. Those who acquired such knowledge, either through their work in the bureaucracy or because as members of the underground they deliberately sought it for themselves, had to make an effort to imagine what it meant. Because what they had to imagine was unprecedented, they were not always able to conceive the monstrous dimensions of the crime. Despite mentioning hundreds of thousands of victims, or referring to these acts as the worst crime in history and an unparalleled phenomenon, it seems that even they could not and did not grasp its incredible magnitude. Thus, what became known as *the Holocaust* was an inconceivable and therefore unbelievable reality even for those anti-Nazis who deliberately sought information.

As for the vast majority, they heard rumours; and, the more the information had been filtered in its passage from person to person, the less precise it had become. The lack of specific descriptions of how the murders were perpetrated made people try to imagine it for themselves – which explains the stories of gassing-tunnels and mass electrocution. Hans Mommsen is right, then, in saying that we should ask not who knew but who wanted to believe.[80] Germans sensing the gravity of the crime committed by their nation were caught between feelings of guilt and an urge to deny responsibility. Soldiers could not repress what they saw on the Eastern Front: even when relegated to the subconscious, it kept seeping into consciousness. Those in Germany who obtained the information in a roundabout way were able to submerge it. The next two chapters will show that the vast majority of the population appear to have consciously avoided such knowledge, especially when fear of retribution triggered guilt feelings, or awareness of guilt gave rise to fear of the consequences.

7

Public Responses to Antisemitism, 1939–1943

At first sight the SD reports create the impression of full public support for the Nazi antisemitic measures, emphasizing the insatiable demands for a more stringent anti-Jewish policy. The exceedingly antisemitic dispositions to which the reports testify overshadow the few, trivial cases they mention in which positive attitudes towards Jews were demonstrated – generally by individuals who defied the authorities by providing Jewish families with articles of food that they were not allowed to buy, such as fruit, pastry and chocolate.

Nazi records show the population not only endorsing the persecution, but insisting on the clarification of unsettled issues of anti-Jewish policy and pressing for that policy to be sharpened. Reporters provide numerous examples of public dissatisfaction with the inconsistencies of Jewish policy. Members of the professions, for example, asked the politicians to make a decision about paying Jews for public holidays. Physicians protested that in writing to a Jewish doctor they had to address him by his title, as if he were a colleague. If an academician became a criminal, they argued, his title was taken away; the same should hold for a Jew since he was an arch-criminal responsible for starting the war.[1] Unspecified social elements were surprised that Jews and the Jewish community were still listed in the new telephone book (in the summer of 1940 Jews had been ordered to include the official Jewish designations of 'Sarah' and 'Israel' in the telephone directory). Some people expressed anger that Jewish children received the same milk ration as Germans, or that Jewish houses remained unmarked. Others took issue with orders relating to public transport: since Jews were permitted to travel third class, workers and soldiers could not avoid them; they suggested that instead Germany should emulate Slovakia and make Jews travel in special wagons. There were those who asked that Jews should be banned from public transport altogether, except when travelling to work.

The regulations on shopping-hours for Jews also served as a source of complaint. It was suggested that Jews and Poles should buy their products after regular hours, when Germans had finished shopping, or that they be assigned to separate stores. Others asked that Jews be marked, as in Poland, so that they would not come to markets and so that 'Jewish-looking' Germans would face no threat of attack. On the whole, many concurred that the antisemitic measures taken fell short of the desired state of affairs and that the best solution would be to evacuate all Jews immediately.[2]

It must be pointed out that such hostility was not reserved solely for Jews. A general xenophobia prevailed in Germany during the war. The SD reports furnish information on similar attitudes towards slave labourers. Germans sharply criticized the fact that they had to sit with foreign workers in the same waiting-rooms for doctors and dentists, or that they had to share the same hospital rooms. They objected to foreign workers' using the same trains, asking that their travel be restricted or that special wagons or sections be allotted to them.[3]

Did these attitudes faithfully reflect popular opinion? Were these demands to radicalize anti-Jewish policy a dominant trend, or did they merely mirror the opinions of party members and Nazi sympathizers? When an SD report states that people 'from all over' or 'the majority' supported the antisemitic line, was this true, or did the Nazi reporter exaggerate?

The nature of the sources admittedly makes a conclusive answer difficult. Nevertheless, a few comments may prove helpful. To begin with, the SD reports cannot be taken at face value. An incident in Bielefeld casts doubt on the reliability of the surveys.

In 1941, a Bielefeld SD reporter told of a storm of indignation. Whereas until then the Jews had been allowed to shop between 8 and 9 a.m., the local administration had changed the shopping hours to 11 a.m. to 4.30 p.m. This change, he claimed, had sparked public anger: the population complained that if German women did not want to mingle with Jews they had to shop at the coldest hours of the day – either in the early morning or late evening – whereas the Jews could go shopping during the warmer hours in between. This indirect criticism of the local-government measure elicited a letter of protest from the city administration to SD headquarters, denying the alleged public outcry. In his reply, the SD chief admitted that the outcry had been limited to one case, involving a few village women.[4] This example demonstrates the danger of taking the surveys' generalizations at face value, since they can be highly biased. It is therefore important to use other sources when available, as a control or to correct distortions. Regrettably, however, additional material does not always put us on more solid ground.

Some non-Nazi surveys of the German situation and of public attitude towards Jews do not stand up to critical scrutiny. Such is the case with the *Inside Germany Reports* released by German exiles who wanted to foster an image of 'another Germany'. Much of what they say is consequently a projection of their own wishes and contrasts sharply with the SD's version of events. Typical of this uncritical and apologetic approach is the picture of a country in which at the end of 1940 assistance to Jews was apparently more common than hostility – a country in which there were *thousands* of instances of non-conformist behaviour, and Jews were secretly helped in every conceivable way: by neighbours and acquaintances who procured them clothing with their own ration cards; by shopkeepers who arranged to supply them with goods they were not permitted to buy; by neighbours who managed to smuggle milk to elderly Jews – when normally it was only available to the sick and to children; and by fellow employees who shared their food with Jews. Such acts of succour were the rule, rather than the exception. What is more, people's entire attitude towards the Jews had changed, to the extent that Jews now received frequent visits from their non-Jewish acquaintances. The report that suggests all this ends with the allegation that the growing difficulty in securing emigration to the United States was partly due to the fact that American consuls were aware of the friendly treatment tendered to Jews.[5] Obviously this picture, which contradicts any other available source, must be interpreted as German exiles' apologetics.

Though for different reasons, similar caution ought to be exercised with the post-war recollections of Jews who emigrated. First, memory lapses result in discrepancies and contradictions in the accounts. Secondly, many of these memoirs, whether consciously or unwittingly, 'touch up' the past: they are characterized more by what they repress than by what they remember. Their frame of perception leads to omissions, confusions and generalizations on the basis of isolated incidents. Here we must bear in mind the warning of experts in the field of oral history, that memory is not a reproduction of reality but rather a symbolic mediation and elaboration of meaning with the imagination guiding the perception of reality. Hence, the recollections of German Jews who emigrated should in most cases be used simply to illustrate or add colour to an account based on less subjective sources – allowing us to feel the pulse of events by adding atmosphere to the historian's detached and analytical reconstruction.[6]

What about personal testimonies? Although much more adequate as a historical record, many of them, too, fail to put us on firmer ground – even if recorded during the events. Let us consider a few examples. A Jewish businessman who left Germany in March 1941 told his British interviewer that Jews were not hated by the middle and working classes and that even army officers opposed antisemitic policy.[7] A more measured and judicious appraisal, but still along the same lines, was furnished by another emigrant, who left in August 1941. He thought that the mass of Germans disliked the Nazis' clamorous, terrorist antisemitism and wanted nothing to do with it, but did not dare to raise their voices or take any action against it. Fear had become so great that many tried to avoid speaking to Jews on the street, but would gladly go to their homes in the evening.[8] According to a third witness, who left Berlin for Switzerland in February 1942, the public attitude was sometimes hostile but mostly neutral and reserved. There had been individual expressions of sympathy, such as a Jewish family finding fruit, pastry and chocolate at the door of its flat. There were still friendly relations between Jews and non-Jews in many buildings.[9] These testimonies must be taken with a grain of salt – even if their assessment was accurate. Jews were matchless confidants: with them Germans could give vent to their anxieties and discontent without fear of being denounced. At the same time, those who expressed criticism to Jews were not necessarily representative of the majority of the German population.[10]

With these methodological precautions in mind we can draw the following conclusions from a careful evaluation of the available empirical data: SD reports; diaries; letters, and diplomatic and Allied intelligence reports.

Many who comprehended the significance of the Nazi policy and were well placed to attempt some form of organized rescue operation did nothing. This was generally the case with the churches. When Helmuth von Moltke realized that merely 20 per cent of the deported Jews survived the killings in the east, he was spurred to action and raised the topic in discussions with Bishop Konrad von Preysing of Berlin. The bishop, however, like the rest of the Catholic hierarchy, chose to remain silent.[11] Only a small minority displayed a sense of decency and moral stature. These were mainly people who had been deeply affected by the persecution of the Jews and who consequently devoted themselves to helping them for purely altruistic reasons. Some who were motivated by religious beliefs extended help in organized ways. This was true of Carl and Eva Neumann of Mannheim, for example, members of the German Society of Friends, who sent parcels to deportees in Poland and were arrested for helping Jews;[12] and of the nuns who helped Jews in the convent in which the 'Jewish ghetto' outside Munich was created.[13] A few in small clandestine networks, such as those to which Ursula von Kardorff and Ruth Andreas Friedrich belonged, fed Jews and brought them clothing.[14] Some helped without being linked to any anti-Nazi organization – among them the few anonymous Germans who brought food to the Jews rounded up in assembly camps prior to their deportation,[15] and Lili Hahn, who attempted to save individual Jews during the deportations by furnishing some of her father's patients with certificates that they could not be moved on medical grounds.[16]

The vast majority cannot be characterized as having a sense of solidarity with the victims. True, there were other instances of goodwill; but, all told, they involved only a tiny fraction of the population. Isolated expressions of individual pity derived from various motives, including Christian ethics. In most cases, however, even for antisemites, it was simply a matter of helping personal acquaintances. This was the case with Lili Hahn's father, for example: basically an antisemite, he took risks for 'his' Jews.[17] Such people usually drew a line between their convictions and approval of a policy on the one hand, and the implementation of that policy in their own environment on the other. There is considerable evidence, especially in post-war German apologetic writings, of people helping 'their Jews' by appealing to high-ranking personalities to intercede on their behalf. Some even mention the intercession of high-ranking Nazis: for example, Hans Lammers, head of the Reich Chancellery, protected one of his workers, the half-Jew Dr Leo Killy.[18] The American journalist Louis Lochner asked a Nazi official in the Ministry of Propaganda, Rudolf Semmler, to help a Jewess get to the United States. According to Semmler, Goebbels himself had agreed to ask for the necessary exit papers.[19] If we pursue this line of thinking, however, we would have to include even Hitler, for his alleged intervention to help his former family doctor to emigrate, or to Aryanize his dietician, who had Jewish ancestors.[20] As historians have rightly noted, we cannot blur the distinction between resistance and non-conformist behaviour. These manifestations of occasional sympathy were individual acts that infringed the norms but did not necessarily question the system as a whole. They are, therefore, historically irrelevant from the point of view of their effect on the Nazi regime.[21]

A small minority suffered moral anguish. Some, such as Lisa de Boor of Marburg, were paralysed by shame and guilt;[22] others, such as Ursula von Kardorff in Berlin, were spurred on to action in the underground. For some, maintaining social links with Jews was a way of showing opposition to the system; and for the same reason some people went out of their way to help Jews, as noted by neutral observers who visited Berlin.[23] For many, objecting to the persecution of Jews was a way of manifesting dissent, though not out of dislike of antisemitism: their motive, rather, was a concern for law and order, which were being violated by the Nazi barbarity. As we have seen in previous chapters, many documents suggest that the population's approval in principle of the Nazi world view reached its limit when the actual policy began to violate basic values of law and order. People were shocked by the brutality and turned away from the Nazis, especially after 1938. A Swiss who visited Germany in 1941 said, after meeting German industrialists, that the savage attack on Jews had been the first of Hitler's measures that had profoundly disappointed them.[24] A similar view was conveyed by another visitor to Germany. He mentioned that his friends in Berlin were horrified at the Gestapo's activity, starting with *Kristallnacht*.[25]

It goes without saying that the positive attitudes towards Jews did not always rest on religious or humanitarian grounds, personal reasons or shame. There were cynical, material benefits to be gained. Even the *Inside Germany Reports* acknowledged that many employers treated their Jewish workers decently out of ulterior motives. They were glad to get workers who would do their jobs, without any danger of interference from Nazi Party obligations or military service. The exiles also conceded that the friendliness of the general public was not free of greed – that is, a desire to profit from the advantages which formerly wealthy Jewish families still enjoyed.[26]

The majority, however, seem to have been openly hostile. The Nazi policy succeeded because it was anchored in deeply rooted anti-Jewish sentiments which permeated all classes. The general feeling was that a solution had to be found to the Jewish question. Yet, the more isolated the Jews were, the less they suffered from public harassment. Whereas converts, half-Jews and Jews who for one reason or another still maintained contact with the general population felt the hostility, most Jews lived in a social ghetto which enabled them to avoid it. In order to understand this point, let us consider the reality for the Jews in wartime Germany.

Isolation was systematically pursued: Jewish families were compelled to move to overcrowded communal apartments and houses occupied solely by Jews. They were transferred from various city neighbourhoods, lived in a kind of ghetto and were obliged to display a star of David on their front doors. The administration of these houses was turned over to the Jewish community. Jews were not seen in cinemas, concerts, museums, libraries, parks. They were not seen in shops, since only the scantiest food was allowed them and they had to buy their goods (and particularly their provisions) at certain shops and at fixed times. They were not seen at work. In order to extract the last ounce of work from them before they were deported from the Reich, all Jews between the ages of sixteen and sixty-five, fit or unfit, were drafted into forced labour, usually in segregated companies. Also, those assigned to a particular factory were organized into a single group and put to work in such a way as to make contact with German workers almost impossible. In factory canteens, Jews could not take their meals together with other workers. Later on they were forbidden to enter canteens altogether, taking their meals in special kitchens organized by the Jewish community in the factory area. Jews were not seen in business, for beginning in autumn 1941 they were prohibited from engaging in any kind of business whatsoever. The exceptions to this rule were a few physicians, dentists and lawyers, who, however, were not allowed to be known by the customary designation, but had to have a professional title, such as 'medical adviser', 'legal adviser', rather than 'physician', 'attorney', or the like. Such professionals could cater only to Jews. On the other hand, non-Jewish doctors and lawyers were prohibited from having Jewish clients. Jews were seldom seen on public transport, since they were forbidden to use trams and could travel on the railways only by special permit, which was seldom granted. A curfew was established prohibiting Jews from being on the streets after 8 p.m. during the winter and 9 p.m. during the summer.[27]

Let us consider the situation of those who did maintain contact with the German population, the converts. The SD report of 24 November 1941 furnishes an interesting account of the reactions in the churches to the Jews' yellow badge. The population was thoroughly astonished by the number of Jews still around. Some people told their priests that they wished neither to pray with Jews nor to take Communion with them. In order not to deter Germans from coming to church, converted Jews wearing the yellow star were asked to refrain from attending services or to make themselves inconspicuous. Such incidents prompted the Confessing Church in Breslau to disseminate throughout the Reich leaflets urging Christians not to discriminate against converted Jews. It suggested that, to protect converted Jews from violence in church, they should be seated on special benches with trustworthy churchgoers next to them. Due to pressure from the Nazi Party and the population, the Evangelical Consistory in Silesia dissociated itself from this leaflet.

The situation in Catholic communities was no different. In big cities the public and some clergymen proposed establishing a separate Jewish Christian community to avoid offending German Christians. When this came to the notice of Cardinal Adolf Bertram, he insisted that any measures offensive to Jewish converts should be avoided – though he conceded that, if this raised problems, the church should consider separate services.[28] This embarrassing situation is further corroborated by the diaries and recollections of converts. It is staggering what they had to endure, precisely because they still had, or wanted to have, contact with the surrounding society.

This disgraceful state of affairs, encapsulated in a few dry sentences in a laconic SD report, is reproduced in stark detail in the notes of Emma Becker Kohen. Her notable record makes only too clear the public's entanglement in the Nazi web, showing that not only the Nazi terror apparatus was to blame. The public did not simply conform, granting sanction through silence, but demonstrated antisemitic behaviour themselves – even towards converts.[29]

Having converted and married a Catholic, Becker was detached from Jewish society and protected from official persecution. She was not spared, however, for the public was harsher than the state. In January 1940 Germans openly expressed their distaste at living next to Jews, and the only acquaintance of hers who dared to visit was her priest, who in consequence was insulted by her neighbours. Becker also describes the utter hatred she encountered in the shelter during bombing-raids. A clear example of the inroads of antisemitism into everyday life is the fact that she celebrated Christmas alone. She relates how on the evening which symbolizes Christian values of love and charity nobody wanted to be with a convert. She asserts that at the end of August 1941 attitudes in Berlin had visibly deteriorated. The party's reign of terror was strict: someone who wished to speak to her on the street received a warning from the local Nazi chief. But not only party supervision restricted her contact with Germans: non-party people also took the initiative. Before long even the church-going population had ostracized her. She had to leave the church choir because the other singers did not wish to be with a convert; Christians flatly refused to kneel next to a Jew or take Communion with her, and even priests abstained from contact with converted Jews. She was particularly shocked when people of her own social milieu – the educated civil servants – expressed deep hatred for Jews.

Although it could hardly have consoled someone such as Becker, it should be pointed out that such manifestations of antipathy were not specifically anti-Jewish: they instead reflected the extreme racialist sentiments of the German population towards Jews and other 'inferior' races. Many SD reports reveal that attending church with Polish slave workers aroused lively public discussions, as did the special services the Catholic Church granted to foreign – mainly Polish – workers, because of the German church-going population's refusal to pray with them.

In contrast, Jews who were isolated, their ties with the German population totally severed, were less exposed to offences. A Jewish schoolteacher who remained in Berlin until the end of October 1942 had the impression that general attitudes towards Jews were more neutral and reserved. In her view, most people gave little thought to Jews and every Jew had his good Aryan. In the street and on public transport, there was no harassment. Now and again surprise was expressed that Jews were still around.[30]

When compared to the converts' stories, her comments suggest that anti-semitic attitudes were in direct proportion to the degree of Jewish exposure. If so, then how did the public react when Jews were removed from isolation and made visible to the public? Did this exacerbate antisemitic attitudes? What was the attitude to the policy that had exposed the Jews to the public? Was acceptance of the policy's legitimacy reason enough to support it? If there were no objections to the antisemitic principle, did this ensure co-operation? Let us consider these questions by examining the reactions to two cases in which the public was personally confronted by the fate of the Jews: the imposition of the yellow badge, which suddenly made all the Jews visible; and the deportations to the east.

REACTIONS TO THE YELLOW BADGE

When the yellow star was introduced, in September 1941, there were still some 150,000 Jews in Germany. 70,000–80,000 of them lived in Berlin, and in such areas their presence could not pass unnoticed. Although it is true that by this time social links with Jews had been almost totally severed, it is reasonable to assume that the marking of Jews lent antisemitism concrete expression. The stigma attached to them was clearly evident and could no longer be ignored.

According to the SD national summaries, which were based on reports from different cities of the Reich, the introduction of the yellow badge was favourably received. People were surprised how many Jews still lived in Germany, and praised the labelling, which brought them into the open. When criticism was voiced, it was directed not at the measure in principle but at its partial nature or practical effect. Thus, the SD reports reveal that the public was not fully satisfied and wanted stricter measures, preferring a radical solution to compromise. It viewed the labelling not as a final measure but as an intermediate step toward the elimination of the Jewish problem through the removal of all German Jews. Negative reactions to the measure are mentioned only in passing. There are objections to the labelling of a specific 'good' Jew who sells products cheaply or distinguished himself in the First World War. There are incidents of Germans buying food for Jews and merchants bringing products to Jewish homes. But the main recurring note of dissent is the consequence labelling could have for Germans abroad. In particular, Catholics and the bourgeoisie complained of the introduction of medieval practices, adding that Germans abroad would be marked with a Swastika in retaliation. Such reactions were not necessarily grounded in remorse: in most cases they were probably based on a psychological transference of aggression blended with some residue of human concern.[31]

How does this picture, based entirely on an intrinsically problematic Nazi source, compare with other documents? Post-war recollections of German Jews almost unanimously maintain that the predominant public response was a display of sympathy. Ernst Bukofzer, Klaus Scheurenberg, Leo Baeck, Jacob Jacobson and Inge Deutschkron, for example, assert that the typical German in Berlin reacted with a mixture of sympathy and shame. Gentiles, Bukofzer said, tried to outdo each other in rendering small favours and services to Jews, supplying them, whether openly or otherwise, with food.[32] We cannot, however, draw conclusions solely on the basis of such material, which hardly constitutes firm historical evidence. Many of these post-war accounts are marred by distortion. Their accuracy is impaired not only by the passage of time but sometimes also by a process of reinterpretation which makes for exaggeration. Nevertheless, the picture that they present seems to be generally confirmed by a group of documents that are not subject to the limitations of retrospection: the eyewitness accounts delivered at the time of labelling or immediately thereafter. A few examples will suffice.

A Jewish schoolteacher who was in Berlin until the end of October 1942 and wrote her account immediately after leaving Germany for Palestine notes that initially the labelling caused quite a stir. In time, however, people got used to it, though reactions varied. There were antisemitic remarks, especially from children who showed contempt for Jews. But adults turned away, apparently in shame. In the public transport system, she emphasizes, there were comments such as 'I wish you would remove this rubbish.'[33] Equally revealing are the testimonies of two other refugees who made their way to Switzerland in February 1942. They said that after the yellow badge had been introduced many Jews committed suicide, fearing insults and physical violence in the streets. This was corroborated by Carl B. Peters, *New York Times* correspondent in Berlin, who returned to the United States at the end of November 1941. One week after the yellow badge was ordered, he stated, sixteen Jews took their lives in Charlottenburg alone. The suicides, he added, had an unsettling effect on decent Germans, eliciting criticism of the measure.[34] The same sources stated, however, that Jewish fears proved to be completely unjustified. There were only isolated instances of aggression and offensiveness. In some cases, the yellow star attracted spiteful stares; in others, pity and sympathy; but on the whole there was no jeering in public. On the contrary, people were often demonstratively kind. Many displayed forms of disobedience, offering Jews cigars and cigarettes, giving children sweets, or standing up for Jews on trams and underground trains.

Another witness, a Jewish mechanic who was employed in a large Hamburg plant, supports this picture. One of his fellow workers reacted to the yellow star by saying, 'We'd like to put one of those things on too and then it would be clear to everyone that we are decent fellows!' The mechanic also said that in his apartment building, where most of the residents were businessmen and civil servants, hardly a night passed without his finding a parcel of food in front of his door.[35] Some rare responses went beyond ordinary sympathy. Such is the notable story of a Viennese Jewess who ended up in Stockholm. Arriving at a German railway station at 2 a.m. she could not go to a hotel, because she was wearing the yellow star, and she could not stay at the station, because it was now closed. One of the porters told her to remove the badge, took her home with him, gave her a clean bed and food, and refused to accept any payment.[36]

How are we to evaluate these testimonies? If we were to object that Jewish refugees have a tendency to highlight positive experiences, magnifying them against the background of general suffering, then let us consider a third group of documents: the impressions of non-Jews, mainly foreigners, who would have no reason to overstate expressions of sympathy. Let us look at comments on internal conditions in Germany written by neutral observers from neighbouring countries.

To be sure, many anti-Nazis found the labelling morally abhorrent, as letters and personal diaries show.[37] What is astonishing is that it appears to have been not only opponents of Nazism that disavowed the labelling. Ruth Andreas Friedrich, a realistic observer, estimated that the majority of Germans were not pleased with the new decree. Almost everyone she met was as ashamed as she was.[38] Similar observations were made by numerous foreign journalists serving as their papers' correspondents in Germany. The Swedish correspondent in Berlin, Advin Fredborg, concluded that the labelling was a huge failure, provoking negative reactions: many Germans hung their heads when encountering a Jew in the streets. In addition, since offering a seat on a tram to a Jew was punishable, some Germans let Jews get on first so that they could have the seats without their being offered.

It seems that in Germany as in France, the star was a subject of ridicule. It was popularly called 'yellow star of honour' or 'pour le sémite'. Fredborg also said that even people associated with the Nazis considered it counterproductive.

A clandestine pamphlet which probably stemmed from conservative circles was distributed among foreign correspondents in Berlin, asking them to understand that the measure had not been authorized by Hitler. It was the act of irresponsible people, the pamphlet claimed, not of the real leaders who were fighting at the front. It concluded by condemning the order as treason to the German people and accused the Ministry of Propaganda of playing into enemy hands.[39] Ivar Andersson, chief editor of *Svenska Dagbladet*, was similarly impressed by what he saw in Berlin in October 1941. 'A quite remarkable thing which was very noticeable', he commented, 'was the treatment of the Jews. Apart from certain exceptions, Jews were treated with consideration.' Twice he saw young Germans give their seats to old Jews in a crowded tramcar, to the general approval of the other passengers.[40] Lastly, the *Zürcher Tages-Anzeiger* correspondent concluded that labelling the Jews had elicited sympathy and condolence from most Germans: people averted their eyes and were decent to old Jews travelling by public transport.[41]

The predominantly negative reaction to the badge was confirmed by visitors, diplomats and Germans interviewed abroad. For example, both the Dutch chargé d'affaires in Stockholm, who met mostly with people from the industrial sectors, and a Swedish woman who returned from Bavaria received the impression that the German public did not approve of the measure. 'Everybody hated the idea of the star and tried to show how ashamed he was.'[42] People were so bewildered by the positive attitudes towards Jews that a theory was put forth at the time that the deportations had been accelerated because Germans persisted in acting humanely towards the Jews in spite of the propaganda and threatened penalties. Some even asserted that the reason why Jews were forbidden to use the tram was that Germans, 'pitying those over-tired men, gave up their seats to them.'[43]

Which of the opposing reports of the public reaction to the yellow badge are we to believe? The SD version or the eyewitness accounts?

If we weigh the available evidence against the SD reports, the scale appears to tip in favour of the eyewitness accounts. A negative reaction to the labelling seems to have been the more typical public response to the antisemitic measure. Indeed, the negative reactions caught Goebbels' attention, to the extent that the Nazi propaganda apparatus deemed it necessary to come to grips with the situation. Goebbels, it seems, was taken by surprise and realized that the truth was the opposite of what the SD digests conveyed. Albert Speer tells of an incident at a lunch he attended at the Chancellery. During the conversation, Goebbels began to complain about Berliners. 'The introduction of the Jewish star has had the opposite effect from what we intended…. People everywhere are showing sympathy for them [the Jews]. This nation is simply not yet mature; it's full of all kinds of idiotic sentimentality.'[44]

These attitudes certainly underlay the initiatives taken at this time to discourage expressions of pity or sympathy towards Jews. The decree of 24 October 1941, meant to intimidate anyone who took issue with the labelling, called for three months' incarceration in a concentration camp for Germans who publicly displayed sympathy towards Jews. Goebbels also handled the matter in a most unusual manner. The need he felt to address the issue was indicated by the leaflet sent to German families together with their monthly ration card. The black leaflet, bearing a yellow star and the inscription 'German, this is your mortal enemy', sought to convince the public that the war was part of the Jewish conspiracy and that German Jews, spiritually connected to the Jewish complot, should be destroyed. Complementing this was his caustic editorial 'The Jews are Guilty!' on 16 November in *Das Reich*, castigating those who out of a 'false sentimentalism' felt pity for German Jews. To involve the public in the persecution, the editorial sought to persuade Germans of Nazi views. In part it read,

If Mr Bramsig or Mrs Knöterich feel a stir of pity at the sight of an old woman wearing the yellow star, let them kindly not forget that the Jews planned the war and started it. The death of every German soldier is on the head of the Jews…. Everyone who wears the Jewish star is thus branded as an enemy of the people…. Everyone who associated privately with Jews belonged to them and must be considered as a Jew and treated as a Jew. He has to earn the scorn of the entire nation. He is deserting his nation in cowardice and shame in the hour of its greatest trial and is taking his place on the side of those who hate his own flesh and blood. Whoever takes the part of the Jews has gone over to the side of the enemy in the midst of war.... Everyone owes a duty to the anti-Jewish regulations of the state and must support them.[45]

A subsequent vitriolic onslaught published by the *Stuttgart NS-Kurier* acknowledged that expressions of compassion for Jews were not unusual:

As the wife of a sergeant remarked in the tramcar that a Jew could easily get up from his corner seat and offer it to her, her fellow passengers criticized her loudly. Such cases of unsuitable compassion for Jews are not unusual. In one section of Stuttgart there are two homes for Jewish old people. Every evening when the shops close and the traffic is heaviest, the old Jewesses use the tramcars together with racial comrades and, although they wear the Star of David, people get up to give their seats. There was another incident: a German met a Jew wearing the yellow star on the street and said to him, 'It really requires more courage to wear the star than to go to war.'[46]

Continuing his effort to eradicate all criticism of the badge, Goebbels enclosed the above diatribe with the following month's ration cards. Finally, it is reasonable to surmise that it was Goebbels who circulated the rumours that the United States government secretly required all Americans of German origin to carry a black Swastika on their left side – as if the yellow star had been forced upon Germany as a countermeasure to compel Jews in the United States to stop persecuting Germans.[47] This tale naturally took hold among those predisposed to hate Jews, but it presumably also soothed the conscience of many ordinary Germans who were not necessarily Nazis and sought an escape from guilt. Thus, we learn from a repatriated American,

Whenever he expressed sympathy for the Jews who were singled out for humiliation, his German acquaintances invariably replied in self-justification that the measure was not at all unusual. It was merely in keeping with the way the American authorities treated German nationals in the United States, compelling them to wear a large Swastika sewn onto their coats.[48]

The available documents would thus cast doubt on the accuracy of the SD reports. This conclusion raises another problem: such a display of sympathy for Jews and manifest disapproval of Nazi policy is a conspicuous exception to German conduct in general. We must consider what occasioned the public's unexpected change of attitude towards Jews – a shift from indifference to persecution to overt kindness – before the pendulum swung back to indifference, as we shall see below.

If we take the pogrom of 1938 as a point of reference, we may find a certain correspondence with the reasons for the criticism vented in 1941. In both instances the negative public reaction seems to have derived from obvious suffering. People confronted with what they didn't want to see felt prompted to alter their everyday ethic. As in November 1938, they were again made uncomfortably aware of what supporting the Nazi regime implied. If it is true that the acceptance of antisemitism as a social norm undermined resistance to the coming persecution in the Third Reich, it is equally true that the public gradually grew accustomed to the reality of antisemitism and ceased to notice it. It is further the case that such acceptance of 'mild' persecution paved the way for harsher measures. On the other hand, ordinary Germans clearly could not tolerate actions which outraged their sense of decency, even towards stigmatized Jews. As long as the Jews were 'merely' segregated and in most cases not plainly perceived, the public could claim ignorance and deny the reality created by the antisemitic policy. As long as Germans indulged in the abstractions of a mythical Jewish power they could take refuge in their private lives and withhold sympathy for the victims' tribulations. As long as anonymous Jews were persecuted, the population could remain emotionally distant from the moral consequences of the affliction they had helped to cause, easily coming to terms with persecution since shame and guilt were not involved. Labelling the victim, however, made him an accusing public witness who testified to the cost of conformity and adjustment in a murderous system. Suddenly the average German in Hamburg, for example, was forced to see 3,000 marked old men and women queuing in front of a single shop to buy food. Suddenly the escape route of inner emigration was blocked, and the ordinary German had to face his conscience.

These disturbing feelings obviously did not last long. As had happened with other measures, the penalties exacted from those who sympathized with Jews, plus mounting insensibility to what became a common sight, produced increasing apathy and insensitivity. Eventually most Germans slid into acceptance of the labelling. They adapted to it, justifying and preserving their value system. The acts of charity towards Jews recorded by eyewitnesses show that the labelling aroused dormant moral habits in certain – probably small – segments of the population. The majority, however, seem to have segregated the information in a psychological process of defensive dissociation that in the end hardened their attitudes. Given that inner consistency is integral to an untroubled mind, it was certainly easier to adjust to a criminal normality than to continue manifesting non-conformity, especially when this adjustment brought social gratification and a positive pay-off.

People try to avoid conflicting loyalties and permanent dilemmas. Moreover, long-term exposure to unpleasant stimuli often leads to inurement: they become just another fact of life. This mental process is well illustrated by two examples of everyday attitudes in the Third Reich just one year after the introduction of the yellow star. The first example is furnished by a foreigner who visited Germany in 1942 and left with an enduring and utterly depressing image of Jews wearing their badges. They looked undernourished and walked miles, since they were only allowed to use public transport over a certain distance. And, although people sometimes gave up their seats to Jews, he witnessed a young Nazi girl order an elderly Jewess to stand up in the underground. The old lady got up, but nobody paid any attention to the incident. He found the public's passivity disheartening.[49] The second example is provided by Anna Haag. Her diary shows the metamorphosis that attitudes towards the yellow badge underwent within a year of its introduction and the norms of behaviour that the population used to master practical life. She recounts an experience in Stuttgart on 5 October 1942, exactly one year after the publication of the *Stuttgart NS-Kurier* article which complained of philosemitic attitudes on the city's public transport:

I travelled on the tram. It was overcrowded. An old lady got on. Her feet were so swollen that they bulged out of the top of her shoes. She carried the David star on her dress. I stood up to allow the lady to sit. Then I got – how else – the 'popular fury'. 'Out!' shouted a whole choir. From the voices I heard the angry words 'Jew slave!', 'Person without dignity!' The tram stopped. The driver ordered, 'Both of you get out!'[50]

This trivial incident, so vividly portrayed by Anna Haag, captures the extent to which vicious antisemitism was woven into everyday life. It shows how the German public not only came to terms with Nazi antisemitic policy and adjusted to the new social ethics, but actively participated in injustice and adopted a violent way of life. The tram passengers' attitude can justifiably be seen as a modest contribution to the Holocaust. Incidents of this sort substantiate the contention that day-to-day contact with a virulent, antisemitic atmosphere progressively dulled people's sensitivity to the plight of their Jewish neighbours. In Nazi Germany the process of repression created collective indifference and apathy. However, these were attitudes deriving not from concern over everyday needs, but from a diminished capacity to identify with others' suffering. They resulted from conscious decisions. Similar conclusions hold for the German public's reactions to the deportations.

REACTIONS TO THE DEPORTATIONS

Were the German public aware of the deportations and what they meant for the deportees? How did they react, and were their reactions uniform? The SD national summaries do not adequately represent public opinion on the deportations, being too succinct and laconic: they give the false impression that the public was *a priori* uninterested in what was happening to the Jews.

The local reports, by contrast, expose the manifold positions and diverse views of a fragmented society. Similarly, the situation portrayed in the SD national summaries diverges so strikingly from that of contemporary diaries, eyewitness reports and other non-Nazi material that we must seriously question the Nazi source. The local reports and eyewitness accounts are then more likely to render a faithful picture.

A recurrent legend is that the German population was not aware of the deportations. For example, what remained engraved in the mythical memory of the interviewees in an oral-history project conducted in the Ruhr in the 1970s is that Jews 'just disappeared'.[51] Some scholars explain this lack of awareness by arguing that for the majority of Germans the Jewish issue was of minor importance and hence earned little notice.[52] To be sure, many of the antisemitic ordinances were unknown to the general population since they were not announced in the general press but only within the Jewish community, new regulations usually being given during synagogue services.[53] This was not the case with the deportations, which could not have escaped the attention of the general population.

That people were not aware of the deportations is clearly untenable from the wealth of available evidence. An American journalist commented in the autumn of 1941 that in Berlin it was an open secret, although correspondents were not allowed to publish it, that the entire Jewish population was to be removed to Poland in the near future.[54] Furthermore, by the end of 1941 the deportations were accompanied by newspaper announcements that Germany would be cleared of Jews by 1 April 1942, in order that the country might be *Judenrein* by the end of June. And, although by the middle of December 1941 the deportations had temporarily ceased because of a significant overburdening of transport, people were talking about their resumption on a larger scale.[55]

Deportations in small communities could hardly go unremarked: in such places people do not just vanish unnoticed. Kurt Maier, for instance, remembers that the deportation of Jews in a small village in Baden elicited comment and praise from his teacher in class.[56] Nor were the deportations ignored in the big cities. Various sources report that Jews could be seen on the streets carrying heavy packs to the call-up points and that this sight was a subject of public discussion. In Frankfurt-am-Main the deportees were required to march through the streets in groups to the central market hall. In Berlin all evacuees under the age of sixty made their way from the synagogue on Levetzowstrasse to the Grunewald railway station on foot, the Jewish community official Hermann Samter wrote in January 1942.[57] There was nothing clandestine about the deportation: people could plainly see how Jews were herded into the synagogue and deported to the east. One of the witnesses, Hilde Mekley, observes that many Germans watched when Jews were deported from Berlin to Riga in August 1942. Jubilant SS men leaned out of their barrack windows, jovially welcoming the departure of a truckload of old Jews.[58] Albert Speer remembers that repeatedly during the daily drive to his office he could see crowds of Berlin Jews on the platform of the Nicolasee railway station awaiting evacuation.[59] The same applies to other places. Deportations from Vienna are described with much sensitivity by Ludwig Haydn. He notes in his diary that 'Jews were taken on open trucks like animals to the slaughter. The aged who could not walk were put on trucks while seated on their chairs. As to the reactions to the expulsion, most people looked away, ashamed; others laughed and enjoyed the view.' This scene, he adds, indelibly stamped itself on his memory, tormenting him for a long time.[60]

Not only could the deportations be observed, but they aroused interest. Although it is true that the Jewish issue may not have been a factor in shaping public opinion, the circumstances of deportation definitely helped the public to relate to it. Abandoned Jewish property, for example, or Jewish belongings put up for public auctions were coveted by party officials and private individuals. If during the process of Aryanization in 1938 there was a barely disguised scramble for the spoils, and obvious evidence of graft and peculation on the part of political bosses, this was even more the case during the deportations, when so much property was abandoned by Jewish owners. In 1938, rumours circulated that syndicates had been formed to dispose of the real estate and art works confiscated from Jews, and that the profits were divided between high-ranking party officials. Abundant documentation points to the fact that, after the Jews were sent to the east, the question of who would profit from the plunder became a bone of contention among the authorities – the Gestapo, the Ministry of Finance, the Civil Housing Bureau and other agencies. Nor was it confined to bureaucratic correspondence. Local SD reports and private diaries reveal how unscrupulous members of the general public also coveted a share. People grumbled that the best things had been taken by party bosses and that the flats of deported Jews had not been put at the public's disposal.[61] Besides, it was common knowledge that, when disabled war veterans, who received preferential status in purchasing the remaining Jewish property, could not afford to do so, they served as straw men for real-estate sharks, who resorted to all sorts of legal finagling.[62]

In considering responses to the deportations, one should not rule out the possibility that the early deportations, in 1940, elicited a different response from those of 1941–3. In 1940, weeding Jews out of German society was in harmony with the desires and expectations of large segments of the German public. People not only subscribed to the measure but expressed the wish that German Jews should be sent away, just as Czech and Austrian Jews had been removed to Lublin.[63] But what did people think in 1941–3, when many of them knew, or at least surmised, that deportation meant death? Did they still advocate and endorse deportation, or did they protest or simply show indifference? Was knowledge of these events divorced from emotional and moral significance? The available evidence does not provide a conclusive answer. Whereas in 1941, with the deportation of Berlin Jews, Helmuth von Moltke speaks of considerable unrest,[64] Ursula von Kardorff describes reactions a year later as marked by sheer indifference.[65]

Let us examine these contradictory perceptions, first by using the reports of local SD stations. A few of them tell enough about public reactions to allow us to sketch a map of responses. It is plain that the deportations were significant enough to affect parts of the population, and they became a theme on which non-conformist attitudes did evolve. It was reported from the town of Lemgo, for example, that the deportation of the last Jews sparked a heated debate. It even became a topic of discussion in the town market, revealing public ambivalence. Some people said that German Jews were destined to die in any case and such stringent steps were unnecessary. Church circles feared divine retribution for sending Jews to their death and couched their dissent in theological terms.[66]

The account from neighbouring Bielefeld is similar. The deportation of the local Jews to Riga in December 1941 also prompted serious reservations which were aired in a lively discussion. Dissenters raised a wide gamut of objections, ranging from moral concern to fear of reprisals. On the one hand, the Nazi population – in the reporter's estimation the majority – naturally favoured the evacuation: 'We have to thank Hitler for freeing us of this pest', they said. Their only reservations centred on the fact that the Jews were transported to the railway station in comfortable buses! Other sectors of the public both approved and dissented. Some people objected to the regime's policy or aspects of it, protesting not against the principle of deporting Jews but against a particular aspect of the measure. This was true of people who advanced the well-known objection that 'some of my best friends are Jewish.' They defended the local Jews whom they esteemed, but thought that other Jews should all be deported. Here we also find a few overt instances of moral condemnation, with some people identifying with the Jews' plight. This occurred when the Jews were rounded up and brought to an assembly hall, two days prior to their removal. According to the report, church circles and the liberal bourgeoisie, especially among the older generation, were bothered by the expulsion of the Jews. Since Nazi policy violated the basic principles of these groups, they did not conceal their true opinions. Some objected to the deportation out of Christian humanitarianism and moral sensibility. All men, including Jews, were created by God, they said, and it was barbarous to treat them in such a fashion. Others added to these views a variety of other arguments: that the Jews were old and harmless; that many would not survive the trip in the winter; and that these were people who had established themselves in the area over many years. After the deportation, the SD suspected these circles of being the source of information of what befell the deportees. They allegedly spread the rumour that the Jews had travelled to Warsaw in passenger wagons and had then been transferred to cattle wagons and taken to Russia; there, the healthy had been enslaved, the aged and sick shot.

Here, too, we find those who voiced pragmatic concerns rather than ethical and humanitarian ones. They questioned the political wisdom of deporting Jews, citing the negative consequences of *Kristallnacht* and the alleged retaliatory marking of Germans in America with a Swastika. As with the yellow-badge order, the antisemitic policy triggered apprehensions that Germans in neutral countries, particularly in the United States, would suffer reprisals.[67]

The mixed reactions found in this area were apparently echoed elsewhere. A similar range of viewpoints was recorded in a report submitted by Bremen's Gestapo headquarters for November 1941, touching on the animated discussion stimulated by the deportation of Bremen's Jews. Whereas Nazi sympathizers greeted the imminent evacuation, church and industrial circles objected to it. Firms employing Jews asked for them to be spared since they were vital to production. Catholics, and Evangelicals of the Confessing Church, protested on humanitarian and religious grounds. One of the local churches, with members drawn mainly from the middle-class intelligentsia, even dared to react against the deportation by materially assisting the Jews, and appealing to the mayor, the Minister of Churches, and the chancellery of the German Evangelical Church. As in Bielefeld, punitive measures were taken against those who felt the need to uphold humane values and give practical help by providing the Jews with food.[68]

The small body of local SD reports conveys a more complex picture than the national summaries, allowing a more subtle classification of public responses. On this basis, the following tentative conclusions may be drawn. First, criticism was voiced, but by small circles. For the large majority, the theme was not important enough to turn criticism, if they had any, into full-scale opposition. Second, it would be wrong to conclude that all objections were motivated by purely humanitarian considerations. Some undoubtedly were, but many smacked of undisguised self-interest. This was the case with the appeals of industrialists or those who feared Allied retribution. Heavy air raids made the theme of Jewish retribution crop up with greater frequency. As an Allied victory hovered over their heads, many Germans were haunted by the spectre of a mythical Jewish retribution. Even then, however, remorse was not the logical consequence of these fears. As for the industrialists' appeals, the reason for their objections was far from ethical. Manpower was scarce as a result of conscription and the demands of the armament industry for higher production levels. The industrialists wanted to retain their Jewish workers, who were paid the lowest salaries and stripped of labour rights.

Other sources give different insights on deportation. Eyewitness comments confirm the local SD reports in showing that there was neither uniform approval for the expulsions nor simple black-or-white reactions. Nor do the eyewitnesses suggest a dichotomy between those who approved the deportations out of consistent Nazi zeal and those who opposed it on resolute moral grounds. At the one extreme, we have considerable evidence on confirmed antisemites who obviously applauded the actions against the Jews. In Berlin, for instance, they greeted the deportation with euphoria, clamouring, 'Look at the insolent Jews', 'Now they laugh but their last hour has rung.'[69] When referring to the reactions of the Nazis a word of caution is in order. One must not misinterpret the impressions of the correspondent of the Swedish newspaper *Svenska Dagbladet*, Arvid Fredborg, that high-ranking Nazis opposed the deportations.[70] It was not the deportations they opposed but their manner of execution, which defied a sense of propriety. They merely lamented the absence of 'proper', 'decent', 'clean' and 'Germanic' conduct in the elimination of the Jews. A notable case which encapsulates the Nazi mentality illustrates this point.

On 4 March 1943, SS Lieutenant-Colonel Rudolf Brandt, of Himmler's personal staff, received a letter from the editor of the SS official organ *Das schwarze Korps*. The journal's editorial office was located on the Zimmerstrasse next to the Clou cabaret, which served as an assembly hall for Jewish deportees. The editor complained that his staff, as well as employees from the Eher publishing-house, including women and foreigners, were subjected to what he called a 'degrading and shameful' ('entwürtigend und beschämend zugleich') sight: Jews were brutally lashed by a Gestapo official in the course of deportation. He thought such treatment intolerable and politically sheer madness. An SS captain whose attention was called to the incident also deemed the act intolerable. The writer emphasized that his criticism had nothing to do with humanitarian or sentimental feelings, but with his sincere conviction that things had to be done in a properly German manner, for 'after all, we do not want to look like frenzied sadists' ('wir wollen ja nicht den Anschein blindwürtiger Sadisten erwecken').[71] The author of the letter, like many other members of the SS, shared Himmler's own views as expressed in his notorious speech of 4 October 1943 in Posen. He idealized the way in which the criminal act was to be carried out, emphasizing that the interference of private passions was a breach of discipline. The elimination of the Jews was to be perpetrated in a methodical, cold-blooded way that displayed and reinforced discipline.

At the other end of the spectrum a small minority passively objected to the deportations. Lisa de Boor's diary reveals that the fate of the deportees, particularly children, kept weighing on her conscience.[72] For this minority the deportations can perhaps be said to have encouraged the social bonds with Jews which by this period were to have been dissolved. We learn from a letter of July 1942 from Berlin that since the onset of the deportations the population had behaved quietly towards the Jews, some people even seeking to show kindness or express sympathy through good wishes or handshakes.[73] The Swedish correspondent, Arvid Fredborg, even mentions several cases of active opposition to Jewish round-ups. He maintains that in a house near the foreign press club all the tenants staged a protest when two Jews were taken away. The same thing happened at another building, and a girl was accidentally shot.[74] There is, however, no corroborating evidence of these events.

The reactions of the public to the notorious *Fabrikaktion* (factory action) or round-up of Jewish workers detailed for Poland – an operation which started on 27 February 1943 and deported over 2,500 Jews to Auschwitz – are typical of the attitudes to deportations in general. Ursula von Kardorff evokes a noisy scene in the Rosenthalerplatz, where German women gathered to protest against the deportation of their Jewish husbands. The round-up was accompanied by strife and beatings, but, apart from those directly concerned and the few who dared to tell the Gestapo men to go to fight on the front and leave old Jews alone, most observers, she notes, were completely indifferent. One self-exculpating remark she overheard seems to be characteristic: 'Why should I care about the Jews? The only thing I think about is my brother in Russia.'[75] This woman, like most other people apparently, abjured moral responsibility when confronted by a moral challenge. Most illuminating is the portrayal of the same deportation by the Spanish counsellor Fermín Lopez Robertz, who happened to be in Berlin at the time. After the air raid of 1 March 1943, he says, thousands of homeless people with what furniture and belongings they had saved sat on the kerbs, waiting for transportation. They complained bitterly when it did not come, and were wildly indignant when long strings of lorries filed past them full of Jews, since all available lorries had been commandeered for that purpose. Some tried to stop the lorries and take possession of them and the police had to intervene. As he rightly notes, the clamour was due to selfish considerations rather than to sympathy for the Jews.[76]

Here again, the local SD stations mention the liberal bourgeoisie and certain church circles as the groups who manifested pro-Jewish dispositions. Goebbels' and Hitler's comments refer to artistic circles who disapproved of the deportations.[77] These manifestations of sympathy account for the assessment of a German correspondent in Stockholm who returned from a visit to Berlin. In his view the massive round-up of Jews in Berlin at the end of April

1943 was not made public because people were displaying a fair degree of sympathy for the Jews.[78] This was also the assessment of a Jewish escapee who left Berlin at the end of October 1943 and managed to get to Switzerland. He said that many Germans objected to the maltreatment of Jews, especially the deportations, but they did not dare to do anything; and, if anybody said something in the heat of the moment when coming across such scenes, he was immediately arrested and put into a concentration camp. This observer also mentioned that there was much antagonism between the German population and the workers from occupied territories. Many Germans privately asked each other why Jews were deported when foreign workers, who were regarded as worse, had to be brought in to replace them. He added that this attitude seemed to be rather general with the older generation, but did not apply to younger Germans who had been brought up under the Nazis.[79] Whether these were actually the social sectors that most vehemently objected to the deportations is difficult to determine. In an impressionistic evaluation, Ursula von Kardorff thought that ordinary folk behaved much better than the educated or semi-educated.[80] Jacob Jacobson held a similar view: when the transport passed through a workers' quarter, the workers expressed sympathy for the Jews and aversion for the regime.[81] Since these are no more than personal impressions, they do not allow us to draw conclusions. Further research may yield more information on the reactions of various social groups to the deportations.

The present state of knowledge seems to show that sympathy was expressed by small groups, while the masses remained unperturbed, except to lament briefly the fate of well-known personalities. Countless Jews committed suicide rather than be deported, but the impact of such suicides on the public was ephemeral: they aroused passive disaffection and perhaps concern if the person involved was a celebrity. This was the case with Joachim Gottschalk, one of the most celebrated German actors, who was married to a Jewess and refused to divorce her. The night before his wife and son were to be deported they all committed suicide.[82] When a less popular figure, such as Jochen Klepper, committed suicide with his family, the event passed unnoticed.

As with the yellow badge, the overwhelming majority were not indifferent to a marginal issue but deliberately indifferent to a criminal act. Most Germans consciously chose indifference because they were unwilling to admit participation in committing injustices, which would have led to feelings of guilt and shame. The statement of a Swiss journalist who was in Berlin up to September 1943 sheds light on what may have been an attempt to overcome those guilt feelings. He notes that the Germans did not fully realize the extent of what was done to the Jews, and they 'treated the Jews very well, doing their best to see that families were sent away together.'[83] If his assessment of public behaviour was a correct one, this certainly was an attempt to dispose of guilt and harmonize behaviour with morality. The Gestapo certainly did try to send families together, but in order to facilitate the deportation.[84] That the general public claimed to be doing their best to send families together was not only a banal response to criminal policy, but in fact a grotesque ploy to evade moral responsibility.

8
Image and Reality – the End

This chapter closes the circle: having begun by analysing image and reality in the early years of the Third Reich, we shall now explore the same topic during the war years.

Relying mainly on the SD reports, historians have argued that the remarkable success of propaganda in depersonalizing the Jews was a decisive enabling factor in the Nazi regime's murderous policy. The largest sections of the German population accepted discrimination and expulsion; having internalized the mythical image of the Jew, they were convinced of the need to find a final solution to the Jewish question. As for the reactions to propaganda, some scholars point out the decreasing interest in the Jews and the progressive privatization and hardening of attitudes through which the Jews were excluded from the collective consciousness. The Jewish question was of marginal importance in shaping public opinion, since it ranked very low on the value and priority scale of most Germans.[1] Other scholars highlight the effect of Nazi propaganda, asserting that it so penetrated public consciousness that its images were internalized and its argument for the elimination of the Jews accepted. They see the effect of the abstraction of the Jewish question in what they believe were the responses to the introduction of the yellow badge and the deportations.[2] Still other scholars advance the view that most people applauded the conduct of traditional policy through peaceful means. Hence popular support for antisemitic policy came to an end with *Kristallnacht* when these means were abandoned.[3] Martin Broszat notes the increased passivity towards anti-Jewish propaganda and policy in the war years, for example, but offers a slightly different explanation. He calls this phenomenon *Resistenz*, a kind of amoral self-alienation (he interprets morality as a structural process rather than a normative code) coupled with retreat into a protective isolation.[4]

Our sources lead us to draw the following conclusions. From 1941 on, there was a massive withdrawal from antisemitic propaganda despite the prevalence of basic antisemitic sentiments in German society. Second, this public response regulated social reality not only at the end of the war, when Hitler's integrative power had almost totally vanished, but as soon as the Germans started to suffer defeats, news arrived of the mass killings in the east, and large segments of the German population – feeling collective guilt – began to fear retaliation from Jewish or Allied powers.

That antisemitic propaganda was especially potent when it appealed to deep-seated anti-Jewish sentiments is beyond dispute, as is the fact that it served as an efficient, socially integrative force as long as the Nazis were successful. Two examples illustrate how antisemitic propaganda fell on particularly fertile ground when Germany was at the height of its military success; at that point the public's euphoria made it most susceptible to such mobilization rhetoric.

Comments on the screening of the notorious documentary film *Der ewige Jude* ('The Eternal [Wandering] Jew'), shed light on reactions to the propaganda at this time. When it was first shown in Berlin at the end of November 1940, the SD national abstracts reported that the film had been eagerly awaited throughout the Reich. The tremendous propaganda campaign in newspaper and radio advertisements prior to screening attracted a large initial audience. According to the surveys, spectators commented that the film was more informative and convincing than many antisemitic tracts. People were particularly impressed by the cartographic and statistical material on the expansion of world Jewry, the repugnant scene comparing Jews to rats, and the material on the Jewish influence in the United States. The Bielefeld SD reported that a worker had commented on the film, 'Here you see the Jew as he really is. I would gladly break his neck.' An SD man from Munich noted that the public had warmly applauded Hitler's appearance, in which he delivered his notorious speech prophesying the extermination of the Jews. In contrast we also learn from SD reports that the film aroused criticism for its heavy-handedness, though not for its subject. The fact that the documentary was shown a short time after the successful film *Jud' Süß* ('The Jew Süss'), reduced the number of spectators. Some people commented they were tired of being bombarded with antisemitic propaganda: 'we've already seen *The Jew Süss* and we've had enough of the Jewish trash.' Many who had seen the film were thoroughly disgusted by the scenes of ritual slaughter.[5]

The account of a Jewish refugee captured the intensity of antisemitic sentiments in German society. She had been transported to Lublin but managed to escape to the Russian sector of Poland, where she was able to tell her story. She asserted that people believed the propaganda that the English plutocracy and world Jewish capital had plunged the peace-loving Nazi Reich into war. Noting bitterly that her friends had left her, she added that those who had shown any feelings of solidarity had either changed their minds under the pressure of propaganda or no longer dared to speak to her – all this in spite of the fact that the winter saw a wave of discontent with the war and, along with hatred for the English, the first stirrings of a strong sense of indignation towards those responsible for the war.[6]

To be sure, we cannot argue that anti-Jewish propaganda was ineffective because people were not antisemitic. Whilst the body of documents for this period is not large, it is possible to delineate some general tendencies. We do find documents such as the letter written by a Jewess from Barcelona at the end of October 1941, stating that during her passage out of Germany she and her husband, 'like everyone else, had only the best experiences. All classes of the population behaved wonderfully, and one can write with satisfaction that they condemn these monstrous measures.'[7] It would be safer to treat such reports of sympathy towards Jews with caution, for most of the evidence points to the people's antisemitism. Anti-Jewish sentiments might have been reinforced by incessant doses of hatred. Let us look at three representative instances from the available material.

A Swedish girl returning from a visit to Germany was startled by the antisemitic feelings she encountered in the streets. She formulated her impressions in straightforward terms: the public mood was impregnated with bitterness only against the Jews, not against England.[8] This mood was also perceived by the Spanish Jesuit Juan Rodriguez Torres. Upon his return from Germany, he made reference to the omnipresence of antisemitism, under which not only Jews but also Christians of Jewish descent were considered enemies of the Reich.[9] The newsreels on the pogroms in Riga were received enthusiastically, and those showing Jewish POWs triggered reactions such as 'These should be shot straight away.'[10] The prevailing sentiments are poignantly summarized by a Swedish musician who, returning from Dortmund, reported that the Jews were blamed for everything. They had more or less disappeared from the Ruhr and yet everyone he met, even non-Nazis, was still violently antisemitic.[11]

If prior to 1941 the propaganda effectively shaped and sharpened these antisemitic attitudes, what effect did it have on the average German after the reverses on the front and with the rapid deterioration of conditions at home? Was it still welcomed, harmonizing with deep-rooted anti-Jewish sentiments?

As the euphoria of military success began to wane, ordinary Germans were no longer impressed by the propaganda and the continued indoctrination fell short of its mark. The population's enthusiasm for Hitler's victories was offset by rumours of heavy losses and apprehensions of an extended war. Goebbels' casuistry did little to compensate for the social and economic dislocation, the disruption of everyday life and the vanishing prospects of quick victory. Hence the role of antisemitic indoctrination in shaping public opinion should not be overemphasized. Here again it must be remembered that the contention that the propaganda had little resonance does not apply to the Nazi public. They were reassured by it. For them the Jewish problem was always associated with every conceivable negative experience: in normal times with cultural, economic and social misfortunes; in wartime with defeat. It was therefore natural for them to toe the propaganda line which blamed the Jews for the military losses and the devastation inflicted by the Allied bombing on German cities.

The Russian campaign worsened the war situation. Operation Barbarossa generated ambivalent attitudes. Combined with deep anxiety about losses at the front there was war weariness. Actual defeatism and doubts about winning the war were still rare. Contrary to expectations, however, the campaign was prolonged and heavy losses increased feelings that people were going to war as cannon-fodder.

By the end of 1941 the public mood had taken a discernible downward turn, and, although the extent to which there actually was a change in attitudes defies precise measurement, the available data show unmistakable indications of a shift. At the end of 1941, the Ministry of Propaganda orchestrated one of its virulent antisemitic campaigns. These drives usually accompanied Allied measures, which the Nazis interpreted as part of the Jewish war against Germany. The adoption of the Lend–Lease Bill, for example, provided the Nazis with an excuse to renew their anti-Jewish propaganda. Elisabeth Freund describes the scope and scale of the anti-Jewish campaign in Berlin in the winter months of late 1941: 'Over 200 antisemitic rallies, posters, Jews, Jews all over.'[12] This campaign was coupled with the start of systematic deportations. Unlike in previous years, the antisemitic propaganda gave rise to a paradoxical situation: the public distanced itself from anti-Jewish indoctrination, despite the fact that it was imbued with intense antisemitic feelings.

Alert neutral observers who returned from Germany in 1941 commented on the increasingly conscious alienation from the intensive indoctrination. One foreign observer who realized that the massive propaganda caused satiation and political weariness rather than convincing people noted, 'the Germans tended to ignore the newspapers and continual news broadcasting.'[13] In similar vein the Swedish ambassador commented to Anthony Eden,

A visitor to Berlin is struck by the lack of correspondence between the imposing and widely spread propaganda in the newspapers, films, radio and posters and, on the other hand, the complete apathy displayed by the people, who were entirely absorbed by the material difficulties of every-day life. Lack of goods and of manual labour, blackouts and other inconveniences were their chief interest, and not the questions of international Jewry, Freemasonry and Bolshevism. [All these topics] met with complete lack of interest from the public.[14]

These were not isolated responses at the end of 1941 but instances of a behavioural pattern which became dominant in the following war years. The material for 1942 and 1943 shows similar responses to the massive antisemitic propaganda initiated to tighten the grip on public opinion, strengthen people's faith in Nazism and maintain a heightened political consciousness.

The magnitude of the anti-Jewish campaign in the early months of 1942, with widespread publicity blaming the Jews for the war, was so impressive as to stupefy visitors to Berlin.[15] In the exhibition of the 'Soviet Paradise' in the Lustgarten in Berlin, for example, there was a hall lit with dull reddish light, giving the impression of an inferno, full of grotesque caricatures of Jews who occupied important positions throughout the world. Some of those who wandered about the exhibition were horror-struck by the card-backed images of mutilated civilian corpses, and swallowed the message. Others remained indifferent. There is compelling documentary evidence of a steady decline of interest in all types of Nazi preaching as people erected mental barriers to prevent the Nazi world view from intruding on their own. The apathy had an inner momentum and eventually produced a cumulative effect – a reaction against the rhetoric which aimed to mobilize antisemitic feelings. Not only foreign visitors perceived that the public had enough: the security services, too, made no bones about the fact that the population had grown weary of this systematic, external propulsion towards an inner awakening. For example, one SD station lamented that a series of articles in the *Thüringer Gauzeitung* on Jewish influence evoked no response in the population. The public labelled the monotonous stereotyped rhetoric shallow propaganda.[16]

A homework exercise that a teacher who was also an SD informer set twelve- and thirteen-year-old children in a workers' neighbourhood in Bochum provides valuable evidence on the public mood in 1942.[17] The constant hammering on Jewish culpability clearly helped intensify the anti-Jewish sentiments of many, yet not all the public bought it. 'What do people say about the war?' she had astutely asked the children, aiming not at the children's views but at their parents' and relatives'. The themes which recur are food shortages, war-weariness and the question of who was to blame. On the last, the children stated that some people said the Jews wanted war but others did not hesitate to blame Hitler. This document reflects in miniature both the divergence of public opinion and the decline of confidence in Hitler.

This background also casts light on the dissenting reactions to Hitler's speeches. Surveying the comments on one of Hitler's addresses, one SD reporter notes that a few, whose sense of human dignity was violated, were unambiguously critical: 'Nobody has the right to exterminate another people', they said. Others, however – even some who held anti-Jewish prejudices and endorsed Hitler's total war against the Jews – tempered their enthusiasm with caution and objected, 'Germany could have solved the Jewish question differently, more humanely'; 'Obviously, the Jews were malignant but we could have let them leave after 1933'; 'Germans in America will suffer because of it.'[18] This singular ambivalence is also mirrored in the words of a Guatemalan who left Berlin in 1943. He noticed that 'feelings were certainly strong against Jews in general, but what the regime had done to them was considered by nearly everyone to be excessive.'[19] While exercising all due caution, we should not underestimate these comments, especially since they were made in the face of state terror. It is reasonable to assume that what the SD reports presented was not the whole story. In private, people also expressed themselves much more sharply.

Goebbels tried to counteract this criticism, which obviously gave the authorities cause for concern, by setting the massive propaganda apparatus into action. In the autumn of 1943, for example, under direct instructions from Hitler, it renewed its attempts to bolster the nation's will-power and faith in Nazi antisemitic policy.[20] The Nazi media and official speakers pointed out intermittently that, in spite of the successful elimination of the Jews, there was still a Jewish problem. Goebbels even resorted to absurd anachronisms, lashing out in long, monotonous disquisitions against the Jews who were no longer in Germany. The reappearance of articles on race and race defilement in Nazi propaganda illustrate the new emphasis particularly well.[21] A huge campaign was also launched to change Jewish and biblical first names.[22] Such arguments did not achieve their aim, however. This form of indoctrination antagonized the public, increasing alienation and political fatigue. It is hardly surprising to find the SD reports recording the waning of confidence in the German media and of interest in newspapers and radio.[23] The same went for antisemitic propaganda. Goebbels' tactic was now interpreted by many as an attempt to divert public attention from war difficulties that the leaders could no longer overcome. The overuse of the Jewish campaign not only caused fatigue, but generated scepticism and a credibility gap. Supersaturated with propaganda and lacking hope for the future, the population demanded concrete facts, not empty clichés. This situation, laconically portrayed in SD reports, was concisely summarized by a Swede who returned from Germany. The Jewish problem, he said, no longer existed because (1) no Jews were left, and (2) no one reacted to antisemitic propaganda any more.[24]

The diary of Rudolf Semmler, a senior official in the Ministry of Propaganda and Goebbels' press officer, sheds interesting light on the reactions to antisemitic propaganda. One of Semmler's duties was to submit periodic reports on letters from private citizens to the Ministry of Propaganda. Goebbels used these letters as an index of the public's mood. The criticism shows what really preoccupied the public. Dissatisfaction with the progress of the war became more widespread and more openly expressed. Over 10 per cent of the letters received in mid-August 1943 openly protested against the mounting antisemitic campaign. Some complained that antisemitism was irrelevant when people had other concerns to worry about. Others protested that the Germans were being punished for the way they treated the Jews.[25]

Goebbels had good reason to believe that the letters were merely the tip of the iceberg, and he must have realized that they were, at best, symptomatic of a discredited propaganda; at worst, a sign that people were losing faith in the regime. Since public opinion no longer displayed the uniformity of a successful totalitarian system, he took steps to tighten social control and counteract dissenting opinions on the war and antisemitic policy. The project was far from new, but its intensity and scale were.

This tension between withdrawal from antisemitic propaganda and displays of deep anti-Jewish dispositions is well documented in our sources. We must try to elucidate this paradox of how a population that was basically antisemitic rejected anti-Jewish propaganda. How are we to account for the fact that, at this stage, Nazi propaganda produced not the desired result but indifference?

Ian Kershaw has suggested that people's normal daily concerns sapped their energy, leaving only indifference towards the Jews.[26] Martin Broszat has advanced the view that the passive and apathetic responses of the German public were not merely incidental, but were motivated by people's awareness of being accomplices who shared responsibility for crimes.[27] I think Broszat is right. Criticism of Nazi antisemitic policy and propaganda gained considerable momentum after the first defeats.

In early 1942 German troops suffered major defeats on the Russian Front. By the middle of the year the Russian offensives on the Eastern Front, the British and American operations in North Africa, and the nervous strain caused by air raids had produced considerable consternation and widespread disillusionment. A compromise peace now seemed wishful thinking. The public withdrew from propaganda because it offered no reliable information on these developments or their significance. Until then many believed that Germany would obtain peace on favourable terms, but now no rhetorical pyrotechnics could dissipate the gloom of a hard reality. Furthermore, chilling stories, enhanced by rumours on the fate of the Jews in Russia, were in circulation. Soldiers on leave made no secret of the massacres perpetrated by the *Einsatzgruppen*, providing grounds for comment on the fate awaiting deported German Jews. People chose to turn a deaf ear to antisemitic preaching in order to bury their unpleasant awareness of the extermination. They made a conscious decision to withdraw from it, suppress it and make it taboo, in the belief, whether conscious or not, that they could absolve themselves of collective guilt by dissociating themselves from the social consensus that had sanctioned so horrible a crime.

The aim of propaganda is to mobilize the public to the highest pitch of consent. In this case the campaign on the Jewish issue interfered with the public's wish to escape from feelings of shame and guilt. Rather than succumb to it, Germans chose to alienate themselves from it. In other words, they relegated the Jewish issue to a marginal position neither because of concern with daily troubles, nor because they had internalized the antisemitic preaching to such a degree that they did not need articulate responses to the antisemitic policy, but mainly because according attention to the antisemitic propaganda entailed an unpleasant awareness of the atrocities committed in the name of solving the Jewish question. This background makes it easy to understand why, when the prospects of a quick victory began to vanish, people started to fear Russian and Jewish vengeance for the massacres in the east. The journalists who commented that Germans feared possible Jewish retribution had correctly assessed the public mood. There is abundant evidence that fear of the consequences and anxieties over Jewish retribution were a recurring theme in the public's reactions to information on the extermination policy.

To be sure, repression was natural for Jews who did not want to believe what awaited them, and for German anti-Nazis who refused to acknowledge the inextricable involvement of their people in such crimes. But what was the response of the average German conformist, of the silent majority? Unlike the impression we gain from the SD abstracts, our source material reveals that fear of the consequences, which in turn led to submergence of knowledge, was typical. The common post-war claim that the German people did not know was a laborious pretence to deny guilt. During the war the public sensed collective guilt, since its awareness of the killing-operations exceeded mere suspicion. Outward passivity and apathy were the way the public chose to minimize discomfort. These were attitudes which stemmed from awareness of the Jews' fate without entailing any affective implications. Beneath the apparent insensitivity, however, were fright and fear. The population sensed the catastrophic end of the regime that they had brought to power and supported and in whose crimes so many were implicated as accomplices. Although the public made ceaseless and strenuous efforts to bury the unpleasant Jewish issue, it re-emerged when guilt fed fears of retribution. These apprehensions and anxieties were articulated when the earliest news of the extermination reached the German public. Everything it sought to ignore, repress or marginalize because of the unwillingness to confront the knowledge of mass murder surfaced in the face of fear of punishment. Since this news arrived during the first setbacks on the Russian Front, which eroded confidence in final victory, it engendered anxieties which led to the resurgence of repressed fears. This point must be elaborated and illustrated.

First, let us keep in mind that the heavy bombing of 1943 deeply affected the public, considerably increasing its fears. The destruction brought more dismay and helplessness, and forced the population to seek some remedy to relieve its pent-up emotions. At this point, when people were searching for a way to explain their own suffering, the repressed knowledge of the Jews' fate rose again to the surface. Documents of various sorts attest that many interpreted the bombing as retaliation for what they had done to the Jews. Deportations and the burning of synagogues on *Kristallnacht* – perceived symbolically as the first step on the road to crimes of mass murder – were believed to be the cause of their afflictions. On 3 March 1943 Ursula von Kardorff noted in her diary that everyone in Berlin was saying that the bombing-raid was a reprisal for the deportation of the Jews a few days earlier. Various reports mentioned that the raids were being linked to *Kristallnacht* and the deportations. In Ochsenfurt, for example, a reporter wrote, 'Some suspected that Würzburg was not bombed because the local synagogue was not burned, while others predicted that it will be bombed because the last Jew had lately been expelled from there.'[28]

But did this re-emergence of the topic imply sincere regret, soul-searching or self-condemnation? Not necessarily. There were those who clung to a primitive instrumentalism: their second thoughts about the deportations lacked a moral dimension. For some, the notorious Nazi idea of using the Jews as hostages offered a way out which had been forfeited through deportations. Had the Jewish question been solved by concentrating the Jews in ghettoes in the German cities, they claimed, the Jews could have served as living shields to prevent Allied bombing.[29] Others voiced similar utilitarian arguments, claiming that what was done to the Jews in 1938 was a mistake. The error lay not in persecuting the Jews but in destroying their property on *Kristallnacht* since it was badly needed in wartime.[30]

The reports contain instructive instances of a punishment-oriented morality. Many saw in the destruction of Cologne cathedral divine retribution for the burning of synagogues in November 1938.[31] The inroads of antisemitic views can be gauged from people's efforts to explain the bombing as the work of a mythical Jewish power. Those Germans who refused to admit that they had fathered their own adversity found relief in blaming their misfortunes on the image of the powerful Jew. It was obvious to them that Jewish interests directed the bombing. These typical guilt projections found expression in a rumour among Schweinfurt workers that the city was not bombed because of

Swedish and Jewish industries there.[32] In Nuremberg some attributed the fact that Frankfurt and Fürth were spared to their being Jewish cities. Those who voiced such speculations connected the Allied air raids with the extermination in a relation of cause and effect, but still sought a reasonable explanation why certain cities were bombed and others were spared. Even Catholic circles who understood that Nazism was to be blamed for Germany's calamities shared the myth that a Jewish hand was behind the bombing. They reacted to the destruction in Kiel, Essen and Hamburg by claiming that, if the Jews had not been expelled from Germany, they would not have retaliated in this manner.[33]

It seems that these fears of retribution and vengeance were also strong among German soldiers.[34] One of them put it clearly after having witnessed the mass murder of Jews in a Lithuanian village: 'God forbid we lose the war. If revenge comes upon us, we'll have a rough time.'[35] But not only soldiers and witnesses of the murders in the east manifested these apprehensions: they featured prominently among the civilians in Germany, too. As early as November 1941, a Swedish professor who returned from a congress in Berlin said that, whereas members of the Nazi Party sought to justify antisemitic policy, nearly all the scientists he had met agreed that the Jewish question was being solved in a horrible and inhuman manner, and feared Jewish revenge.[36] The Nazi reports make clear just how widespread these apprehensions were. Nazi propaganda itself cultivated them. These fears inform the reactions to the notorious Goebbels article 'Die Juden sind schuld' ('The Jews are Guilty'), published in *Das Reich* in November 1941. The SD summarized public responses by simply stating that the article had great resonance, without specifying of what sort. However, Catholic circles, by commenting that the article did not convince but merely aroused fears, clarified the sort of resonance it had.[37]

It is also interesting to examine how the public reacted to the excerpts from Theodore Kaufmann's book *Germany Must Die* which appeared in the Nazi press. SD agents noted that during the initial victories in Russia the excerpts triggered antisemitism in groups where it had not previously existed. By early October 1941, press and radio discussions of the book had deeply impressed the public, who now voiced concern about their fate should Germany lose the war.[38] In spring 1942 the Detmold SD station noted that, whereas at the beginning of the war people had believed that the conflict was between Germany and England, after the invasion of the Soviet Union they recognized that it was a war against the Jews. Kaufmann's book, the commentator added, helped make people realize the magnitude of Jewish vengeance a defeat might bring. Equally revealing is a letter from the Dortmund SD appended to a special report on public attitudes. The letter states that the population was convinced that the Jews had started the war and were therefore responsible for the suffering it inflicted. Everyone, including those who did not sympathize with Nazism, agreed that Jewish revenge left no alternative but victory.[39]

The report by Spanish counsellor Fermín Lopez Robertz corroborates this uneasiness with regard to the Jews.[40] On the one hand, people attempted to exculpate themselves, saying they were helpless and that what the government did with the Jews was not their concern. At the same time, the majority feared that, whether Germany won or lost the war, they would be made answerable for the atrocities. Similarly, the district governor of Swabia reported that rumours about the fate of Jews sent to the east aroused fear of retribution by Germany's enemies or, after a German defeat, by returning Jews.[41] These feelings also prevailed among the Nazis themselves, but in their case, as the example of Hans Frank shows, the fear of reprisals drove them to further killing. They had gone so far that they could not turn back. Since what was done could not be undone, continuing the extermination became necessary in order to justify it.[42] Albert Speer recalled that from the German defeat at Stalingrad in late 1942, and to an ever-increasing extent thereafter, he and other Nazis were haunted by a fatalist feeling that there was no return – though these apprehensions were never discussed, not even among friends.[43] Goebbels also noted in his diary that, having burned all their bridges, their only option was to continue with the policy on the Jewish question. Moreover, he made clear to the German people their irreversible involvement in the Nazi policy. Since he believed that those who knew they had burned their bridges would fight with greater determination, he increasingly used this theme in propaganda. Precisely this view explains the Nazi leaders' campaign of 'strength through fear'.

This line of propaganda could also boomerang, however, since the combination of feverish encouragement, exhortation and frankness could induce pessimism. This menacing possibility made it imperative not only to strengthen the confidence of the SS, as Himmler tried to do in his notorious speech of 4 October 1943, for example, but also to reassure the public of the correctness of the Nazi line. The leadership became alarmed about the danger posed by increasing apprehensions, since they could breed defeatism and internal disruption rather than the determination to fight. The SD abstract of 12 August 1943 cautioned that the articles on the enemies' plans, such as one on Jewish world rule printed by the *Völkischer Beobachter*, were counterproductive, as they deepened worries that, should Germany lose the war, a terrible fate awaited every German, particularly children.[44] For this reason the Nazi press heightened its efforts to bolster public morale by disproving current opinions about the war and antisemitic policy. For similar reasons Hitler empowered Martin Bormann to remove the extermination policy from the public agenda by ending all discussions of it.[45]

From September 1943 it was a commonplace of Nazi propaganda to argue that defeat could be avoided only through the continued resistance of the German population. In a 'backs to the wall' campaign, the propaganda consistently tried to persuade the German public that it stood or fell with Hitler, since in the event of defeat the German nation would be annihilated. This line of argument merely aggravated fears of retribution, which, in turn, the propaganda had to address. Without a doubt these public anxieties were directly linked to the themes the propaganda dealt with at this time.

Direct evidence of a body of vocal criticism can be obtained from the SD reports and from the counterarguments advanced by the Nazi press. The propaganda's tone suggests that the leadership feared that defeatism would spread. The articles in the *Stuttgart NS-Kurier* in September and October 1943 are good examples of the attempts by the press to deal with public apprehensions. One writer in fact referred to the gap between the press and its public. The editor of the paper listed fourteen points of 'what might be said' and tried to rebut them. He was at pains to contradict the second one: the widespread argument that world Jewry would not have fought Germany had it not so radically solved the Jewish question.[46] In *Das Reich* Goebbels himself published 'Thirty Articles of War for the German People', number 17 being 'Do not criticize things beyond your judgement.'[47] Finally, Hitler gave authoritative expression to these arguments in his speech in Munich on 8 November 1943. 'This great speech has answered all the questions that interest the German nation', reported the communiqué of the German News Bureau.[48]

Goebbels' backlash apparently did not arrest the downward trend or successfully refute the criticism. He had reached the limit of his influence on the attitudes of the masses. His rhetorical pirouettes could not stiffen German morale. A misrepresentation of the true state of affairs could produce exhilaration only until the troubles of daily life reasserted themselves. Moreover, the average German's anxieties could not be met by preaching that there was no retreat. The argument that the Jews would show no mercy if their lackeys, the Allies, conquered Germany perhaps worked for fanatical Nazis, but for ordinary people it only magnified fears.

From the late spring of 1943 the contagion of low morale meant that even party officials, who had access to confidential information which revealed the true state of affairs, had to be warned against lapsing and seeking alibis. In May, Robert Ley told party leaders that 'Every National Socialist burns his boat on entering the party. The return to the old world is no longer possible.'[49] Equally threatening was *Gauleiter* Wegener of Bremen. He warned that the Nazi ship had sailed a long way: 'Anyone who wants to disembark now will be the first to be drowned.'[50] The same point was made on 1 August 1943, in an article in the *Hakenkreuz Banner*:

There is no party member who has not come to the sober conclusion that, in the event of a plutocratic victory, he and his comrades would be the first to be liquidated by Jewish hangmen. By taking the National Socialist oath we consciously burned our bridges. These bridges have been burned behind the whole German people.[51]

In order to tighten the net so that people would fight desperately, the party made it clear that supporting the system was far preferable to falling victim to the Gestapo, or, worse, in the case of defeat, to Jewish vengeance.

It goes without saying that threatening propaganda, which many interpreted as a confession of failure, was insufficient: it was coupled with an ever-more-ruthless use of the machinery of repression. Towards the end of August 1943, Himmler succeeded Frick as Minister of the Interior, thus bringing all the resources of party and state into action against every manifestation of subversive criticism. Publication of some of the numerous death sentences for relatively trivial offences provided cautionary examples.

By briefly summarizing the complex social reality described in the last three chapters we may gain a clearer perspective. From 1941 onwards, the failure of Nazi promises to materialize drove a wedge between the population and the regime. The disenchantment sprang from growing pessimism about the war, the unease surrounding the euthanasia programme and the conflict with the Catholic Church in the campaign to remove crucifixes. By 1942 war fatigue was widespread. Admittedly, for the convinced Nazis fear of the consequences of defeat acted as a strong consolidating factor. For many non-committed average Germans, however, declining hopes of victory and spiralling presentiments of a bitter end issued in a move to distance themselves from propaganda in general and from the Jewish issue in particular. The greater the fear of Jewish or Allied reprisals the more people withdrew, seeking a protective shield of isolation. In seeking to heighten antisemitic feelings the Nazis did not relax the tension of public anxieties, but increased it by posing the moral implications of Hitler's extermination policy. Hitherto the antisemitic policy had been familiar but had not provided a focus of irritation, especially when the Jews' persecution had a semblance of legality. Many may even have disliked the physical persecution, yet consented to the use of terror to eliminate the Jews from German life. It seemed a reasonable price to pay to achieve a utopian *Volksgemeinschaft*. Ordinary Germans knew how to distinguish between an acceptable discrimination, even using emergency terrorist measures, and the unacceptable horror of genocide. They realized that in the summer of 1941 they were entering a danger zone. To applaud antisemitic discourse at this stage, or to be receptive to fantastic arguments which entailed mass murder, was to link themselves irrevocably to the annihilation programme as passive accomplices. To my mind this also explains the dialectical tension between Nazi propaganda and public reactions to it: the more that Goebbels raised the issue, the more the public manifested fatigue; the more that news of mass murder filtered through, the less the public wanted to be involved in the final solution to the Jewish question.

Conclusion

In this book I have attempted to indicate the practical limitations of the Nazi propaganda which sought to change and mould the attitudes of the German population. While that propaganda is widely considered to have been a decisive factor in mobilizing massive support for the regime, we have seen from the responses to it that the regime's ability to manipulate was limited. The party's aestheticization of politics, its dynamism, rituals and cult of symbols all certainly attracted the population. Nevertheless, in the short run these external trappings failed to captivate the public. Instead, Nazi politics became ritualized, the populace politically satiated. Though the party assumed that incessant rallies, bombardment with propaganda and shrill loudspeakers could radically change the public's basic opinions, traditional mental patterns persisted beneath the outward signs of conformity. Large sections of the population continued to adhere to independent positions despite the party propaganda, the terror and repression. Recurrent calls by commentators to step up indoctrination campaigns, and reports on the public's reluctance to participate in party rallies and read the official press point to the shortcomings of the propaganda machine.

While many studies emphasize the importance of the media in fostering a Nazi mentality and legitimizing the regime, this study clearly shows that the Germans preferred to expose themselves to propaganda with which they already agreed, and their interest in the information disseminated continued to be selective. This point was examined in depth by focusing on the extent to which Nazi doctrine penetrated various sectors of the population: the workers, the educated middle-class and the peasants. The Third Reich destroyed the channels of expression of these social groups, but their basic modes of behaviour remained more or less untouched despite the Nazi pressure.

To the extent that there were changes in the attitude of the population, they are attributable to the influence of overall developments and the time factor, which affected one's satisfaction or dissatisfaction with the Nazi order. The achievement of political stability, decreasing unemployment, pride in the state's renewed military power and an improvement in Germany's international status were all welcomed. On the other hand, the cumulative effect of the brutalization of politics, the tedium and stagnation of daily life, and particularly the fear of war during international crises resulted in disaffection. However, since the Nazi regime created a sense of security and satisfied the social aspirations of many groups, it enjoyed a broad and basic public consensus, and the expressions of discontent were never translated into effective political opposition.

These attitudes also prevailed in wartime, in striking contrast to the image peddled by the media of a united, fanatical national community. Despite the propaganda, which increasingly sought to galvanize the nation to action rather than merely enlighten it, from the winter of 1941 onwards the German people began to be plagued by misgivings. The Allied advances in 1942 shattered their confidence in the Nazi regime. By 1943 growing numbers of people realized that Hitler was not going to win the war and saw less and less point in contributing to a lost cause. As the fifth year of war dawned, with constant retreats on the Russian Front, low morale and fear of defeat became widespread. Food-rationing, restrictions of all kinds, an acute shortage of manual labour, poor communications and endless blackouts were the order of the day. Goebbels' call for 'total war' discouraged the citizenry still further and gradually cracks appeared in the wall of public support for the regime. Many people simply wanted a speedy return to normal living-conditions, whether through a German victory or not. As war fatigue grew, the Nazi propaganda machinery countered with two complementary arguments: the encouraging words that the fortunes of war would swing in Germany's favour, and the warning that Germans had no alternative. Goebbels' exhortations of optimism did little to stir the public, however. The Nazi slogans encountered a bulwark of apathy, and gradually lost their effectiveness.

This same background applies to the public's reactions to antisemitic propaganda. These reactions can be understood only in the wider context of the public's responses to Nazi indoctrination because the dynamic processes that characterized German society's relationship to the Nazi order also affected the Jewish question to a considerable degree. Yet, if the success of Nazi doctrine to penetrate the German population has been exaggerated, why then was Nazi antisemitism so effective with the public? Are we to suppose that the propaganda met with indifference when it sought to change thinking on political, religious and other issues but succeeded with the Jewish question? Nazi antisemitism was successful not because the German population changed course and suddenly became devotees of racial theory: it was effective because large sectors of German society were predisposed to be antisemitic. It reinforced deep-seated anti-Jewish feelings, harnessing them to the ideals embodied in Nazi doctrine. There is no doubt that on the whole the public did not assign antisemitism the same importance as the Nazis did. Nevertheless, eradicating the Jews had broad backing and reflected popular aspirations and social norms; dissenting attitudes stemmed mainly from personal annoyance. Agreement in principle is one thing, active involvement another.

On the Jewish question, as with other issues, the radical impulses of the Nazi movement reached a temporary compromise with the moderating demands and pragmatic considerations of political forces and economic groups which sought to stabilize the regime. This compromise received formal expression in the state's antisemitic legislation. It is clear, however, that the handling of the Jewish question rather than antisemitism itself was the point of friction between the dynamic–vitalist component of Nazism and the nationalist–conservative elite groups. Antisemitic policy acted both as an integrative and as an alienating factor. It was integrative for the party, because the Jewish question fulfilled the function of rallying party activists to action and maintaining the revolutionary momentum of Nazism. It unleashed lurking forces: party activists found in antisemitic violence an instrument of self-expression and a means of achieving a high revolutionary pitch. Through antisemitic activities, the radical elements of the SA, in particular, expressed their aspirations for permanent revolution and sought to justify their existence as a political entity. For the population, antisemitic drives were for the most part an alienating factor, because violent anti-Jewish activism worked against its political socialization.

While aggressive antisemitic policy gained the enthusiasm and support of party radicals and kindred spirits, among the public it often met with misgivings and antagonism. Yet here, as with the reactions to antisemitic propaganda, we found scarcely any trace of humanitarianism behind the objections to antisemitic policy – so broad was the consensus on ridding Germany of its Jews. The conflict between the regime and the population revolved not around antisemitism as an avowed political aim but around the measures adopted. Opposition to the antisemitic campaigns surfaced when they endangered individual safety and public law and order, or Germany's image and economic interests; even if the SA's outrages hardly constituted a social model, the principle behind these actions enjoyed wide approval. On the whole, critical reactions to antisemitic policy seem to have been inspired by personal annoyance and vested interest rather than by humanitarian considerations. The objections here as with other issues did not indicate opposition to Nazism but instead reflected a society which voiced selective criticism while basically accepting the regime. Hence, apart from isolated, exceptional cases, there was no active opposition to state antisemitism itself. Objections to the handling of the Jewish issue never resulted in direct confrontation with the state, as happened with the question of the Catholic Church. Since the Nazis were merely carrying out programmes of political antisemitism which had been in circulation for half a century, the exclusion of Jews from the German nation did not contradict the basic values of a society which was 'traditionally' antisemitic.[1] Thus the bulk of Germans endorsed antisemitic policy fully aware that a pure racial community could not be achieved if one were unduly sensitive to morality. The majority reacted by opposing not antisemitism itself, but the terror – whose dangerous consequences would only cease once a legal solution to the Jewish question was in place. Even the 'other Germany' consciously avoided critical reflection, suppressing private feelings that conflicted with political necessities.

The policy of deportations and mass murder succeeded because the public displayed moral insensibility to the Jews' fate. It is true that in wartime dissent remained passive because of the fear of state terror; that the hardening of attitudes blurred moral boundaries; and that social atomization precluded a collective response. It is equally true, however, that, since most Germans were 'traditionally' antisemitic and did not reject persecution of Jews on principled grounds, their level of resistance to genocidal means was very low. The lack of committed opposition to the persecution of Jews largely explains why so many deliberately sought refuge from the consciousness of genocide and tried to remain as ignorant as possible: because it salved their conscience. Knowledge generated guilt since it entailed responsibility, and many believed that they could preserve their dignity by avoiding the horrible truth. This deliberate escape into privacy and ignorance did not save the public from being aware of the Third Reich's criminality. Knowledge of the mass shootings and gassings filtered through to it, increasing the concern about the consequences of the Nazis' criminal deeds. Yet the population chose to shirk responsibility for the crimes by deflecting it onto others. When Nazi antisemitism again exceeded acceptable limits, it once more proved to be an alienating factor: induced by the prospect of impending defeat and the fear of severe retribution, awareness of the extermination caused dissent. The Nazis' exhortations to endorse their solution to the Jewish question thus failed. The public withheld its support, fearing the possible repercussions from the kind of struggle waged against the Jews. As Melita Maschmann so poignantly put it in her recollections, everything she saw and heard about the Jews sickened her, because the Jews' wretchedness 'offered the spectacle of a human fate which might, for all one knew, be some day one's own as well.'[2]

Notes

The abbreviations used are listed at the beginning of the Bibliography.

INTRODUCTION

1 On the methodological problems of researching past public opinion see L. Benson, 'An approach to the scientific study of past public opinion', *Public Opinion Quarterly*, 31 (1967–8), pp. 522–67; R. A. Kann, 'Public opinion research: a contribution to historical method', *Political Science Quarterly*, 73 (1968), pp. 374–96.

2 This approach was espoused by H. Arendt in *The Origins of Totalitarianism* (Meridian, New York, 1969), pp. 305–40. See also the essays in C. J. Friedrich (ed.), *Totalitarianism* (Grosset and Dunlap, New York, 1964), esp. pp. 88–140; and J. L. Talmon, *The Myth of the Nation and the Vision of Revolution* (Secker and Warburg, London, 1980).

3 For a discussion of this issue see H. Mommsen, 'Nationalsozialismus', in *Sowjetsystem und demokratische Gesellschaft. Eine vergleichende Enziklopädie* (Freiburg i.B., 1971), vol. IV, p. 702; I. Kershaw, *The Nazi Dictatorship* (Edward Arnold, London, 1985), pp. 20–3.

4 O. D. Kulka, 'Die deutsche Geschichtsschreibung über den Nationalsozialismus und die "Endlösung"', *Historische Zeitschrift*, 240 (1985), pp. 600–9.

5 See in particular the following works by M. Broszat: *Der Nationalsozialismus. Weltanschauung, Programmatik und Wirklichkeit* (DVA, Stuttgart, 1960); *Der Staat Hitlers* (DTV, Munich, 1969); 'Soziale Motivation und Führer-Bindung des Nationalsozialismus', *Vierteljahrshefte für Zeitgeschichte*, 18 (1970), pp. 393–409.

6 W. S. Allen, *The Nazi Seizure of Power* (Quadrangle, Chicago, 1965).

7 Studies trying to show German public resistance to the Nazis draw heavily on reports on the public mood. See for example H. J. Steinberg, *Widerstand und*

Verfolgung in Essen 1933–1945 (Verlag für Literatur und Zeitgeschehen, Hanover, 1969); H. P. Görgen, *Düsseldorf und der Nationalsozialismus* (Schwann, Stuttgart, 1969); K. Klotzbach, *Gegen den Nationalsozialismus. Widerstand und Verfolgung in Dortmund 1933–1945* (Verlag für Literatur und Zeitgeschehen, Hanover, 1969). The first printed collection of some of these sources was J. S. Steward, *Sieg des Glaubens. Authentische Gestapoberichte über den kirchlichen Widerstand in Deutschland* (Thomas, Zürich, 1946). This was followed by several further collections, including B. Vollmer, *Volksopposition im Polizeistaat: Gestapo und Regierungsberichte 1934–1936* (DVA, Stuttgart, 1957); F. J. Heyen, *National-sozialismus und Alltag. Quellen zur Geschichte des Nationalsozialismus im Raum Mainz-Koblenz-Trier* (Boldt, Boppart/Rh. 1967); T. Mason, *Arbeiterklasse und Volksgemeinschaft. Dokumente und Materialien zur deutschen Arbeiterpolitik 1936–1939* (Westdeutscher Verlag, Opladen, 1975); R. Thevoz et al. (eds), *Die geheime Staatspolizei in den preußischen Ostprovinzen 1934–1936. Pommern 1934–1935 im Spiegel von Gestapo Lageberichten und Sachakten* (Grote, Cologne and Berlin, 1974). Among the studies based on these documents see M. Broszat et al. (eds), *Bayern in der NS Zeit*, 6 vols (Oldenbourg, Munich, 1977–83); T. Klein (ed.), *Die Lageberichte der Geheimenstaatspolizei über die Provinz Hessen-Nassau 1933–1936* (Böhlau, Cologne, 1986). For an analysis of these reports see H. Witetschek, 'Die bayerischen Regierungspräsidenten Berichte 1933–1939', *Historisches Jahrbuch*, 87 (1967), pp. 355–72.

8 M. Steinert, *Hitler's War and the Germans* (Ohio University Press, Athens, Ohio, 1977). L. D. Stokes, 'The Sicherheitsdienst (SD) of the Reichsführer SS and German Public Opinion, September 1939 – June 1941', (PhD dissertation Johns Hopkins University, Baltimore, 1977). I. Kershaw: 'Antisemitismus und Volks-meinung. Reaktionen auf die Judenverfolgung', in Broszat et al., *Bayern in der NS Zeit*, vol. II, pp. 281–348; 'The persecution of the Jews and German popular opinion in the Third Reich', *Yearbook of the Leo Baeck Institute*, 26 (1981), pp. 261–89; *Popular Opinion and Political Dissent in the Third Reich* (Clarendon Press, Oxford, 1984); 'German popular opinion and the "Jewish Question", 1939–1943: some further reflections', in Arnold Paucker (ed.), *Die Juden im nationalsozial-istischen Deutschland* (Mohr, Tübingen, 1986), pp. 365–86; *The 'Hitler Myth'* (Clar-endon Press, Oxford, 1987); 'German popular opinion during the "Final Solution": information, comprehension, reactions', in Asher Cohen et al. (eds), *Comprehending the Holocaust* (Peter Lang, Frankfurt a.M., Bern, New York and Paris, 1989), pp. 145–58; O. D. Kulka: 'The "Jewish Question" in the Third Reich' (PhD disser-tation, Hebrew University, Jerusalem, 1975: in Hebrew); '"Public opinion" in National Socialist Germany and the "Jewish Question"', *Zion*, 40 (1975), pp. 186–290; F. Wiesemann, 'Judenverfolgung und nichtjüdische Bevölkerung', in Broszat et al., *Bayern in der NS Zeit*, vol. I, pp. 427–86.

9 See for example R. Darnton, 'The Grub Street style of revolution. J. B. Brissot, police spy', *Journal of Modern History*, 40 (1968), pp. 301–27.

10 L. Lenk, 'Revolutionär-kommunistische Umtriebe im Königreich Bayern. Ein Beitrag zur Entwicklung von Staat und Gesellschaft 1848–1864', *Zeitschrift für bayerische Landesgeschichte*, 28 (1965), pp. 555–622. On the link between the Munich police and the Nazis see H. Witetschek et al. (eds), *Die kirchliche Lage in Bayern nach den Regierungspräsidenten Berichten 1933–1943* (Grünewald, Mainz,

1966) vol. I, p. xxiv; S. Aronson, *Reinhard Heydrich und die Frühgeschichte von Gestapo und SD* (DVA, Stuttgart, 1971).

11 J. Schadt, *Verfolgung und Widerstand unter dem Nationalsozialismus in Baden* (Kohlhammer, Stuttgart, 1976) p. 28.

12 Reichsminister des Innern an alle Landesregierungen, 7 July 1934, Berichterstattung in politischen Angelegenheiten, GStA, REP/90P; RP Aachen, an den Reichsminister des Innern, 5 Aug. 1934, HStA D, RAP 1049; G. Plum, 'Staatspolizei und innere Verwaltung 1934–1936, *Vierteljahrshefte für Zeitgeschichte*, 13 (1965), pp. 208–22; OP Rheinprovinz, 17 Jan. 1934, HStA D, RA 23758.

13 Ministerpräsident Goering, Erlaß, GStA, REP/90 P; Plum, 'Staatspolizei', p. 223.

14 Stellvertreter des Führers, 31 Oct. 1934, Richtlinien für die Anfertigung der 'politischen Lageberichte' und der 'fachlichen Tätigkeitsberichte', StA M, NSDAP 983.

15 Frankfurt a.M., 3 July 1935, StA Da, Abt. G 12 B, Nr 21/17.

16 P. Diehl-Thiele, *Partei und Staat im Dritten Reich. Untersuchungen zum Verhältnis von NSDAP und allgemeiner innerer Staatsverwaltung 1933–1945* (Beck, Munich, 1969) pp. 230–1.

17 Ibid. For an analysis of this material see A. Unger, 'The public opinion reports of the Nazi Party', *Public Opinion Quarterly*, 29 (1965), pp. 565–82.

18 Gestapo an Staatspolizeistellen, Berlin, 4 Nov. 1933, HStA D, RA 23758. Cf. Gestapo, Berlin, 26 July 1933, Mitteilungen Nr 8, BA, R 58/1068; Staatspolizei Aachen an Landräte und Polizeipräsidenten, Aachen, 21 May 1935, HStA D, RA 23758; LHA, 403/16915. Early reports can be found in the *Gestapo Nachrichtenblatt*, R 58/1083.

19 F. Zipfel, *Gestapo und Sicherheitsdienst* (Arani, Berlin, 1960), p. 155. Heydrich's instructions on accuracy in reporting in BA, R 58/243. On the functions of the SD see H. Boberach, *Meldungen aus dem Reich. Auswahl aus den geheimen Lageberichten 1939–1944* (Luchterhand, Neuwied and Berlin, 1965), p. xii.

20 Steinert, *Hitlers War*, pp. 14–18.

21 F. Kersten, *The Kersten Memoirs 1940–1945* (Hutchinson, London, 1956), p. 211; L. D. Stokes, 'Otto Ohlendorf, the Sicherheitsdienst and public opinion in Nazi Germany', in George L. Mosse (ed.), *Police Forces in History* (Sage, London, 1975), p. 250.

22 Boberach, *Meldungen*, p. 533.

23 Ibid.

24 'Otto Ohlendorf', p. 250. On the changes introduced due to the pressure on the SD see NAW, T 175 R 267 F 2762298, and Chef des SIPO an alle Statthalter, Regierungspräsidenten und Landesregierungen, 2 Oct. 1944, BHStA, MA 106663.

25 Sopade, Apr.–May 1934, B 5–8.

26 SD Monatsbericht über Linksbewegung, Feb. 1937, BA, R 58/266.

27 Gestapo Berlin, report for first quarter of 1939, BA, R 58/446.

28 *Trial of the Major War Criminals* (International Military Tribunal, Nuremberg, 1949), vol. LI, p. 355.

29 Ibid., vol. XXXI, pp. 324–5.

30 H. G. Seraphim, *Das politische Tagebuch Alfred Rosenbergs* (DTV, Munich, 1964), p. 139.

31 Boberach, *Meldungen*, p. xxiv.

32 RSHA, Berlin, 3 Nov. 1941, Auswirkungen der 'Meldungen aus dem Reich' auf dem Gebiete des Rechtslebens, BA, R 58/990.

33 Staatsministerium des Innern, Munich, 26 Nov. 1937, BHStA, MA 106669.

34 Reichs und Preußischer Wirtschaftsminister an Landesregierungen, Berlin, 25 Aug. 1936, GStA, REP/90 P,

35 W. A. Boelcke, *Kriegspropaganda 1939–1941* (DVA, Stuttgart, 1966), p. 211. On Goebbels' attitude to the SD abstracts see L. Lochner, *The Goebbels Diaries* (Award, New York, 1971), p. 37.

36 Boelcke, *Kriegspropaganda*, p. 757.

37 Ibid., p. 711. Many more examples in Stokes, 'The Sicherheitsdienst', pp. 212ff.

38 Kersten, *Kersten Memoirs*, p. 39.

39 Ibid., p. 211.

40 Ibid., p. 300; Stokes, 'Otto Ohlendorf', p. 250. The influence of the reports on policy-making is fully elaborated in Stokes, 'The Sicherheitsdienst', ch. 4.

41 Kersten, *Kersten Memoirs*, p. 300.

42 F. Wiedemann, *Der Mann der Feldherr werden wollte* (Blick und Bild, Dortmund, 1964), pp. 89–90.

43 H. Picker, *Hitlers Tischgespräche im Führerhauptquartier 1941–1942* (Seewald, Stuttgart, 1977), 25 Mar. 1942.

44 M. Domarus (ed.), *Hitler Reden und Proklamationen 1932–1945* (Loewit, Wiesbaden, 1973), 1 Sep. 1939.

45 Ibid., p. 974; H. von Kotze and H. Krausnick (eds), *'Es spricht der Führer'. Sieben exemplarische Hitler-Reden*, (Mohn, Gütersloh, 1966), p. 296.

1   IMAGE AND REALITY IN THE THIRD REICH

1 For a similar reality in other totalitarian regimes see A. P. L. Liu, *Communications and National Integration in Communist China* (University of California Press, Berkeley, Calif., 1975), pp. 111–12; A. Inkeles and R. Bauer, *The Soviet Citizen. Daily life in a totalitarian society* (Harvard University Press, Cambridge, Mass., 1959), pp. 172–3; G. H. Hollander, *Soviet Political Indoctrination. Developments in Mass Media and Propaganda since Stalin* (Praeger, New York, 1972), pp. 163ff.

2 RP Niederbayern und Oberpfalz, report Apr. 1934, BHStA, MA 106676.

3 RP Aachen, report Sep. 1934, BA, R 18/1555; Vollmer, *Volksopposition*, p. 104.

4 Gestapo Düsseldorf, report October 1934, GStA, REP/90 P.

5 Gestapo Münster, report June 1935, ibid.

6 Gestapo Aachen, report July 1935, BA, R 58/662; Vollmer, *Volksopposition*, p. 255.

7 *Documents on German Foreign Policy* (Her Majesty's Stationery Office, London, 1957), series C, vol. I, p. 114. See also K. D. Bracher, M. Sauer and G. Schulz, *Die nationalsozialistische Machtergreifung* (Westdeutscher Verlag, Cologne, 1960), p. 906, n. 34.

8 Gestapo Hannover, report Feb. 1935, BA, R 58/1128; Gestapo Münster, report June 1935, GStA, REP/90 P; RP Königsberg, report Aug. 1934, BA, R 58/1563.

9 RP Minden, report Aug. 1935, BA, R 18/1566.

10 Allen, *The Nazi Seizure of Power*, pp. 241–67.

11 Gestapo Erfurt, report Apr. 1935, GStA, REP/90 P; OP Königsberg, report Aug. 1934, BA, R 58/1563.

12 Gestapo Trier, report Aug. 1934, GStA, REP/90 P.

13 Gestapo Kiel, report May 1935, BA, R 58/480.

14 Gestapo Lübeck, report Aug. 1934, GStA, REP/90 P.

15 RP Magdeburg, report Sep. 1934, YVA, JM/2834.

16 RP Koblenz, report Nov. 1934, BA, R 18/1564. Cf. RP Wiesbaden, report Oct. 1935, YVA, JM/2834; RP Minden, report Aug. 1935, BA, R 18/1566.

17 Gestapo Trier, report May 1935, BA, R 58/510.

18 On the Hitler cult see D. Schoenbaum, *Hitler's Social Revolution* (Anchor, New York, 1967), pp. 73ff.

19 Gestapo Münster, report May 1935, BA, R 58/510.

20 Gestapo Bielefeld, report May 1935, YVA, JM/2834.

21 RP Oppeln, report Apr.–May 1935, GStA, REP/90 P.

22 Gestapo Berlin, report May 1935, BA, R 58/436. At the same time the Gestapo stations at Düsseldorf, Münster and Osnabrück reported that participation in the elections for workers' councils was expected to be poor, owing to the critical mood among workers. Similar problems were experienced at other times: for example, the Gestapo at Braunschweig reported that in May 1938 (BA, R 58/449) most of workers gathered for rally left the assembly place, and only with difficulties were a third of them reassembled.

23 RP Osnabrück, report Aug. 1934, BA, R 18/1569.

24 Gestapo Aachen, report Oct. 1934, HStA D, RAP 1025; Vollmer, *Volksopposition*, p. 108.

25 Reichsleitung für Kommunalpolitik, Vertrauliche Berichtauszüge, Gau Hessen-Nassau, report Mar. 1935, BA, NS 25/85, fo. 1.

26 Report on Gau Köln-Aachen, ibid.

27 Gestapo Düsseldorf, report Sep. 1934, GStA, REP/90 P; RP Minden, report Oct. 1934, BA, R 18/1566; Gestapo Köslin, report July 1935, GStA, REP/90 P.

28 In the analysis of this theme I found the newspaper collection of Borge Maciejewsky (YVA, JM/3454 1–105) most helpful. It comprises eighty volumes of newspapers covering the years 1921–45. From the large body of literature dealing with the press and its impact see esp. J. Hagemann, *Die Presselenkung im Dritten Reich* (Bouvier, Bonn, 1970); F. Sänger, *Politik der Täuschungen. Mißbrauch der Presse im Dritten Reich, Weisungen, Informationen, Notizen, 1933–1939* (Europa, Vienna, 1975); Z. A. B. Zeman, *Nazi Propaganda* (Oxford University Press, London, 1973); W. A. Boelcke, *'Wollt ihr den totalen Krieg?' Die geheimen Goebbels Konferenzen 1939–1943* (DVA, Stuttgart, 1967); H. Bohrmann and G. Toepser Ziegert (eds), *NS Presseanweisungen der Vorkriegszeit* (Saur, Munich, 1985–7).

29 Hagemann, *Presselenkung*, p. 201, a view shared by H. Storek, *Dirigierte Öffentlichkeit. Die Zeitung als Herrschaftsmittel in den Anfangsjahren der nationalsozialistischen Regierung* (Westdeutscher Verlag, Opladen, 1972). On the limitations of the media in other totalitarian regimes see W. Pye (ed.), *Communication and Political Development* (Princeton University Press, Princeton, NJ, 1963); N. Wessel, 'The Credibility, Impact and Effectiveness of the Soviet Non-Specialized Newspaper' (PhD Dissertation, University of California, 1972),

pp. 166ff.; Hollander, *Soviet Political Indoctrination*, pp. 59ff.; A. Buzek, *How the Communist Press Works* (Pall Mall, London, 1964).

30 Arendt, *Origins of Totalitarianism*, p. 351.

31 OP Rheinprovinz, report Nov. 1934, BA, R 18/1563.

32 Gestapo Aachen, report Aug. 1934, BA, R 58/660; Vollmer, *Volksopposition*, p. 79.

33 OP Westfalen, report Sep. 1934, GStA, REP/90 P; Gestapo Köln, report January 1935, BA, R 58/681; Gestapo Aachen, report May 1935, BA, R 18/1555.

34 Minister des Innern, Oldenburg, report Nov. 1934, BA, R 18/1568.

35 Gestapo Aachen, report Sept. 1934, HStA D, RAP 1024; Vollmer, *Volksopposition*, p. 94.

36 Gestapo Aachen, report Dec. 1934, HStA D, RAP 148; Vollmer, *Volksopposition*, pp. 134–5; RP Aachen, report May 1935, R 18/1555.

37 Gestapo Aachen, report Dec. 1934, HStA D, RAP 148; Vollmer, *Volksopposition*, pp. 134–5.

38 Gestapo Aachen, report July 1934, HStA D, RAP 1049; Vollmer, *Volksopposition*, p. 48.

39 Gestapo Düsseldorf, report March 1935, BA, R 58/381.

40 RP Kassel, report Sept. 1934, BA, R 18/1561.

41 RP Minden, report Aug. 1934, BA, R 18/1566.

42 Ibid.

43 Gestapo Frankfurt a.d. Oder, report Apr. 1935, GStA, REP/90 P; RP Osnabrück, report Apr. 1935, BA, R 18/1569.

44 Gestapo Aachen, report July 1935, BA, R 58/662; Vollmer, *Volksopposition*, p. 255.

45 RP Aurich, report Sep. 1934, YVA, JM/2834.

46 RP Koblenz, report Oct.–Nov. 1934, BA, R 18/1564. During 1934 the total circulation of the party press decreased by a million copies and the trend continued in 1935. This assessment is based on the Nazi sources themselves: see O. J. Hale, *The Captive Press in the Third Reich* (Princeton University Press, Princeton, NJ, 1964), pp. 57, 145–6, 231.

47 RP Wiesbaden, report Feb. 1935, YVA, JM/2834.

48 Gestapo Aachen, report Sep. 1934, BA, R 58/660; Vollmer, *Volksopposition*, p. 94.

49 Gestapo Aachen, report Mar. 1935, BA, R 58/514; Vollmer, *Volksopposition*, p. 186.

50 For a detailed report on the German press see Sopade, June 1936, B 10–55.

51 Gestapo Hannover, report Mar. 1935, BA, R 58/386. Sopade, Feb. 1935, A 72.

52 RP Pfalz, report Mar. 1935, BHStA, MA 106675.

53 F. Morstein Marx, 'State propaganda in Germany', in Harwood L. Childs (ed.), *Propaganda and Dictatorship* (Princeton University Press, Princeton, NJ, 1936), pp. 11–34.

54 Gestapo Köln, report Jan. 1935, BA, R 58/681.

55 Gestapo Hannover, report Mar. 1935, BA, R 58/386.

56 Ibid.

57 Gestapo Düsseldorf, report Feb. 1935, BA, R 58/1127.

58 Gestapo Bielefeld, report Mar. 1935, BA, R 58/100; RP Minden, report Apr. 1935, BA, R 18/1566.

59 RP Minden, report Mar.–Apr. 1935, BA, R 18/1566.

60 Gestapo Aachen, report Apr. 1935, BA, R 58/661.

61 SD Oberabschnitt Süd, May 1935, NAW, T 175 R 271 F 2768198; Gestapo Aachen, report Dec. 1934, HStA D, RAP 148; Vollmer, *Volksopposition*, p. 159; Sopade, June 1936, B 28.

62 Hale, *The Captive Press*, p. 143. On the limited effect of this measure see Gestapa Sachsen, report Jan. 1935, StA N, Polizei Direktion Nürnberg-Fürth 430.

63 Polizei Direktion Augsburg, report Mar. 1935, BHStA, MA 106675.

64 RP Pfalz, report Apr.–May 1935, BHStA, MA 106675.

65 Polizei Direktion München, report Sep. 1935, BHStA, MA 106677.

66 Gestapo Potsdam, report May 1935, GStA, REP/90 P.

67 Gestapo Aachen, report Mar. 1935, BA, R 58/100; Vollmer, *Volksopposition*, p. 181. Gestapo Aachen, report June 1935, HStA D, RAP 1029; Vollmer, *Volksopposition*, p. 237; Sopade report, June 1936, B 29.

68 Gestapo Aachen, reports on June and July 1935, BA, R 58/662; Vollmer, *Volksopposition*, p. 255.

69 RP Minden, report July–Aug. 1935, BA, R 18/1566.

70 Gestapo Münster, report May 1935, BA, R 58/510.

2 INSTITUTIONALIZATION AND RADICALIZATION

1 Gestapo Wesermünde, report May 1935, BA, R 58/510.

2 Gestapo Wilhelmshaven, report May 1935, BA, R 58/480.

3 Gestapo Münster, report May 1935, BA, R 58/510.

4 *Der SA Mann*, 27 Jan. 1934; Cf. Sopade, May–June 1934, A 46. On permanent dynamism as the dominant trait of the SA see for example the notes in Horst Wessel's personal diary: 'the dynamic force of the young movement was incredible…. One meeting followed the next, each more tempestous than the other. Street demonstrations, newspaper propaganda operations, propaganda trips to the province, all these created an atmosphere of activism and high tension which served the movement' (quoted in Bracher et al., *Die nationalsozialistische Machtergreifung*, pp. 843–4).

5 Gestapo Aachen, report Aug. 1934, BA, R 58/660; Vollmer, *Volksopposition*, p. 79; Gestapo Aurich, report Sep. 1934, YVA, JM/2834.

6 Gestapo Aachen, report Oct. 1934, HStA D, RAP 1025; Vollmer, *Volksopposition*, p. 108.

7 OP Rheinprovinz, report Nov. 1934, BA, R 18/1563.

8 Polizei-Präsident Stettin, report July 1935, GStA, REP/90 P; Der Führer, SA Brigade 151 (Westpfalz-Saar), Kaiserslautern, 17 Jan. 1935, report for third quarter of 1934, BA, NS 23/265.

9 Gestapo Erfurt, report Oct. 1934, GStA, REP/90 P. This provided useful background to Sopade reports of a decrease in SA ranks (see for example Sopade, Nov.–Dec. 1934, A 39), and the appeals in the SA organ for discipline (see for instance H. Sommer, 'Selbstdisziplin', *Der SA Mann*, 18 Aug. 1934; 'Seid Aktivisten durch euer Verleben', ibid., 22 Sep. 1934).

10 RP Minden, report Sep. 1934, BA, R 18/1566. All in all, from Sep. 1934 to Oct. 1935 the SA was reduced from 2.6 million to 1.6 million men. The process continued, and by 1938 the SA was down to 1.2 million members.

11 Gestapo Kassel, report Feb. 1935, BA, R 58/1128.

12 Gestapo Aachen, report Oct. 1934, HStA D, RAP 1025; Vollmer, *Volksopposition*, p. 108; Polizei Direktion Dresden, report Nov. 1934, StA N, Polizei Direktion Nürnberg-Fürth 429. In Berlin for example the units were reduced from 130,000 to 60,000 men. In the Rhine region 60–5 per cent of the units' membership was sacked (Sopade, Nov.–Dec. 1934, A 39). See also H. G. Schumann, *National-sozialismus und Gewerkschaftsbewegung* (Norddeutsche Verlagsanstalt, Hanover, Frankfurt a.M. and Hamburg, 1958), pp. 89–90. C. J. Fisher, 'The occupational background of the SA's rank and file membership during the Depression years 1929 to mid 1934', in Peter D Stachura (ed.), *The Shaping of the Nazi State* (Croom Helm, London, 1978), pp. 131–59. But see R. Bessel and M. Jamin, 'Nazis, workers and the use of quantitative evidence', *Social History*, 4 (1979), pp. 111–16.

13 Führer der Gruppe Kurpfalz SA der NSDAP, report for second quarter of 1934, Mannheim, 27 Aug. 1935, BA, NS 23/265. This information is corroborated by the reports of Catholic exiles in *Deutsche Briefe*, 12 (24 Dec. 1934). The contribution of frustrated upward mobility to political militancy has been investigated in an illumi-nating study of the *Gauleiter* by R. Rogowski: 'The Gauleiters and the social origins of fascism', *Comparative Studies in Society and History*, 19 (1977), pp. 399–430.

14 Gestapo Harburg-Wilhelmsburg, report Feb. 1935, BA, R 58/1128; Polizei Direktion Augsburg, report Feb. 1935, BHStA, MA 106675.

15 Gestapo Köln, report Feb. 1935, BA, R 58/1128; Gestapo Harburg-Wilhelmsburg, report Feb. 1935, BA, R 58/386; Gestapo Kassel, report Feb. 1935, ibid.

16 V. R. Berghahn, *Der Stahlhelm. Bund der Frontsoldaten* (Droste, Düsseldorf, 1966), pp. 239ff.

17 Gestapo Wilhelmshaven, report Mar. 1935, BA, R 58/432. On the SA's aspirations note SA leader Wagner's comments: 'the SA will not see its duty in the future limited to propaganda activities and the provision of security men at rallies: it will be the reservoir of a German national army' (quoted in Bracher et al., *Die nationalsozialistische Machtergreifung*, p. 851).

18 On the rumours around Feder's retirement see Gestapa Sachsen, report 22 Dec. 1934–4 Jan. 1935, StA N, Polizei Direktion Nürnberg-Fürth 430. Reports from Bavaria, Saxony and Silesia, as well as surveys of the socialist and Catholic exiles, testify to the crisis in the winter months of 1934 and the inner strife in the party. See for example Sopade, Nov.–Dec. 1934, A 35–9; *Deutsche Briefe*, 9 (30 Nov. 1934). The purges were accompanied by a hard line against 'leftist' elements in the Nazi Party and the closure of the periodical *Der Reichswart*, published by Ernst zu Reventlow. In his articles he frequently voiced his disappointment at the failure of the Nazi Party to realize its 'socialist' ideals, and blamed the party leadership for yielding to the demands of the conservative right (see Schumann, *Nationalsozial-ismus*, p. 106).

19 Gestapo Düsseldorf, report Oct. 1934, GStA, REP/90 P; Gestapa Frankfurt a.d. Oder, 15 Oct. 1934, ibid. According to the socialist reporter in Berlin, 'The atmos-phere resembles the one that preceded 30 June. The mood is particularly negative within the party organization' (Sopade Nov.–Dec. 1934, A 6ff.). A similar situation prevailed in southern Bavaria: 'lately there is plenty of talk of a new 30 June. The

whole atmosphere is charged; people are waiting for a catastrophe' (ibid.). For further reports of the same kind see *Neuer Vorwärts* (published in exile), 23 and 30 Dec. 1934, and other Nazi reports of the period. Small wonder that people spreading rumours on an imminent takeover by the army were arrested (RP Koblenz, report Dec. 1934 – Jan. 1935, BA, R 18/1565; RP Minden, report Dec. 1934, BA, R 18/1566). It is more than plausible that the meeting of the military and the political leadership on 3 Jan. 1935 is to be seen against this background. See *The Times*, 3 January 1935.

20 RP Wiesbaden, report Dec. 1934, YVA, JM/2834.
21 RP Koblenz, report Dec. 1934 – Jan. 1935, BA, R 18/1565; Gestapo Koblenz, report Feb. 1935, BA, R 58/1128.
22 Gestapo Düsseldorf, report June 1935, GStA, REP/90 P; Gestapa Sachsen, report Feb. 1935, StA N, Polizei Direktion, Nürnberg-Fürth 430; Gestapo Frankfurt a.d. Oder, report July 1935, BA, R 58/1588.
23 Der Führer der SA Standarte 22, Zweibrücken, report for third quarter of 1934, BA, NS 23/265.
24 RP Unterfranken und Aschaffenburg, 8 Jan. 1935, BHStA, MA 106675; Bezirksamt Alzenau, report Nov. 1934, StA W, LRA Alzenau 339.
25 OP Rheinprovinz, report Dec. 1934 – January 1935, BA, R 18/1563.
26 Gestapo Köln, report Jan. 1935, BA, R 58/681; *Inprecor*, 5 Jan. 1935.
27 *Jewish Chronicle*, 8 Feb. 1935.
28 Sopade, Sep.–Oct. 1934, A 4; *Inprecor*, 26 Jan. and 2 Feb. 1935.
29 PRO, FO 371/18883.
30 Gestapo Münster, report May 1935, YVA, JM/2834. Cf. OP Rheinprovinz, report 17 Mar. 1934, BA, R 18/1563. He referred to a widespread belief among radicals that, since the state leaders had their hands tied by political considerations, the revolution had to be rolled up from below.
31 G. Warburg, *Six Years under Hitler* (Allen and Unwin, London, 1939), pp. 215–16.
32 K. Pätzold, *Faschismus, Rassenwahn, Judenverfolgung* (Deutscher Verlag der Wissenschaften, Berlin, 1975), pp. 242ff.; O. D. Kulka, 'Die Nürnberger Rassengesetze und die deutsche Bevölkerung im Lichte geheimer NS Lage und Stimmungsberichte', *Vierteljahrshefte für Zeitgeschichte*, 32 (1984), pp. 617–20; R. Rürup, 'Das Ende der Emanzipation: die antijüdische Politik in Deutschland von der "Machtergreifung" bis zum Zweiten Weltkrieg', in Paucker, *Die Juden im Nationalsozialistischen Deutschland*, p. 102.
33 Gestapo Düsseldorf, reports June and Aug. 1935, GStA, REP/90 P; Gestapo Berlin, report Aug. 1935, ibid.; Gestapo Berlin, report May 1935, BA, R 58/436.
34 See the instructions to put an end to the riots despite the fact that some high-ranking Reich leaders were backing them: Oberste SA Führer an Hitler, 22 Aug. 1935, BA, NS 10/78.
35 On the Stahlhelm see H. Diehl, *Paramilitary Politics in Weimar Germany* (Indiana University Press, Bloomington, 1977); R. Lakowski, 'Das Ende des "Stahlhelm". Ein Beitrag zur Geschichte der Stabilisierung der faschistischen Diktatur in Deutschland', *Wissenschaftliche Zeitschrift der Humboldt Universität zu Berlin. Geschichte und Sprachwissenschaft*, 22 (1973), pp. 39–48.

36 Gauleiter Grohé, report Feb. 1935, BA, NS 22/vorl. 583.
37 Gauleiter Grohé, report Mar. 1935, ibid.; *Jüdische Rundschau*, 19 Mar. 1935; *Centralverein Zeitung*, 21 Mar. 1935. On the conflict over Jewish shops and businesses see H. Genschel, *Die Verdrängung der Juden aus der Wirtschaft im Dritten Reich* (Bausteine zur Geschichtswissenschaft, Göttingen, 1966); U. Uhlig, *Die Warenhäuser im Dritten Reich* (Westdeutscher Verlag, Cologne, 1956); R. Gellately, 'German shopkeepers and the rise of National Socialism', *Wiener Library Bulletin*, 28 (1974–5), pp. 31–40; H. A. Winkler, 'Der entbehrliche Stand. Zur Mittelstandspolitik im "Dritten Reich"', *Archiv für Sozialgeschichte*, 17 (1977), pp. 1–40, and 'From social protectionism to National Socialism. The German small-business movement in comparative perspective', *Journal of Modern History*, 48 (1976), pp. 1–18.
38 Gestapo Düsseldorf, report Feb. 1935; Genschel, *Die Verdrängung*, p. 87.
39 Gestapa Sachsen, report Jan. 1935, StA N, Polizei Direktion Nürnberg-Fürth 430.
40 Polizei-Präsident Berlin, report May–June 1935, YVA, JM/2834.
41 Gestapo Berlin, report Aug. 1935, GStA, REP/90 P.
42 Ibid.; RP Koblenz, report Aug.–Sep. 1935, BA, R 18/1565; Gestapo Aachen, report July 1935, BA, R 58/662; Vollmer, *Volksopposition*, p. 255.
43 Gestapo Aachen, report July 1935, BA, R 58/662; Vollmer, *Volksopposition*, p. 255.
44 Gestapo Düsseldorf, report Aug. 1935, GStA, REP/90 P; Gestapo Berlin, report July 1935, ibid.; Gestapo Münster, report July 1935, ibid.; Gestapo Osnabrück, report July 1935, BA, R 58/672; RP Minden, report July–Aug. 1935, BA, R 18/1566; Sopade, Aug. 1935, A 3, 5, 27, 35, 89; *Deutsche Briefe*, 43 (26 July 1935), 48 (30 Aug. 1935).
45 Gestapo Breslau, report July 1935, GStA, REP/90 P; Gestapo Köln, report Aug. 1935, ibid.; Gestapo Aachen, report July 1935, BA, R 58/662.
46 Gestapo Dortmund, report July 1935, GStA, REP/90 P; Gestapo Magdeburg, report July 1935, ibid.; G. W. Allport, *The Nature of Prejudice* (Doubleday, New York, 1958); G. W. Allport and L. Postman, *The Psychology of Rumor* (Henry Holt, New York, 1947).
47 Gestapo Dortmund, report July 1935, GStA, REP/90 P; Gestapo Magdeburg, report July 1935, ibid.
48 Gestapo Aachen, report July 1935, BA, R 58/662; Sopade, July 1935, A 3, (Rheinland-Westfalen), and Aug. 1935, A 26–7 (Berlin).
49 Gestapo Kassel, report Aug. 1935, GStA, REP/90 P.
50 Gestapo Magdeburg and Schneidemühl, reports on July 1935, GStA, REP/90 P; Sopade, Aug. 1935, A 26–7.
51 Gestapo Aachen, report July 1935, BA, R 58/662; RP Koblenz, report June–July 1935, LHA, 401/28263; see also the rumours in Leipzig mentioned by Gestapo Sachsen, report July 1935, StA N, Polizei Direktion Nürnberg-Fürth 430.
52 Sopade, Aug. 1935, A 3 (Bayern), A 5 (Südwest), A 6 (Rheinland-Westfalen), A 7 (Nordwest), A 9 (Berlin), A 11 (Sachsen), A 27 (Schlesien).
53 RP Koblenz, report July 1935, LHA, 401/28263, On the nationalist–conservatives' expectations of a Stahlhelm takeover see Gestapo Dortmund, report Feb. 1935, BA, R 58/1127; and G. van Roon, 'Widerstand und Krieg', in Jürgen Schmädeke and Peter Steinbach (eds), *Der Widerstand gegen den National Sozialismus* (Piper, Munich, 1986), p. 56.

54 Sopade, July 1935, A 3 (Düsseldorf), A 5 (Schlesien); Gestapo Frankfurt a.d. Oder, report Aug. 1935, GStA, REP/90 P.

55 Gestapo Aachen, report July 1935, BA, R 58/662; RP Minden, report July–Aug. 1935, BA, R 18/1566.

56 *Reichsgesetzblatt*, I, 1935, pp. 1146–7.

57 B. Lösener, 'Das Reichsministerium des Inneren und die Judengesetzgebung', *Vierteljahrshefte für Zeitgeschichte*, 9 (1961), pp. 262–313; Lösener's testimony was taken at face value by many scholars: see for example R. Hilberg, *The Destruction of the European Jews* (Quadrangle, Chicago, 1961), p. 46; L. Dawidowicz, *The War against the Jews* (Bantam, New York, 1976), p. 89. For a more critical approach see Kulka, 'Die Nürnberger Rassengesetze'; L. Gruchmann, ' "Blutschutzgesetz" und Justiz. Zur Entstehung und Auswirkung des Nürnberger Gesetzes vom 15. Sep. 1935', *Vierteljahrshefte für Zeitgeschichte*, 31 (1983), pp. 418–42.

58 *Völkischer Beobachter*, 10 Jan. 1935.

59 *The Times*, 27 Apr. 1935, *Jüdische Rundschau*, 30 Apr. 1935.

60 Gestapo Königsberg, report May 1935, YVA, JM/2834.

61 *Jewish Chronicle*, 30 Aug. 1935.

62 J. Walk (ed.), *Das Sonderrecht für die Juden im N. S. Staat* (Müller, Heidelberg and Karlsruhe, 1981), p. 105.

63 Warburg, *Six Years*, pp. 209–11.

64 N. H. Baynes (ed.), *The Speeches of Adolf Hitler* (Oxford University Press, London, 1942), vol. I, p. 732.

65 Ibid., p. 449.

66 *Jüdische Rundschau*, 17 Sep. 1935.

67 British Consul in Munich to Foreign Office, 17 Sep. 1935, PRO, FO 371/18880.

68 E. Phipps to Samuel Hoare, 16 Sep. 1935, PRO, FO 371/18883.

3 INTERNAL CRISIS AND FOREIGN POLICY

1 M. Broszat, 'Soziale Motivation und Führerbindung des Nationalsozialismus' *Vierteljahrshefte für Zeitgeschichte*, 18 (1970), pp. 393–409; L. Herbst, 'Die Krise des nationalsozialistischen Regimes am Vorabend des Zweiten Weltkrieges und die forcierte Aufrüstung', ibid., 26 (1978), pp. 347–92.

2 H. Mommsen, 'National Socialism. Continuity and change', in Walter Laqueur (ed.), *Fascism. A reader's guide* (University of California Press, Berkeley, Calif., 1976), pp. 179–210.

3 Tim Mason, 'Intention and explanation: a current controversy about the interpretation of National Socialism', in Gerhard Hirschfeld and Lothar Kettenacker (eds), *Der 'Führerstaat'. Mythos und Realität* (Klett-Cotta, Stuttgart, 1981), p. 39.

4 K. Hildebrand, 'Monokratie oder Polikratie? Hitlers Herrschaft und das Dritte Reich', in Hirschfeld and Kettenacker, *Der 'Führerstaat'*, p. 82, and 'Innenpolitische Antriebskräfte der nationalsozialistischen Außenpolitik', in Manfred Funke (ed.), *Hitler, Deutschland und die Mächte. Materialien zur Außenpolitik des Dritten Reiches* (Droste, Düsseldorf, 1976), pp. 223–38.

5 Kulka, 'The "Jewish Question" ', vol. I, pp. 223–30; S. Aronson, 'Die dreifache Falle', *Vierteljahrshefte für Zeitgeschichte*, 32 (1984), pp. 45–8.

6 H. Rauschning, *Gespräche mit Hitler* (Europa, Zürich, 1940), pp. 102–3.

7 H. Heiber (ed.), *Hitlers Lagebesprechungen im Führerhauptquartier 1942–1945* (DVA, Stuttgart, 1962), p. 287.

8 British Embassy in Berlin, 30 Dec. 1935, PRO, FO 371/19883; *Le Peuple* (Brussels), 15 Jan. 1936; R. Diels, *Lucifer ante portas* (DVA, Stuttgart, 1950), pp. 80–5. For the background to this step, see J. T. Emmerson, *The Rhineland Crisis, 7 March 1936. A study on multilateral diplomacy* (Temple Smith, London, 1972); G. L. Weinberg, *The Foreign Policy of Hitler's Germany* (University of Chicago Press, Chicago, 1970), pp. 245–6; E. M. Robertson, *Hitler's Prewar Policy and Military Plans, 1933–1939* (Longman, London, 1963), pp. 202–5.

9 E. M. Robertson, 'Zur Wiederbesetzung des Rheinlandes 1936', *Vierteljahrshefte für Zeitgeschichte*, 10 (1962), p. 203; M. Funke, '7 März 1936. Studie zum außenpolitischen Führungsstiel Hitlers', *Aus Politik und Zeitgeschichte*, 3 Oct. 1970, p. 6. See also I. Kershaw, *The Hitler Myth*, pp. 75ff.

10 Sopade, Nov. 1935, A 3 (Rheinland-Westfalen), A 5 (Sachsen 1): 'Summing up it may be said that the attitudes towards the regime have worsened to such an extent that only a spark is needed to blow up the gunpowder barrel.'

11 Sopade, Nov. 1935, A 14 (Bayern).

12 Sopade, Dec. 1935, A 1.

13 Gestapo Berlin, report Jan. 1936, BA, R 58/1146.

14 Gestapo Dortmund, report Feb. 1936, BA, R 58/1151.

15 Gestapo Aachen, report Jan. 1936, ibid.; Vollmer, *Volksopposition*, p. 341.

16 Gestapo Berlin, report Jan. 1936. BA, R 58/1146.

17 Gestapo Kiel, report Jan. 1936, BA, R 58/1148; Gestapo Koblenz, report Jan. 1936, ibid.; Gestapo Münster, report Jan. 1936, BA, R 58/1149; Gestapo Dortmund, report Jan. 1936, BA, R 58/1147; Gestapo Frankfurt a.M., report Jan. 1936, YVA JM/2834.

18 Gestapo Köln, report Jan. 1936, BA, R 58/604; Gestapa Sachsen, report Sep. 1935, StA N, Polizei Direktion Nürnberg-Fürth 430.

19 Gestapo Berlin, report Feb. 1936, BA, R 58/1150.

20 Ibid.

21 Gestapo Düsseldorf, report Feb. 1936, BA, R 58/1151.

22 Gestapo Münster, report Feb. 1936, BA, R 58/1147.

23 Gestapo Wesermünde, report Feb. 1936, BA, R 58/1147.

24 Gestapo Frankfurt a.M., report Feb. 1936, BA, R 58/1151.

25 Landrat Bad Kreuznach, report Jan. 1936, LHA, 441/28265.

26 Gestapo Koblenz, report Jan. 1936, BA, R 58/1148.

27 Gestapo Kiel, report Jan. 1936, BA, R 58/1148.

28 RP Ansbach, report Feb. 1936, BHStA, MA 106680.

29 NS Frauenschaft, Krefeld Ost, Gau Düsseldorf, report May 1936, BA, NS 22/vorl. 860.

30 Sopade, July 1936, A 25–6 (Sachsen 1).

31 Sopade July 1936, A 27 (Rheinland-Westfalen 1), A 29 (Bayern), A 30 (Schlesien); June 1936, A 17 (Bayern), A 17a (Nordwest).

32 Ibid., A 1, A 14 (Westfalen).

33 M. Domarus, *Hitlers Reden*, vol. I, p. 647.

34 Sopade, Feb. 1937, A 1.
35 British Embassy in Berlin to Foreign Office, 27 Apr. 1937, PRO, FO 408/67.
36 Sopade, Sep. 1937, A 17 (Bayern).
37 Ibid.
38 British Embassy in Berlin to Foreign Office, 27 Apr. 1937, PRO, FO 408/67.
39 Ibid.
40 Sopade, Sep. 1937, A 6–8; June 1937, A 9.
41 Sopade, Feb. 1938, A 2.
42 Ibid., A 4–5.
43 NS Frauenschaft, Gau Weser-Ems, report May 1937, BA, NS 22/vorl. 860. Cf. Sopade, Jan. 1938, A 15.
44 NS Frauenschaft, Gau Baden, report May 1937, BA, NS 22/vorl. 860.
45 NS Frauenschaft, Gau Westfalen Nord, report Aug.–Sep. 1937, ibid.
46 NS Frauenschaft, Kreis Bentheim, Gau Baden, ibid.
47 Sopade, July 1937, A 9.
48 Ibid., A 10.
49 Sopade, July 1937, A 8 (Sachsen 2).
50 Ibid.; British Embassy in Berlin to Foreign Office, 27 Apr. 1937, PRO, FO 408/67.
51 Sopade, Feb. 1947, A 28 (Schlesien 1); Nov. 1937, A 7; Jan. 1938, A 1.
52 Sopade, Nov. 1937, A 6 (Bayern 1); Apr. 1937, A 5; Feb., A 28 (Pfalz); July, A 7–9.
53 Situation report of Central Division II–1 for Jan. 1938, BA, R 58/999; Kulka, 'The "Jewish Question"', doc. 28.
54 BA, R 58/717; Kulka, 'The "Jewish Question"', doc. 18.
55 Von Kotze and Krausnick, '*Es spricht der Führer*', p. 147.
56 Ibid.
57 Domarus, *Hitlers Reden*, vol. I, pp. 759–60.
58 *Akten zur deutschen Auswärtigen Politik 1918–1945* (Vandenhoeck and Ruprecht, Göttingen, 1971), serie D, vol. I, p. 87.
59 Broszat, *Der Staat Hitlers*, pp. 423–42; Kulka, 'The "Jewish Question"', pp. 200–27.
60 H. R. Trevor Roper, *Hitler's Table Talk 1941–44* (Weidenfeld and Nicolson, London, 1973), p. 141. On the centrality of the Jewish question in Nazi ideology see E. Jaeckel, *Hitlers Weltanschauung: Entwurf einer Herrschaft* (DVA, Stuttgart, 1986); H. V. Thamer, *Verführung und Gewalt. Deutschland 1933–1945* (Siedler, Berlin, 1986), pp. 695ff.
61 W. Baumgart, 'Zur Ansprache Hitlers vor den Führern der Wehrmacht 22 August 1939', *Vierteljahrshefte für Zeitgeschichte*, 16 (1968), pp. 120–49; H. Boehm, 'Zur Aussprache Hitlers vor den Führern der Wehrmacht am 22 August 1939', ibid., 19 (1971) pp. 294–300.
62 *Trial of the Major War Criminals*, vol. XXXII, PS-3358.
63 Situation report of Central Division II–1 for Jan. 1938, BA, R 58/991; Kulka, 'The "Jewish Question"', doc. 28.
64 Sicherheitshauptamt, annual report for 1938, BA, R 58/1094.
65 S. Esch, 'Between discrimination and extermination. The fateful year 1938', *Yad Vashem Studies*, 2 (1958), pp. 79–94.

4 PUBLIC RESPONSES TO ANTISEMITISM, 1933–1938

1 J. Tomaszewski, 'The situation of the Jews in Germany in spring 1933 as reflected in reports of the Polish Republic Legation and Consulate General in Berlin', *Biuletyn Żidowskiego Instytutu Historycznego*, 139–40 (1986), pp. 131–42; H. J. Robinsohn, 'Ein Versuch sich zu behaupten', *Tradition*, 3 (1958), pp. 197–206; R. Weltsch, 'First of April 1933', *World Jewry*, 1 (1958), p. 11; Uhlig, *Warenhäuser*, p. 84; Genschel, *Die Ausdrängung*, p. 52; report of the Italian Embassy in Berlin, 6 Apr. 1933, CDJC, CDL–15; diaries of Mally Dienemann and Max Riener, LBI, entries for 3 April 1933. Riener noted that in Berlin people just moved away from the SA men and went into Jewish shops. There was no sympathy for the Jews but people complained that a government could not sanction such political manoeuvres.

2 H. Rumbold to Foreign Office, 5 and 13 April 1933, PRO, FO 408/62.

3 J. Noakes and G. Pridham, *Nazism 1919–1945* (Exeter University Press, Exeter, 1984), vol. II, p. 225.

4 F. Stern, *Dreams and Delusions. The drama of German history* (Knopf, New York, 1987), p. 180.

5 Ibid., p. 181.

6 Sopade, Feb. 1937, A 22.

7 Noakes and Pridham, *Nazism 1919–1945*, vol. II, pp. 642–3.

8 Gestapo Potsdam, report Sep. 1934, GStA, REP/90 P.

9 Gestapo Kiel, report July 1935, ibid. Various party reports indicate the apathy with which calls for participation in the antisemitic drive were received by the populace: see for example Kreispropagandaleiter, Kreisleitung Eichstädt, report Mar. 1935, StA N, NSDAP Nr 8. See also F. Wiesemann, 'Judenverfolgung und nichtjüdische Bevölkerung', in Broszat et al., *Bayern in der NS Zeit*, vol. I, pp. 441, 449.

10 RP Würzburg, report May 1934, YVA, JM/2858. On the old middle class and its attitude to antisemitic policy see C. D. Krohn and D. Stegmann, 'Kleingewerbe und NS in einer agrarisch-mittelständischen Region. Das Beispiel Lüneburg 1930–1933', *Archiv für Sozialgeschichte*, 17 (1977), pp. 1–40; A. von Saldern, *Mittelstand im 'Dritten Reich'. Handwerker- Einzelhändler–Bauern* (Campus, Frankfurt a.M., 1979), pp. 154–82.

11 Gestapo Harburg–Wilhelmsburg, report July 1935, GStA, REP/90 P; Gestapo Königsberg, report Apr. 1935, ibid.; Gestapo Dortmund, report Aug. 1935, ibid.; RP Oldenburg, report July 1935, BA, R 18/1568.

12 Gestapo Kassel, report Aug. 1935, GStA, REP/90 P.

13 Gestapo Kassel, report Sep. 1935, BA, R 58/529.

14 RP Koblenz, report Sep. 1934, BA, 18/1564.

15 Gestapo Aachen, report Mar. 1935, BA, R 58/100; Vollmer, *Volksopposition*, p. 181.

16 Gauleiter Grohé, report Apr. 1935, BA, NS 22/vorl. 583. On the agitative value of antisemitism see Gestapo Wilhemshaven, report Aug. 1935, NAW, T 175 R 313 F 2813141.

17 Gestapo Aachen, report July 1935, BA, R 58/662; Vollmer, *Volksopposition*, p. 255.

18 Gestapo Köln, report Mar. 1935, GStA, REP/90 P.

19 RP Trier, report Apr.–May 1935, LHA, 441/15625.

20 Gestapo Köln, report Mar. 1935, GStA REP/90 P.
21 Gestapo Bielefeld, report Aug. 1935. ibid.
22 Gestapo Potsdam, report July 1935, BA, R 58/1591; Gestapo Königsberg, report July 1935, GStA REP/90 P.
23 Gestapo Köln, report Apr. 1935, ibid.; RP Augsburg, report May 1935, BHStA, MA 106676.
24 Gestapo Wesermünde, report Jan. 1936, BA, R 58/1149.
25 Gestapo Magdeburg, report Aug. 1935, GStA, REP/90 P.
26 Gestapo Münster, report July 1935, ibid.; Gestapo Dortmund, report July 1935, ibid.
27 Gestapo Harburg–Wilhelmsburg, report Aug. 1935, ibid.
28 Gestapo Bielefeld, report July 1935, ibid.
29 Gestapo Kiel, report July 1935, ibid.
30 Gestapo Köln, report May 1935, BA, R 58/480.
31 Gestapo Magdeburg, report July 1935, GStA, REP/90 P.
32 Gestapo Königsberg, report July 1935, ibid.
33 Gestapo Kösslin, report Aug. 1935, ibid.
34 RP Koblenz, report Aug.–Sep. 1935, BA, R 18/1565.
35 Gestapo Bielefeld, report July 1935, GStA, REP/90 P.
36 *Die Weltbühne*, 6 June 1935, pp. 726–7.
37 Gestapo Harburg–Wilhelmsburg, report Sep. 1935, BA, R 58/529.
38 Polizei Direktion München, report Aug.–Sep. 1935, BA, R 58/671.
39 British Consul in Munich, 17 Sep. 1935, PRO, FO 371/18880.
40 RP Koblenz, report Aug.–Sep. 1935, BA, R 18/1565.
41 Sopade, Sep. 1935, A 35 (Sachsen 1).
42 Gestapo Potsdam, report Sep. 1935, BA, R 58/1591.
43 Ibid.; Gestapo Kiel, report Sep. 1935, YVA, JM/2834; Kulka,'Die Nürnberger Rassengesetze', p. 609.
44 Gestapo Bielefeld, report Aug. 1935, GStA, REP/90 P; Kershaw, 'Persecution of the Jews', p. 270; Kulka, ' "Public opinion" ', p. 130.
45 Gestapo Bielefeld, report Sep. 1935, YVA, JM/2834.
46 Gestapo Berlin, report Mar. 1935, BA, R 58/100.
47 Gestapo Berlin, report Sep. 1935, BA, R 58/513.
48 Gestapo Merseburg, report Sep.–Oct. 1935, YVA, JM/2834.
49 Gestapo Trier, report Sep. 1935, ibid.
50 Gestapo Kassel, report Sep. 1935, BA, R 58/529.
51 Gestapo Potsdam, report Sep. 1935, BA, R 58/1591.
52 Gestapo Dortmund, report Sep. 1935, BA, R 58/514.
53 Gestapo Potsdam, report Sep. 1935, BA, R 58/1591.
54 Gestapo Bielefeld, report Sep. 1935, BA, R 58/513; RP Koblenz, report Oct.–Nov. 1935, BA, R 18/1565.
55 Gestapo Koblenz, report Nov. 1935, GStA, REP/90 P.
56 Gestapo Dortmund, report Oct. 1935, BA, R 58/1143.
57 Gestapo Berlin, report Sep. 1935, BA, R 58/513.
58 Ibid.

59 D. Bankier, 'The German Communist Party and Nazi Antisemitism, 1933–1938', *Yearbook of the Leo Baeck Institute*, 32 (1987), pp. 331–3.

60 Ibid.

61 RP Speyer, report Sep. 1935, BHStA, MA 106677.

62 Gestapo Potsdam, report Sep. 1935, BA, R 58/1591.

63 Gestapo Bielefeld, report Sep. 1935, BA, R 58/513; RP Oberbayern, report Aug.–Sep. 1935, BA, R 18/1567.

64 RP Koblenz, report Oct.–Nov. 1935, BA, R 18/1565; Gestapo Hildesheim, report Oct. 1935, BA, R 58/1144; RP Ansbach, report Oct. 1935, YVA, JM/2858. Other issues which remained unclear despite the legislation also confused the public: see Gauamt für Kommunalpolitik, Magdeburg-Anhalt, 25 Oct. 1935, and Schwabe, 31 Dec. 1935, BA, NS 25/85, fo. 1.

65 RP Ansbach, report Mar. 1936, BHStA, MA 106690.

66 Sopade, Dec. 1936, A 11 (Südwest). On the renewal of antisemitic terror following the games see ibid., A 112–27.

67 Sopade, June 1936, A 62 (Mitteldeutschland); Jan. 1936, A 21 (Berlin 3).

68 The Sopade contact man informed that 'People condemn violent antisemitism and persecutions, but the removal of Jews from the civil service, science, arts, etc. is endorsed by almost everyone' (Sopade, Oct. 1936, A6).

69 Sopade, Jan. 1936, A 20 (Berlin 2).

70 Kershaw, *Popular Opinion*, pp. 231–45; S. M. Lowenstein, 'The struggle for survival of rural Jews in Germany 1933–1938: the case of Bezirksamt Weissenburg, Mittelfranken', in Paucker, *Die Juden im nationalsozialistischen Deutschland*, pp. 115–24; Wiesemann, 'Juden auf dem Lande: die wirtschaftliche Ausgrenzung der jüdischen Viehhändler in Bayern', in Detlev Peukert and Jürgen Reulecke (eds), *Die Reihen fast geschlossen. Alltag im Nationalsozialismus* (Hammer, Wuppertal, 1981), pp. 381–96.

71 Sopade, July 1938, A 76.

72 British Consulate General in Vienna, 29 April 1938, PRO, FO 371/21635.

73 Ibid.

74 SD II–112, Berlin, 1 July 1938, BA, R 58/996.

75 British Consulate General in Vienna to British Embassy in Berlin, 7 Oct. and 7 Nov. 1938, PRO, FO 371/21665; Jewish Telegraphic Agency, News Bulletin 88 (14 Apr. 1938).

76 British Consulate General in Vienna, 13 Apr. 1938, PRO, FO 371/21634.

77 Kulka, 'The "Jewish Question"', vol. II, pp. 396–9.

78 Sopade, Feb. 1938, A 60–2.

79 Sopade, July 1938, A 89.

80 Henderson to Halifax, 2 May 1938, PRO, FO 408/68. On the expropriation policy see A. Barkai, '"Schicksalsjahr 1938": Kontinuität und Verschärfung der wirtschaftlichen Ausplünderung der deutschen Juden', in Ursula Büttner (ed.), *Das Unrechtsregime* (Christians, Hamburg, 1986), vol. II. pp. 45–68.

81 Sopade, July 1938, A 94.

82 Sopade, July 1938, A 89–90, 94–5; British Consulate in Hamburg, report June 1938, PRO, FO 371/21635.

83 British Chargé d'Affaires in Berlin to FO, 13 July 1938, PRO, FO 371/21635.

84 Sopade, Feb. 1938, A 67 (Sachsen 2).

85 Sopade, Feb. 1938, A 62.

86 Sopade, July 1938, A 101.

87 It is important to remember that widespread antisemitic rioting preceded *Kristallnacht*. Thus, there were outbursts of violence in the night of 7 Nov., in Rothenburg, Fulda and Vebra: Jewish houses, shops and schools were demolished and acts of terror committed. The synagogue of Bad Hersfeld was burned on the night of 8 Nov. and other synagogues – in Eschwege, Witzenhausen, Fritzlar, Kirchhain and Neustadt (near Marburg) – were destroyed before *Kristallnacht*. See Chef Sicherheitspolizei an Chef Ordnungspolizei, 9 Nov. 1938, BA, R 58/979; also Kulka, 'The "Jewish Question"', vol. II, p. 399.

88 The varied reactions to the pogroms, including the objections, are reflected in most sources. For Nazi reports see for example SD Unterabschnitt Thüringen-Erfurt, Außenstelle Gotha, 24 Mar. 1939, report for first quarter of 1939, BA, NS 29/77; SD Unterabschnitt Württemberg-Hohenzollern, 1 Feb. 1939, report for fourth quarter of 1938, StA L, K110 Bü. 44, and 1 Apr. 1939, report for first quarter of 1939, ibid., Bü. 45. Cf. the impressions of foreign diplomats: for example those of the Italian Consul in Munich, R. Pittalis, contained in his report of 19 Nov. 1938, 'Le ulteriori ripercussioni delle recenti manifestazioni antisemite' (Comunicazioni di diplomatici italiani su misure ed azioni antiebraiche nel terzo Reich. Documenti tratti dagli Archivi del Ministero degli Affari Esteri Italiano, CDEC); the British diplomat Ogilvie Forbes noted in his dispatch of 15 Nov. 1938 (PRO, FO 371/21637) that he heard no expressions of shame or disgust, and that the on-lookers appeared completely passive, but he noticed the 'inane grim which often inadvertently betrays the guilty conscience'. By contrast the British Consul in Cologne noted that Germans who had nothing at stake displayed a certain amount of *Schadenfreude* (report of 14 Nov. 1938, PRO, FO, 371/21638). Cf. also L. Kochan, *Pogrom* (André Deutsch, London, 1957), pp. 93–4. For the subjective dimension as reflected by personal diaries see for example E. Nies, *Politisches Tagebuch 1935–1945* (Ebner, Ulm, 1947), entry for 11 Nov. 1938.

89 On Goerdeler's reactions to the expulsion of Polish Jews see PRO, FO 371/22961; A. P. Young, *The 'X' Documents. The secret history of Foreign Office contacts with the German Resistance 1937–1939* (André Deutsch, London, 1974), pp. 139 (on *Kristallnacht*), 153, 160–1.

90 Gestapo Aachen, 30 Nov. 1938, report Marxism, BA, R 58/446. Cf. the report of the Nazi Teachers' League (NSLB) of Marquenstein, Haslach, Erding, 19 Nov. 1938, StA N, NSDAP 983; Wiesemann, 'Judenverfolgung', p. 470; Sopade, Nov. 1938, A 45 (Rheinland-Westfalen 2). It is noteworthy that, in localities without Jews, demonstrations were staged in front of churches: see Sopade, Nov. 1938, A 35 (Bayern), A 45 (Köln), A 49 (Schlesien 2); RP Mainfranken, report Nov. 1938, BHStA, MA 106694.

91 Gestapo Schwerin, report Nov. 1938, YVA, JM/2834; Gestapo Köln, report Nov. 1938, BA, R 48/446.

92 Sopade, Jan. 1939, A 9.

93 The most common objection was that the destruction of property contradicted the goals of the Four Year Plan: see for example Kommandeur der Gendarmerie, Land

Württemberg, 31 Dec. 1938, StA L, E 151 cII, Bü. 434. See also Kershaw, *Popular Opinion*, pp. 269–70. Kulka, '"Public opinion"', pp. 230–42.

94 SD Unterabschnitt Württemberg, 1 Feb. 1939, report for fourth quarter of 1938, StA L, K 110 Bü. 44, and 1 Apr. 1939, report for first quarter of 1939, ibid., Bü. 45. For a suggestive interpretation of these reactions see W. S. Allen, 'Die deutsche Öffentlichkeit und die "Reichskristallnacht". Konflikt zwischen Werthierarchie und Propaganda im Dritten Reich', in Peukert and Reulecke, *Die Reihen fast geschlossen*, pp. 397–412.

95 PRO, FO 371/21638.

5   WORKERS, PEASANTS AND BUSINESSMEN

1 Gestapo Berlin, report on the Marxist movement, Nov. 1938, YVA, JM/2834; *Vorwärts*, 2 July 1933. For studies of this topic see I. Deak, *Weimar Germany's Left-Wing Intellectuals* (University of California Press, Berkeley, Calif., 1968); D. L. Niewyk, *Socialist, Antisemite and Jew* (Louisiana State University Press, Baton Rouge, 1971); H. M. Knütter, *Die Juden und die deutsche Linke in der Weimarer Republik 1918–1933* (Droste, Düsseldorf, 1971); E. Silberner, *Sozialisten zur Judenfrage* (Colloquium, Berlin, 1962); R. Rürup and W. Kaiser, 'Sozialismus und Antisemitismus in Deutschland vor 1914', in *Jahrbuch des Instituts für deutsche Geschichte*, 2 (1977), pp. 203–25.

2 A selection of documents were published by Tim Mason (*Arbeiterklasse und Volksgemeinschaft*), though with almost no material on our topic. See also Noakes and Pridham, *Nazism 1919–1945*, vol. II, pp. 327–74; Schoenbaum, *Hitler's Social Revolution*, pp. 73ff.; W. Zollitsch, *Arbeiter zwischen Weltwirtschaftskrise und Nationalsozialismus* (Vandenhoeck and Ruprecht, Göttingen, 1990).

3 H. Walter, *Die Weltbühne*, 28 (23 Feb. 1932). Cf. H. von Gerlach, 'Antisemitismus', ibid., 1 Jan. 1920, pp. 7ff. Cf. G. S. Shoham, 'German socialism and anti-semitism: social character and the disruption of the symbiosis between Germans and Jews', *Clio*, 15 (1986), pp. 303–20.

4 Kreuzberger files, LBI, AR 7183, box 1, folder 7; on this phenomenon see also B. Wenke, *Interviews mit Überlebenden* (Theiß, Stuttgart 1980), p. 99.

5 *Organisiert den Massenkampf gegen die faschistische Diktatur*, Halle, 21 Mar. 1933, IfZ, MA 423/867315–16.

6 Gestapo [Hamburg?], report Mar. 1934, BA, R 58/1561.

7 Gestapo Potsdam, report Aug. 1935, GStA, REP/90 P; Gestapo Bielefeld, report Aug. 1935, BA, R 58/1587.

8 *Wir Kämpfen. Organ der KPD, Aug. 1935*, NAW, T 175 R 280 F 2774327.

9 *Wie antworte ich auf Schlagworte der Nazis? Viertes Thema: Die Rassenfrage*, WL, P24. See also K. Mammach, *Die KPD und die deutsche antifaschistische Widerstandsbewegung 1933–1939* (Röderberg, Frankfurt a.M., 1974), p. 240.

10 D. Bankier, 'Die Beziehungen zwischen deutschen jüdischen Flüchtlingen und deutschen politischen Exilierten in Südamerika', in Achim Schrader and Karl Heinz Rengstorf (eds), *Europäische Juden in Lateinamerika* (Röhrig, St Ingbert, 1989), pp. 213–25.

11 Sopade, Feb. 1936, A 5.

12 NAW, T 175 R 317 F 2807458.

13 Sopade, Jan. 1936, A 17–18 (Sachsen 2).

14 Gestapo Köln, report Jan. 1935, BA, R 58/681; Gestapo Düsseldorf, report June 1935, GStA REP/90 P.

15 Gestapo Sigmaringen, report July 1935, GStA, ibid.

16 Gestapo Köln, report Mar. 1935, YVA, JM/2834.

17 IfZ, Fa 382. On similar cases in which workers merely feared the consequences of antisemitic policy on their livelihood see Landratamt Alzenau, report Aug. 1935, StA W, Bezirksamt Alzenau 339; Gestapo Breslau, report Feb. 1935, BA, R 58/1569; RP Ansbach, reports Mar. and Sep. 1933, YVA, JM/2858; Gestapo Bielefeld, report Aug.–Sep. 1934, BA, R 58/1587; Meldungen der Kreiswaltungen der DAF, Kreis Grafenau-Vilshofen, report Dec. 1935; Tätigkeitsberichte der Gauabteilungen der DAF im Gau Bayerische Ostmark 1935–41, 18 Jan. 1936, IfZ, Fa 383.

18 Sopade, Jan. 1936, A 17.

19 J. Aretz, *Katholische Arbeiterbewegung und Nationalsozialismus. Der Verband katholischer Arbeiter und Knappenvereine Westdeutschlands 1923–1945* (Grünewald, Mainz, 1978). Cf. Schumann, *Nationalsozialismus*; D. J. K. Peukert, *Inside Nazi Germany* (Penguin, Harmondsworth, Middx, 1989), pp. 101–24.

20 Sopade, Sep. 1935, A 12 (Bayern).

21 Ibid.; Cf. W. Keil, *Erlebnisse eines Sozialdemokraten* (DVA, Stuttgart, 1947), vol. II, pp. 629–30, 642–3.

22 Sopade, Nov. 1937, A 51 (Wasserkante). It is not surprising to find reports that employers did not want to hire Jews because German workers refused to work with them. See for example Gauamt für Kommunalpolitik, Gau Düsseldorf, report May 1938, BA, NS 25/86.

23 Sopade, Jan. 1936, A 19 (Bayern).

24 Sopade, Feb. 1936, A 5.

25 Sopade, Feb. 1936. The workers' support of Hitler's foreign policy is indicated by many reports. On the plebiscite of 10 Apr. 1938, for example, it is stated that, whereas Catholics voted against the *Anschluß*, working-class districts – former communist strongholds excluded – voted in favour. See RP Niederbayern und Oberpfalz, report Apr. 1938, BHStA, MA 106692. In this context it is worth noting that inquiries by the conspirators of 20 July 1944 showed that the mass of industrial workers were behind the regime. See H. Mommsen, 'Gesellschaftsbild und Verfassungspläne des deutschen Widerstandes', in Walter Schmitthenner and Hans Buchheim (eds), *Der deutsche Widerstand gegen Hitler* (Kiepenheuer und Witsch, Köln, 1966), p. 75.

26 Kershaw, *Popular Opinion*, pp. 240ff.; Lowenstein, 'The struggle for survival of rural Jews', pp. 381–96.

27 Landrat Altenkirchen, report Aug. 1935, LHA, 441/35464.

28 Sopade, September 1935, A 21 (Pfalz 1). On agrarian policy see Broszat, *Der Staat Hitlers*, pp. 230–43.

29 Propagandaleiter, KL Eichstädt, report Mar. 1935, StA N, NSDAP Nr 8.

30 Ibid., report Oct. 1935. The complaint that peasants do not understand the Jewish

question returns stereotypically: see for instance Gestapo Dortmund, report Mar. 1935, BA, R 58/1131; RP Ansbach, report Mar. 1934, BHStA, MA 106672; Landrat Geilenkirchen, report Mar. 1935, HStA D, RAP 1061; Gauamt für Kommunalpolitik, Kurmark, 1 Jan. 1937, and Gau Koblenz-Trier, 1 Feb. 1937, BA, NS 25/85, fo. 1.

31 Sopade, Sep. 1935, A 51 (Südwest 2). Cf. the notes of Friedrich Weil, LBI, printed in M. Richarz, *Jüdisches Leben in Deutschland. Selbstzeugnisse zur Sozialgeschichte 1918–1945* (DVA, Stuttgart, 1882), p. 271–2.

32 NS Lehrerbund, report Haslbach, StA N, NSDAP 983; Wiesemann, 'Judenverfolgung', p. 470.

33 For a discussion and bibliography of the relevant studies see D. Stegmann, 'Antiquierte Personalisierung oder sozialökonomische Faschismus-Analyse. Eine Antwort auf H. A. Turners Kritik an meinen Thesen zum Verhältnis von Nationalsozialismus und Grossindustrie vor 1933', *Archiv für Sozialgeschichte*, 17 (1977), pp. 175–206. In general see Schoenbaum, *Hitler's Social Revolution*, pp. 113ff.; Broszat, *Der Staat Hitlers*, pp. 218–29.

34 Sopade, Sep. 1937, A 14.

35 F. von Papen, *Der Wahrheit eine Gasse* (List, Munich, 1952), p. 321. Cf. W. E. Dodd, *Ambassador Dodd's Diary* (Harcourt Brace, New York, 1941), entry for 1 Nov. 1934; Sopade, Apr.–May 1934, A 10; and the information printed by the organ of the Czech Zionist Organization, *Selbstwehr*, 3 Aug. 1934.

36 Dodd, *Ambassador Dodd's Diary*, entry for 24 May 1934. Cf. von Neurath's warnings to Hindenburg on Germany's isolation, *Trial of the Major War Criminals*, vol. XL, p. 465.

37 Sopade, Sep. 1935, A 28 (Hessen).

38 Gestapo Köln, report Mar. 1935, BA, R 58/386.

39 Gestapo Münster, report Aug. 1935, GStA, REP/90 P.

40 Gestapo Bielefeld, report June 1935, ibid.

41 Gestapo Aachen, report Dec. 1934, HStA D, RAP 148.

42 RP Ansbach, reports on the second half of Sep. 1933, and on Mar. 1933, YVA, JM/2858.

43 Uhlig, *Warenhäuser*, p. 115; Genschel, *Die Verdrängung*, p. 80.

44 Polizei Direktion München, report Sep.–Oct. 1935, BHStA, MA 106677.

45 Gestapo Kassel, report Dec. 1935, GStA, REP/90 P.

46 Polizei Direktion München, report Sep.–Oct. 1935, BHStA, MA 106677.

47 Gauamt für Kommunalpolitik, Gau Schwaben, 12 Nov. 1935, Tätigkeitsbericht, BA, NS 25/351; Gestapo Harburg-Wilhelmsburg, report Sep. 1935, YVA, JM/2834.

48 Gauamt für Kommunalpolitik, Gau Augsburg, report Oct. 1935, BA, NS 25/351.

49 Sopade, Nov. 1938, A 44–50; Dec. 1938, A 27–43; Jan. 1939, A 1–7; Feb. 1939, A 90–101.

6 AWARENESS OF THE HOLOCAUST

1 On these sources see the introduction in H. Boberach (ed.), *Meldungen aus dem Reich*. For a full edition of the SD reports see H. Boberach (ed.), *Meldungen aus dem Reich* (Pawlak, Herrsching, 1984). All further quotations are from this edition.

2 The relevant studies for our topic are: Steinert, *Hitler's War*, pp. 132–47; L. D. Stokes, 'The German people and the destruction of the European Jews', *Central European History*, 6 (1973), pp. 167–91; W. Laqueur, *The Terrible Secret* (Weidenfeld and Nicolson, London, 1980), pp. 17–32; Kulka, '"Public opinion"'; S. Gordon, *Hitler, Germans and the Jewish Question* (Princeton University Press, Princeton, NJ, 1984); Kershaw, *Popular Opinion*, and 'German popular opinion and the "Jewish Question"', pp. 365–86; H. Mommsen, 'Was haben die Deutschen vom Völkermord an den Juden gewußt?', in Werner H. Pehle (ed.), *Der Judenpogrom 1938. Von der 'Reichskristallnacht' zum Völkermord* (Fischer, Frankfurt a.M., 1988), pp. 176–200; H. Mommsen and D. Obst, 'Die Reaktion der deutschen Bevölkerung auf die Verfolgung der Juden', in Hans Mommsen and Susanne Willems (eds), *Herrschaftsalltag im Dritten Reich. Studien und Texte* (Schwann, Düsseldorf, 1989), pp. 374–427.

3 To cite just two examples: H. Schultheis, *Juden in Mainfranken 1933–1945* (Rötter, Bad Neustadt a. d. Saale, 1980), pp. 623–5; H. G. Adler, *Der verwaltete Mensch* (Mohr, Tübingen 1974), pp. 466–7. See also Steinert, *Hitler's War*, pp. 145–6; Stokes, 'The German People', pp. 168–72.

4 M. Balfour and J. Frisby, *Helmuth von Moltke. A leader against Hitler* (Macmillan, London, 1972), p. 218.

5 H. Rosenthal, *Zwei Leben in Deutschland* (Luebbe, Bergisch Gladbach, 1980), p. 54.

6 B. Weil, *Durch drei Kontinente* (Cosmopolita, Buenos Aires, 1948), p. 67.

7 E. H. Boehm, *We Survived: the stories of fourteen of the hidden and hunted of Nazi Germany, as told to Eric H. Boehm* (Yale University Press, New Haven, Conn., 1949), p. 293. Cf. Adler, *Der verwaltete Mensch*, p. 479.

8 See the recollections of Jacob Jacobson, LBI, ME 560, p. 14; and cf. J. Braun-Vogelstein, *Was niemals stirbt: Gestalten und Erinnerungen* (DVA, Stuttgart, 1966), p. 406.

9 L. Hahn, *...bis alles in Scherben fällt. Tagebuchblätter 1933–1945* (Braun, Cologne, 1979), entry for 8 May 1943.

10 U. von Kardorff, *Berliner Aufzeichnungen aus den Jahren 1942–1945* (Biederstein, Munich, 1962), entry for 13 Jan. 1944.

11 Ibid., entry for 15 Aug. 1943.

12 Boehm, *We Survived*, p. 123.

13 YVA, 02/29.

14 *Aufbau* (New York), 27 July 1942.

15 YVA, 02/33.

16 YVA, 02/38.

17 L. Haydn, *Meter immer nur Metter. Das Tagebuch eines Daheimgebliebenen* (Scholle, Vienna, 1946), entry for 29 June 1942.

18 Letter of Hermann Samter dated 26 Jan. 1942, YVA, 02/30.

19 Steinert, *Hitler's War*, p. 83. On public knowledge of euthanasia see the report of a refugee from Württemberg, British Embassy in Washington to Foreign Office, 6 Oct. 1941, PRO FO 371/26508, and the reports of the Bern Legation to Foreign Office, 10 Dec. 1940, PRO, FO 371/26510 and 371/26513. See also Berthold Rosenthal's account in LBI. A rare example of reactions to the euthanasia killings appears in the SD surveys. The reporter mentions a comment on the notorious film

Ich klage an: 'this is what happens in the hospitals where they liquidate the fools' ('wo sie jetzt die Tollen alle Kaputt machen') – Boberach, *Meldungen*, 15 Jan. 1942.

20 L. de Boor, *Tagebuchblätter aus den Jahren 1935–1945* (Biederstein, Munich, 1963), entry for 25 June 1941.
21 PRB Stockholm to PID London, 12 Nov. 1943, PRO, FO 371/34439.
22 Stimmungsbericht, Gauleitung West-Nord, 21 Nov. 1939, StA Mü, Hauptleitung Nr 21.
23 Stokes, 'The German People', p. 179.
24 Boberach, *Meldungen*, 26 Aug. 1940.
25 Der Amtsbürgermeister Sorgentreich, Gauleitung West-Nord, 8 Aug. 1941, StA Mü, Hauptleitung Nr 11; Gauleitung West-Nord, Nov. 1941, ibid.
26 Stokes, 'The German People', pp. 188–9; Gordon, *Hitler*, pp. 180–1.
27 SD Bad Neustadt, 15 Oct. 1943, StA W, SD 14.
28 Vertrauliche Informationen der Parteikanzlei, 9 Oct. 1942, printed in H. Huber and A. Müller (eds), *Das Dritte Reich. Seine Geschichte in Texten, Bilden und Dokumenten* (Desch, Munich, 1964), vol. II, p. 110.
29 D. D. Wall, 'The reports of the Sicherheitsdienst on the Church and religious affairs in Germany 1939–1944', *Church History*, 40 (1971), p. 449.
30 Boberach, *Meldungen*, 19 Apr. 1943, 26 July 1943; SD Würzburg, Außenstelle Bad Brückenau, 16 Apr. 1943, StA W, SD 12; SD Hauptaußenstelle Würzburg, 7 Apr. 1943, StA W, SD 37; Stokes, 'The German People', pp. 186–7; Steinert, *Hitler's War*, p. 143; Kershaw, *Public Opinion*, p. 365.
31 SD Außenstelle Bad Brückenau, 22 Apr. 1943, StA W, SD 12.
32 Postal and Telegraph Censorship Report on Germany, 13 Sep. 1941, PRO, FO 371/26512.
33 Memorandum prepared by the Foreign Office for the PID, Nov. 1941, PRO, FO 371/26515.
34 Testimony of SS *Rottenführer* Pery Broad, in G. Schoenberner (ed.), *Wir haben es gesehen: Augenzeugenberichte über Terror und Judenverfolgung im Dritten Reich* (Rutten-Roening, Hamburg, 1962), p. 277; C. R. Browning, *Fateful months. Essays on the emergence of the Final Solution* (Holmes and Meier, New York, 1985), pp. 82–3.
35 Second manifesto, I. Scholl, *Die Weiße Rose* (Frankfurter Hefte Verlag, Frankfurt a.M., 1952), pp. 91–3.
36 P. Freiherr von Schoenaich, *Mein Finale. Mit dem geheimen Tagebuch 1933–1945* (Christian Wolff, Flensburg and Hamburg, 1947), entry for 29 Nov. 1943.
37 C. Lavabre, *Ceux de l'an 40* (Subervie, Rodez 1981), p. 290.
38 Haydn, *Meter immer nur Metter*, entry for 19 Dec. 1942, and entry for 30 July 1942, mentioning the murder of 100,000 Jews in Poland.
39 British Embassy in Washington to Foreign Office, 24 July 1942, PRO, FO 371/30400.
40 H. and S. Obenaus (eds), *'Schreiben wie es wirklich war!' Aufzeichnungen aus den Jahren 1933–1945* (Fackelträger, Hanover, 1985), pp. 103ff.; Kershaw, 'German popular opinion and the "Jewish Question"', p. 379.
41 Obenaus and Obenaus, *'Schreiben wie es wirklich war!'*, p. 112.
42 Ibid., pp. 113–15.

43 Haydn, *Meter immer nur Metter*, entry for 29 June 1942.

44 O. Buchbender and R. Sterz (eds), *Das andere Gesicht des Krieges. Deutsche Feldpostbriefe 1939–1945* (Beck, Munich, 1982), pp. 13–14.

45 Haydn, *Meter immer nur Metter*, entry for 24 Dec. 1942.

46 Some of these letters are printed in Buchbender and Sterz, *Das andere Gesicht*, pp. 168–73; H. Dollinger (ed.), *Kain, wo ist dein Bruder?* (List, Munich, 1983), p. 35; 'Ausgewählte Briefe von Generalmajor Helmuth Stieff', *Vierteljahrshefte für Zeitgeschichte*, 3 (1954), p. 302.

47 U. von Hassell, *Vom anderen Deutschland, aus dem nachgelassenen Tagebüchern 1938–1944* (Fischer, Frankfurt a.M., 1962). See entries for 19 Oct. 1939, 17 Feb. 1940, 8 Oct. 1940, 4 Oct. 1941, 1 and 30 Nov. 1941, 14 Feb. 1942, 1 Aug. 1942, 26 Nov. 1942 and 15 May 1943. See also F. P. Reck Malleczewen, *Tagebuch eines Verzweifelten. Zeugnis einer innern Emigration* (Fischer, Frankfurt M., 1971), entry for 30 Oct. 1942. In it a soldier who has returned from the Eastern Front tells the author in detail about the shooting and burning of 30,000 Jews.

48 F. M. Buscher and M. Phayer, 'German Catholic bishops and the Holocaust, 1940–1952', *German Studies Review*, 11 (1988), p. 465.

49 M. Brustin Berenstein, 'The process of exterminating Jewish communities in the so called Distrikt Galizien', *Bletter far Geschichte*, 6, no. 3 (July–Sep. 1953), pp. 132–4 (in Yiddish). Detailed accounts of the events appear in *Memorial Book of Jezierna* (Survivors Organization, Haifa, 1971: in Hebrew); *Memorial Book for the Jewish Communities of Trembowla, Strusow, Janow and Vicinity* (Survivors Organization, Benei Berak, n.d.: in Hebrew); *Encyclopaedia of the Jewish Diaspora. Poland series, Tarnopol volume* (Encyclopaedia Co., Jerusalem and Tel Aviv 1955), p. 404 (in Hebrew).

50 PRB Stockholm to PID London, 3 Dec. 1943, PRO, FO 371/34440.

51 PRB Stockholm to PID London, 24 Feb. 1943, PRO, FO 371/34427. The origins of the story about electrocution are unknown. Joshua Wohlfuss also mentions in his diary that in April 1942 rumours went around that the aged and children were murdered by electrocution in Bełżec; see *Memorial Book Rawa Ruska* (Survivors Organization, Tel Aviv, 1973), p. 238: in Hebrew). These rumours also circulated in the west: see 'Nazi execution mill reported in Poland', *New York Times*, 14 Feb. 1944, p. 7.

52 On the French POWs in Rawa Ruska see P. Gascar, *Histoire de la captivité des Français en Allemagne (1939–1945)* (Gallimard, Saint-Amand, 1967), pp. 229–42; Lavabre, *Ceux de l'an 40*, p. 290, also mention the corpses of Jews thrown on the rails. This seriously disturbed the German authorities, as we learn from the appeal of Martin Luther of the German Foreign Office to Heinrich Müller in the RSHA: see S. Spector, 'Operation 1005. Effacing the murder of millions', *Yahadut Zémanenu*, 4 (1987), p. 208 (in Hebrew).

53 PRB Stockholm to PID London, 18 May 1943, PRO, FO 371/34430.

54 Kershaw, *Public Opinion*, pp. 366–7.

55 Stokes, 'The German People', pp. 185–6.

56 PRO, FO 371/30400.

57 British Legation Bern to Foreign Office, 17 Sep. 1941, PRO, FO 371/26513.

58 Hahn, *…bis alles in Scherben fällt*, entry for 30 Nov. 1941.

59 Haydn, *Meter immer nur Metter*, entry for 19 Dec. 1942.
60 British Embassy in Madrid to Foreign Office, 12 Apr. 1943, PRO, FO 371/34429.
61 Lisbon Legation to PID London, 1 Apr. 1943, PRO, FO 371/34429.
62 Lisbon Legation to PID London, 16 June 1943, PRO, FO 371/34431.
63 R. Andreas-Friedrich, *Schauplatz Berlin. Ein deutsches Tagebuch* (Rheinsberg, Munich, 1962).
64 Partei Kanzlei, 8 May, 1943, BA, NS 6/409.
65 Testimony of SS *Rottenführer* Pery Broad, in Schoenberner, *Wir haben es gesehen*, p. 277. Cf. Laqueur, *The Terrible Secret*, pp. 19ff.
66 H. Lindgren, 'Adam von Trotts Reisen nach Schweden 1942–1944', *Vierteljahrshefte für Zeitgeschichte*, 18 (1970), p. 286.
67 Andreas-Friedrich, *Schauplatz Berlin*, entry for 4 Feb. 1944.
68 Hahn, *...bis alles in Scherben fällt*, entry for 1 Mar. 1944.
69 See for example Boberach, *Meldungen*, 3 Sep. 1942.
70 PRB Stockholm to PID London, 27 Mar. 1943, PRO, FO 371/34429.
71 U. Hochmuth, *Streiflichter aus dem Hamburger Widerstand 1933–1945* (Röderberg, Frankfurt a.M., 1969), p. 453.
72 Funk-Abhör Berichte, 11 May 1944, BA, R 58/795; 17 July 1944, BA, R 58/800. Reichsministerium für Volksaufklärung und Propaganda, Erkundungsdienst, 12, 18 and 22 Dec. 1942, BA, R 55/1357. Cf. Lochner, *The Goebbels Diaries*, entries for 13 and 18 Dec. 1942. As early as the beginning of 1940, the BBC announced that 40,000 Jews had died of starvation, severe cold and other sufferings. See the broadcast of 8 Feb. 1940, RSHA, VI B Dienst, Funkbeobachtung des Ref. VI A 6, Bericht Nr 60, 9 Feb. 1940, IfZ, DC 15.24.
73 Obenaus and Obenaus, *'Schreiben wie es wirklich war!'*, p. 126.
74 PRO, FO 371/32681.
75 YVA, 02/154.
76 Funk-Abhör Berichte, 16 June 1944, BA, R 58/795; 3 July 1944, BA, R 58/800; 18 July 1944, BA, R 55/522; 9 July 1944, BA, R 58/800.
77 See the leaflets *Die Ausrottungszone am Bug*, *Christen Deutschlands*, *Warnung* dropped over Germany between 11 Feb. and 9 Mar. 1943, reproduced in K. Kirchner, *Flugblattpropaganda im 2. Weltkrieg* (Verlag D+C, Erlangen, 1977), facsimiles G 94, USG 39, USG 50, G 30.
78 Kardorff, *Berliner Aufzeichnungen*.
79 Manfred Fackenheim memoirs, LBI.
80 Mommsen, 'Was haben die Deutschen gewußt', pp. 199–200.

7   PUBLIC RESPONSES TO ANTISEMITISM, 1939–1943

1 Boberach, *Meldungen*, 15 Aug. 1940; SD Würzburg, Außenstelle Kitzingen, 22 Apr. 1940, StA W, SD 17; Boberach, *Meldungen*, 16 Oct. 1941, 5 Mar., 30 July, 10 and 17 Aug. 1942. For reports on a few who maintained links with Jews see RP Ansbach, 6 Mar. 1942, YVA, JM/2858; SD Würzburg, Außenstelle Kitzingen, 8 Apr. 1940, StA W, SD 17.
2 Boberach, *Meldungen*, 2, 9 and 16 Feb. 1942, 10 Aug. 1942, 19 Jan. 1942. SD

Hauptaußenstelle Bielefeld, 4 Nov. 1941, NAW, T 175 R 577 F 366337; 3 Feb. 1942, NAW, T 175 R 270 F 2766125; 3 Feb. 1942, NAW, T 175 R 577 F 699.

3 On similar attitudes to foreigners see SD Abschnitt Linz, 11 June 1943, BA, NS 6/409; Boberach, *Meldungen*, 20 Aug. and 1 Oct. 1942.

4 This refers to the report of SD Außenstelle Höxter, 19 Jan. 1942. Cf. Boberach, *Meldungen*, 9 Feb. 1942; B. Hey, 'Bielefeld und seine Bevölkerung in den Berichten des Sicherheitsdienstes (SD) 1939–1942', *70. Jahresbericht des historischen Vereins für die Grafschaft Ravensberg* 70 (1975/6), p. 233.

5 *Inside Germany Reports*, 15 (Dec. 1940).

6 Among the studies applying oral-history methods see P. Joutard, *Ces voix qui nous viennent du passé* (Gallimard, Paris, 1983); E. Luchterhand, 'Knowing and not knowing: involvement in Nazi genocide', in Paul Thompson (ed.), *Our Common History. The transformation of Europe* (Humanities Press, Atlantic Highlands, NJ, 1982), pp. 251–72.

7 British Embassy in Washington to Foreign Office, 16 May 1941, PRO, FO 371/26510; 10 Nov. 1941, Experiences and Observations of a Jew in Germany, Aug. 1941, PRO, FO 371/26515.

8 British Legation in Montevideo to Foreign Office, 11 Aug. 1941, PRO, FO 371/26513; memorandum of Capt. H. Cross, Montevideo, 2 Aug. 1941, PRO, FO 371/32681.

9 Report of Käte Cohn, PRO, FO 371/32681.

10 J. W. Wheeler Bennet to British Embassy in Washington, 31 Jan. 1941, PRO, FO 371/26509; British Embassy in Washington to Foreign Office, 16 May 1941, PRO, FO 371/26510.

11 Balfour and Frisby, *Moltke*, entries for 26 Aug., 21 Oct. and 13 Nov. 1941. On motivations for helping Jews see E. Fogelman, 'The Rescuers: a socio-psychological study of altruistic behaviour during the Nazi era' (PhD dissertation, City University of New York, 1987); M. Wolfson, 'Der Widerstand gegen Hitler. Soziologische Skizze über Retter von Juden in Deutschland', *Aus Politik und Zeitgeschichte*, 10 Apr. 1971, pp. 32–9.

12 PRB Stockholm to PID London, 19 Apr. 1944, PRO, FO 371/39060.

13 E. Rosenfeld, *The Four Lives of Elsbeth Rosenfeld as Told by her to the BBC* (Gollancz, London, 1964), pp. 87ff., 95ff.

14 Kardorff, *Berliner Aufzeichnungen*, entry for 28 Dec. 1942.

15 J. Klepper, *Unter dem Schatten deiner Flügel. Aus den Tagebüchern 1932–1942* (DTV, Munich, 1976), entry for 23 Oct. 1941. Cf. entry for 28 Dec. 1942; Andreas-Friedrich, *Schauplatz Berlin*, entries for 19 June, 14 and 26 Aug., 21 Oct. and 13 Nov. 1942.

16 Hahn, *...bis alles in Scherben fällt*, entry for 22 Oct. 1941.

17 Ibid., entry for 31 Oct. 1942.

18 Noakes and Pridham, *Nazism 1919–1945*, vol. II, p. 217.

19 R. Semmler, *Goebbels – the Man Next to Hitler* (Westhouse, London, 1947), entry for 25 Apr. 1941.

20 G. L. Fleming, *Hitler and the Final Solution* (Oxford University Press, Oxford, 1986), p. 8. According to Hitler's personal secretary, Hitler ordered the 'Aryanization' of Marlene von Exener, his assistant dietician, when Jewish blood

was discovered in her mother's ancestral line: see P. Galante and E. Silianoff, *Last Witnesses in the Bunker* (Sidgwick and Jackson, London, 1989), pp. 105–6. For similar 'Aryanizations' see D. Bankier, 'Hitler and the policy-making process on the Jewish Question', *Holocaust and Genocide Studies*, 3 (1988), pp. 11–12.

21 This point is treated in depth in the cited works of Ian Kershaw and Detlev Peukert. See also H. J. Eitner, *Hitlers Deutsche. Das Ende eines Tabus* (Casimir Katz, Gernsbach, 1990).

22 Boor, *Tagebuchblätter*, entries for 8 Apr. and 7 Aug. 1944; Kardorff, *Berliner Aufzeichnungen*, entries for 20 Nov. and 20 Dec. 1942.

23 Political Intelligence memorandum, 15 May 1942, PRO, FO 371/30900.

24 British Consul in Basle, 4 Oct. 1941, PRO, FO 371/26515.

25 PRB Stockholm to Foreign Office, 14 Apr. 1942, PRO, FO 371/30899.

26 *Inside Germany Reports*, 15 (Dec. 1940); British Consul in Basle, 4 Oct. 1941, PRO, FO 371/26515.

27 On living-conditions of Jews in Germany at the time see Jewish refugee to British Consul General in Antwerp, 29 Jan. 1940, PRO, FO 371/24387; Gestapo Bremen, 8 Feb. 1940, StA B, 3-M2h3 Nr 28 (21). For a full list of antisemitic laws and regulations see Walk, *Das Sonderrecht für die Juden im N.S. Staat.*

28 Boberach, *Meldungen*, 24 Nov. 1941.

29 Memoirs of Emma Becker Kohen, LBI. Cf. M. Phayer, 'Margarete Sommer, Berlin Catholics and Germany's Jews 1939–1945', *Remembering for the Future* (Pergamon, Oxford, 1988), vol. I. p. 114. See also Buscher and M. Phayer, 'German Catholic bishops and the Holocaust', pp. 463–85.

30 Irgun Olej Merkaz Europa (ed.), *Die letzten Tage der deutschen Judentums* (Olamenu, Tel Aviv, 1943), p. 31.

31 In addition to the *Meldungen* of 9 Oct. 1941 and 2 Febr. 1942, see the accounts of some local reports, such as SD Außenstelle Minden, 21 Feb. 1942, NAW, T 175 R 577 F 679–80; Reichsfrauenführung, report Sep. 1941, BA, NS 22/vorl. 860, on Gau Hesse-Nassau and Gau Berlin; Bürgermeister Augsburg, 6 Jan. 1942, BA, NS 6/vorl. 416, fo. 1. For conflicting historical interpretations see O. D. Kulka and A. Rodrigue, 'The German population and the Jews in the Third Reich', *Yad Vashem Studies*, 16 (1984), p. 433, and Kershaw, 'German popular opinion and the "Jewish Question"', pp. 372–4.

32 K. Scheurenberg, *Ich will leben: ein autobiographischer Bericht* (Oberbaum, Berlin, 1982), pp. 78–81; E. Bukofzer, *Laws for Jews and Persecution of Jews under the Nazis* (Hübener, Berlin, 1946), p. 11; memoirs of Jacob Jacobson, in Richarz, *Jüdisches Leben*, p. 402; recollections of Leo Baeck, in Boehm, *We Survived*, p. 288. For Inge Deutschkron's experiences see her *Ich trug den gelben Stern* (Wissenschaft und Politik, Cologne, 1978), pp. 85–8.

33 Irgun Olej Merkaz Europa, *Die letzten Tage der deutschen Judentums*, p. 33.

34 See Käte Cohn's experiences, in PRO, FO 371/32681; the experiences of a Jewish professor, in *Inside Germany Reports*, 23 (Nov. 1942); and the report of Carl Peters, who returned to the United States at the end of Nov. 1941, PRO, FO 371/26514.

35 Washington Chancery to Foreign Office, 23 Nov. 1941, PRO, FO 371/26515, reported also in *Inside Germany Reports*, 21 (Feb. 1942). Cf. the impressions of Elisabeth Freund in Richartz, *Jüdisches Leben*, p. 381; PRB Stockholm to PID London, 22 Nov. 1941, PRO, FO 371/26515.

36 PRO, FO 371/26515.

37 See for example Ingeborg Tafel's letter to her husband of 21 Sep. 1941, in H. Dollinger (ed.), *Kain, wo ist dein Bruder?* (List, Munich, 1983), p. 97; Boor, *Tagebuchblätter*, entry for 10 Nov. 1941.

38 Andreas–Friedrich, *Schauplatz Berlin*, entry for 19 Sep. 1941.

39 H. K. Smith, *The Last Train from Berlin* (Knopf, New York, 1943), pp. 195ff.; A. Fredborg, *Behind the Steel Wall. A Swedish journalist in Berlin 1941–43* (Viking, New York, 1944), pp. 69–70. On the hostile reactions of the French public to the introduction of the yellow star in France see M. R. Marrus and R. O. Paxton, *Vichy France and the Jews* (Basic Books, New York, 1981), pp. 234–40.

40 British Ambassador in Stockholm to Foreign Office, 25 Oct. 1941, PRO, FO 371/26508.

41 Cited in *Jüdische Wochenschau* (Buenos Aires), 9 Jan. 1942.

42 British Legation in Holland to Foreign Office, 14 Nov. 1941, PRO, FO 371/26514. See the letter of a Swedish woman dated 14 Oct. 1941, PRO, FO 371/26515; report of the British Military Attaché in Bern, 5 Nov. 1941, PRO, FO 371/26514.

43 Postal and Telegraphic Censorship Report on Germany no. 3, 5 Mar. 1942, p. 19, PRO, FO 371/30898.

44 A. Speer, *Spandau. The secret diaries* (Pocket, New York, 1976), p. 287.

45 PRB Stockholm to PID London, 22 Nov. 1941, PRO, FO 371/26515.

46 *Stuttgart NS–Kurier*, 4 Oct. 1941.

47 Smith, *Last Train*, p. 199.

48 Statement of Edwin van D'Elden, British Embassy in Washington, 24 July 1942, PRO, FO 371/30400.

49 PRB Stockholm to PID London, 11 Sep. 1942, PRO, FO 371/30901.

50 A. Haag, *Das Glück zu Leben* (Bonz, Stuttgart, 1967), entry for 5 Oct. 1942.

51 F. Stern, *The Whitewashing of the Yellow Badge. Philosemitism and Antisemitism in West Germany 1945–1952* (Pergamon, Oxford, 1991).

52 M. Broszat and S. Friedländer, 'A controversy about the historicization of National Socialism', *Yad Vashem Studies*, 19 (1988), p. 21.

53 Hahn,...*bis alles in Scherben fällt*, entry for 14 Dec. 1940; Klepper, *Unter dem Schatten deiner Flügel*, entry for 6 Nov. 1939; PRO, FO 371/26569.

54 PRO, FO 371/24386.

55 *Jewish Telegraphic Agency Reports* (Geneva), 29 Dec. 1941; Postal and Telegraph Censorship Report on Germany no. 3, 5 Mar. 1942, p. 18, PRO, FO 371/30898.

56 Dollinger, *Kain, wo ist dein Bruder?*, pp. 65–6. Cf. M. Mayer, *They Thought They Were Free* (Chicago University Press, Chicago and London, 1974), p. 129.

57 Hermann Samter, 26 Jan. 1942, YVA, 02/30. On Frankfurt see the statement of Edwin van D'Elden, 4 July 1942, British Embassy in Washington to Central Department, PRO, FO 371/30400. On deportations from cities in western Germany see M. Zimmermann, 'Die Deportation der Juden aus Essen und dem Regierungsbezirk Düsseldorf', in Ulrich Borsdorf and Mathilde Jamin (eds), *Überleben im Krieg* (Rowohlt, Hamburg, 1989), pp. 134ff.

58 Schoenberner, *Wir haben es gesehen*, pp. 298–300; Fredborg, *Behind the Steel Wall*, pp. 199–200.

59 M. Schmidt, *Albert Speer. The end of a myth* (Harrap, London, 1985), p. 189.

60 Haydn, *Meter immer nur Metter*, entries for 29 June 1942 and 30–1 July 1942.

61 Obenaus and Obenaus, 'Schreiben wie es wirklich war!', p. 115; SD Gotha, 26 May 1942, BA, NS 29/54; SD Erfurt, May 1942, ibid.; SD Erfurt, 3 June 1942, ibid.

62 Haydn, *Meter immer nur Metter*, entry for 1 August 1942.

63 Kershaw, 'Antisemitismus und Volksmeinung', p. 337.

64 Balfour and Frisby, *Moltke*, letter of 18 Nov. 1941.

65 Kardorff, *Berliner Aufzeichnungen*, entry for 31 Dec. 1942.

66 Außenstelle Detmold, 30 July 1942, NAW, T 175 R 577 F 736.

67 SD Hautaußenstelle Bielefeld, 16 Dec. 1941; SD Außenstelle Minden, 6 and 12 Dec. 1941, NAW, T 175 R 577 F 675.

68 Report of 3 Dec. 1941, StA B, M2h3 Nr 264, printed in R. Bruß, *Die Bremer Juden unter dem Nationalsozialismus* (Selbstverlag des Staatsarchivs, Bremen, 1983), pp. 226–7.

69 Schoenberner, *Wir haben es gesehen*, pp. 298–300.

70 Fredborg, *Behind the Steel Wall*.

71 Facsimile in R. W. Kempner, *Eichmann und Komplizen* (Europa, Zürich, Stuttgart and Vienna, 1961), pp. 118–19.

72 Boor, *Tagebuchblätter*, entries for 28 Dec. 1941, 27 May 1942, 25 Dec. 1942, 1 Jan. 1943, 22 June 1943.

73 Printed by the *Jüdische Wochenschau* (Buenos Aires), 9 Oct. 1942.

74 *Das andere Deutschland*, Montevideo, 3 Mar. 1944; Fredborg, *Behind the Steel Wall*, pp. 199–200.

75 Kardorff, *Berliner Aufzeichnungen*, 3 Mar. 1943.

76 British Embassy in Madrid to Foreign Office, 12 Apr. 1943, PRO, FO 371/34429.

77 Lochner, *The Goebbels Diaries*, entries for 2 and 6 Mar. 1943; Picker, *Hitlers Tischgespräche*, entry for 15 May 1942.

78 PRB Stockholm to PID London, 17 June 1943, PRO, FO 371/34431.

79 Summary of a verbal report given to A. Stieglitz and F. Lichtenstein on the position of Jews in Germany, PRO, FO 371/34362.

80 Kardorff, *Berliner Aufzeichnungen*, 3 Mar. 1943.

81 Jacob Jacobson's memoirs, LBI.

82 Smith, *Last Train*, p. 202.

83 British Embassy in Lisbon to PID London, 11 Oct. 1943, PRO, FO 371/34438.

84 Adler, *Der verwaltete Mensch*, p. 227.

8 IMAGE AND REALITY – THE END

1 See the cited works of I. Kershaw, *Popular Opinion*, pp. 358–72; 'Persecution'; *The 'Hitler Myth'*, pp. 229–52; 'German popular opinion and the "Jewish Question"'; Steinert, *Hitler's War*, pp. 132–47, 335.

2 Kulka and Rodrigue, 'The German Population', pp. 421–35.

3 M. Broszat, 'The Third Reich and the German people', in Hedley Bull (ed.), *The Challenge of the Third Reich* (Clarendon Press, Oxford, 1986), pp. 77–94.

4 M. Broszat, *Nach Hitler. Der schwierige Umgang mit unserer Geschichte* (Oldenbourg, Munich, 1986), pp. 68–91. On public reactions to Nazi propaganda in general see D. Welch, 'Propaganda and indoctrination in the Third Reich: success

or failure?', *European History Quarterly*, 17 (1987), pp. 403–22; R. E. Herzstein, *The War that Hitler Won* (Sphere Books, London, 1980).

5 Boberach, *Meldungen*, 20 Jan. 1941; SD Außenstelle Höxter, 7 Feb. 1941, NAW, T 175 R 505 F 248; Kershaw, *The 'Hitler Myth'*, pp. 242–3. The film was shown in two versions on the advice of Nazi officials: one for women and youth, which excluded the scenes of ritual slaughter; and one for party circles and adults, which included them. See Boelcke, *Kriegspropaganda*, entries for 12 Sep. and 26 Nov. 1940.

6 *Inside Germany Reports*, 13 (July 1940).

7 Postal and Telegraph Censorship Report on Germany no. 3, 5 Mar. 1942. For similar reports on positive attitudes towards Jews see *Sozialistische Mitteilungen*, 1 Jan. 1942.

8 PRB Stockholm to PID London, 21 June 1943, PRO, FO 371/34431.

9 British Vice-Consul in Granada to Foreign Office, 10 July 1943, PRO, FO 371/34434.

10 Boberach, *Meldungen*, 24 July 1941 and 27 Nov. 1941.

11 PRB Stockholm to PID London, 7 June 1943, PRO, FO 371/34431.

12 See the diary of Elisabeth Freund, LBI, printed in Richartz, *Jüdisches Leben*, p. 381.

13 Report of the *New York Times* correspondent in Berlin, Peter Scarlett, 7 Nov. 1941, PRO, FO 371/26514.

14 30 Sep. 1941, PRO, FO 371/26513.

15 See for example the impressions of a Swedish student in Berlin, PRB Stockholm to Foreign Office, 29 Mar. 1942, PRO, FO 371/30898.

16 Boberach, *Meldungen*, 23 Feb. 1942.

17 SD Abschnitt Dortmund, 11 May 1942, StA Mü, Politische Polizei III Reich Nr 381.

18 Boberach, *Meldungen*, 2 Feb. 1942; SD Leipzig, Außenstelle Leipzig, 26 Aug. 1942, BA, NS 29/52. Cf. Kershaw, *'The Hitler Myth'*, pp. 244–5.

19 British Embassy in Lisbon to Foreign Office, 12 Mar. 1943, PRO, FO, 371/34428. We come across a similar mixture of antisemitism with fear of reprisals and apathy towards Nazi propaganda in reports on Vienna. By mid-1943 the public believed that no more than a few dozen Jewish families remained in that city. According to one observer, the Viennese were often heard saying that it was quite a good thing to have got rid of the Jews, but now it was high time for the Nazis to follow. At the same time, the brutal treatment of the Jews had caused many Austrians to turn away in disgust from the Nazi system. Nobody had believed that the Germans would really go to such lengths. According to another report, certainly less reliable, the persecution of Jews was first accepted apathetically, but later it turned everybody against the system and Jews were assisted. A former Nazi concurred with this assessment: 'The persecution of the Jews was at first accepted with apathy, then it made the regime more hated. Deportations are conducted at night and not as a daytime show as before, because Jews are helped. Antisemitic propaganda creates no attraction to the regime.' According to an Austrian lawyer who left in March 1944, and did not hide his antisemitic prejudices, Austrian sentiments towards the Jews had completely changed because 'they never dreamed that the Nazis would

attempt to exterminate the Jews.' PRB Stockholm to PID London, 20 May 1943, PRO FO 371/34431 and 15 June 1943, FO 371/34431; London Bureau of Austrian Socialists, Reports on the Underground Resistance Movement in Austria, May 1943, FO 371/34435; British Embassy in Lisbon to PID London, 24 Oct. 1944, FO 371/39066.

20 10 Sep. 1943, BA, NS 18/225. Cf. Bankier, 'Hitler and the policy-making process', pp. 9–10.

21 *Inside Germany Reports*, 25 Aug. 1943.

22 PRB Stockholm to PID London, 24 Sep. 1943, PRO, FO 371/34438.

23 SD Abschnitt Linz, 23 June 1943, BA, NS 6/409.

24 PRB Stockholm to PID London, 21 Sep. 1943, PRO, FO 371/34438; Cf. Kershaw, 'Persecution of the Jews', p. 286.

25 Semmler, *Goebbels*, entry for 16 Aug. 1943.

26 Kershaw, *The Nazi Dictatorship*, pp. 166–7.

27 M. Broszat, 'Zur Struktur der NS-Massenbewegung', *Vierteljahrshefte für Zeitgeschichte*, 31 (1983), p. 76.

28 Kardorff, *Berliner Aufzeichnungen*. Similar comments were voiced in the Halle area; see Steinert, *Hitler's War*, p. 143.

29 SD Würzburg, Außenstelle Würzburg, 3 Aug. 1943, StA W, SD 23.

30 SD Würzburg, Außenstelle Bad Brückenau, 8 July 1944 StA W, SD 12.

31 SD Würzburg, Außenstelle Bad Brückenau, 7 May 1943, StA W, SD 22; Außenstelle Lohr, 15 May 1944, StA W, SD 19.

32 SD Würzburg, Außenstelle Schweinfurt, 16 Apr. 1943, StA W, SD 22.

33 On these reactions see the files in StA W: SD Würzburg, Außenstelle Schweinfurt, 6 Sep. 1943; Außenstelle Würzburg, 3 Aug. 1943; SD Würzburg, 8 July 1943; SD Hauptaußenstelle Würzburg, 27 July 1943; SD Abschnitt Nürnberg, 7 Sep. 1943, BA, R 58/1130; Kershaw, *Public Opinion*, p. 369.

34 Morale in Germany, 26 Sep. 1942, PRO, FO 371/30901.

35 E. Klee, W. Dressen and V. Riess (eds), *'Schöne Zeiten'. Judenmord aus der Sicht der Täter und Gaffer* (Fischer, Frankfurt a.M., 1988), p. 49.

36 Memorandum prepared by the Foreign Office for the PID, *Germany*, Nov. 1941, PRO, FO 371/26515.

37 Boberach, *Meldungen*, 20 Nov. 1941.

38 For reactions to Kaufmann's book see *Meldungen*, 28 July and 2 Oct. 1941. On the book itself see W. Benz, 'Judenvernichtung aus Notwehr? Die Legenden um Theodore N. Kaufmann', *Vierteljahrshefte für Zeitgeschichte*, 29 (1981), pp. 615–30.

39 SD Außenstelle Detmold, 12 Mar. 1942, YVA, JM/4568; SD Abschnitt Dortmund, Hauptaußenstelle Bielefeld, 15 Mar. 1942, ibid.

40 British Embassy in Madrid to Foreign Office, 1 Apr. 1943, PRO, FO 371/34429.

41 Kershaw, *Popular Opinion*, p. 365.

42 Hilberg, *Destruction of the European Jews*, p. 332.

43 A. Speer, *The Slave State* (Weidenfeld and Nicolson, London, 1981), p. 255; Lochner, *The Goebbels Diaries*, entry for 2 Mar. 1943.

44 Boberach, *Meldungen*, 12 Aug. 1943.

45 Martin Bormann, Führerhauptquartier, circular, 11 July, 1943, BA, NS 19.

46 See the article of Hermann Hirsch in *Stuttgarter NS-Kurier*, 2 Sep. 1943.
47 *Das Reich*, 24 Sep. 1943.
48 *Deutsche Nachrichten Büro*, 10 Nov. 1943.
49 Ibid., 29 May 1943.
50 Research Department, Foreign Office, Memoranda on Axis-controlled Europe, 14 Dec. 1943, PRO, FO 371/34440.
51 Ibid. The warnings were certainly in response to reports that party members had become reluctant to wear their party medals. See Boberach, *Meldungen*, 8 July 1943.

CONCLUSION

1 For a suggestive distinction between 'conventional' and Nazi antisemitism see S. Volkov, 'The written matter and the spoken word', in François Furet (ed.), *Unanswered Questions* (Schocken, New York, 1989), pp. 33–53.
2 M. Maschmann, *Account Rendered* (Abelard-Schuman, London, 1965), pp. 82–3.

Bibliography

ARCHIVES

BA	Bundesarchiv, Koblenz
BHStA	Bayerisches Hauptstaatsarchiv, Munich
CDJC	Centre de Documentation Juive Contemporaine, Paris
CDEC	Centro di Documentazione Ebraica Contemporanea, Milan
DB	Deutsche Bibliothek, Frankfurt a.M.
GLA	General Landesarchiv, Karlsruhe
GStA	Geheimes Staatsarchiv, Berlin
HStA D	Hauptstaatsarchiv, Düsseldorf
HStA Sp	Hauptstaatsarchiv, Speyer
HStA S	Hauptstaatsarchiv, Stuttgart
HHW	Hessisches Hauptarchiv, Wiesbaden
IfZ	Institut für Zeitgeschichte, Munich
LBI	Leo Baeck Institute, New York
LHA	Landeshauptarchiv, Koblenz
NAW	National Archives, Washington, DC
PA	Politisches Archiv des Auswärtigen Amtes, Bonn
PRO	Public Record Office, London
StA B	Staatsarchiv, Bremen
StA D	Staatsarchiv, Darmstadt
StA L	Staatsarchiv, Ludwigsburg
StA M	Staatsarchiv, Munich
StA N	Staatsarchiv, Nuremberg
StA Mü	Staatsarchiv, Münster
StA W	Staatsarchiv, Würzburg
WL	Wiener Library, London and Tel Aviv
YVA	Yad Vashem Archives, Jerusalem

OTHER ABBREVIATIONS USED IN THE NOTES

DAF	Deutsche Arbeitsfront
NSDAP	Nationalsozialistische Deutsche Arbeiterpartei
OP	Oberpräsident
PID	Political Intelligence Department
PRB	Press Reading Bureau
RP	Regierungspräsident
RSHA	Reichssicherheitshauptamt
SD	Sicherheitsdienst

COLLECTIONS OF DOCUMENTS, PERSONAL LETTERS, DIARIES, MEMOIRS

Akten zur deutschen Auswärtigen Politik 1918–1945, Vandenhoeck and Ruprecht, Göttingen, 1971.

Andreas Friedrich, Ruth, *Schauplatz Berlin. Ein deutsches Tagebuch*, Rheinsberg, Munich, 1962.

'Ausgewählte Briefe von Generalmajor Helmuth Stieff', *Vierteljahrshefte für Zeitgeschichte*, 3 (1954), pp. 291–305.

Baynes Norman H. (ed.), *The Speeches of Adolf Hitler*, Oxford University Press, London, 1942.

Bielenberg, Christabel, *The Past is Myself*, Chatto and Windus, London, 1968.

Boberach, Heinz (ed.), *Meldungen aus dem Reich. Auswahl aus den geheimen Lageberichten 1939–1944*, Luchterhand, Neuwied and Berlin, 1965.

——, *Berichte des SD und der Gestapo über Kirchen und Kirchenvolk in Deutschland 1934–1944*, Grünewald, Mainz, 1971.

——, *Meldungen aus dem Reich*, Pawlak, Herrsching, 1984.

Boehm, Eric H., *We Survived: the stories of fourteen of the hidden and hunted of Nazi Germany, as told to Eric H. Boehm*, Yale University Press, New Haven, Conn., 1949.

Boelcke, Willy A., *Kriegspropaganda 1939–41*, DVA, Stuttgart, 1966.

——, *'Wollt ihr den totalen Krieg?'. Die geheimen Goebbels Konferenzen 1939–1943*, DVA, Stuttgart, 1967.

Bohrmann, Hans and Gabrielle Toepser Ziegert (eds), *NS Presseanweisungen der Vorkriegszeit*, Saur, Munich, 1985–7.

Boor, Lisa de, *Tagebuchblätter aus den Jahren 1935–1945*, Biederstein, Munich, 1963.

Braun-Vogelstein, Julie, *Was niemals stirbt; Gestalten und Erinnerungen*, DVA, Stuttgart, 1966.

Buchbender, Ortwin and Reinhold Sterz (eds), *Das andere Gesicht des Krieges. Deutsche Feldpostbriefe 1939–1945*, Beck, Munich, 1982.

Deutschkron, Inge, *Ich trug den gelben Stern*, Wissenschaft und Politik, Cologne, 1978.

Documents on German Foreign Policy, Her Majesty's Stationery Office, London, 1957.

Dodd, William E., *Ambassador Dodd's Diary*, Harcourt Brace, New York, 1941.

Dollinger, Hans (ed.), *Kain, wo ist dein Bruder?*, List, Munich, 1983.

Domarus, Max (ed.), *Hitler Reden und Proklamationen, 1932–1945*, Loewit, Wiesbaden, 1973.

Fredborg, Arvid, *Behind the Steel Wall. A Swedish journalist in Berlin 1941–43*, Viking, New York, 1944.

Haag, Anna, *Das Glück zu Leben*, Bonz, Stuttgart, 1968.

Hahn, Lili,...*bis alles in Scherben fällt. Tagebuchblätter 1933–1945*, Braun, Cologne, 1979.

Hassell, Ulrich von, *Vom anderen Deutschland, aus dem nachgelassenen Tagebüchern 1938–1944*, Fischer, Frankfurt a.M., 1962.

Haydn, Ludwig, *Meter immer nur Metter. Das Tagebuch eines Daheimgebliebenen*, Scholle, Vienna, 1946.

Heyen, Franz J., *Nationalsozialismus und Alltag. Quellen zur Geschichte des National-sozialismus im Raum Mainz-Koblenz-Trier*, Boldt, Boppart/Rh., 1967.

Huber, Heinz and Arthur Müller (eds), *Das Dritte Reich. Seine Geschichte in Texten, Bilden und Dokumenten*, Desch, Munich, 1964.

Irgun Olej Merkaz Europa (ed.), *Die letzten Tage der deutschen Judentums*, Tel Aviv, 1943.

Kardorff, Ursula von, *Berliner Aufzeichnungen aus den Jahren 1942–1945*, Biederstein, Munich, 1962.

Keil, Wilhelm, *Erlebnisse eines Sozialdemokraten*, DVA, Stuttgart, 1947.

Kersten, Felix, *The Kersten Memoirs 1940–1945*, Hutchinson, London, 1956.

Kirchner, Klaus, *Flugblattpropaganda im 2. Weltkrieg*, Verlag D+C, Erlangen, 1977.

Klee, Ernst, Willi Dressen and Volker Riess (eds), *'Schöne Zeiten'. Judenmord aus der Sicht der Täter und Gaffer*, Fischer, Frankfurt a.M., 1988.

Klein, Thomas (ed.), *Die Lageberichte der Geheimenstaatspolizei über die Provinz Hessen-Nassau 1933–1936*, Böhlau, Cologne, 1986.

Klepper, Jochen, *Unter dem Schatten deiner Flügel. Aus den Tagebüchern 1932–1942*, DTV, Munich, 1976.

Kotze, Hildegard von and Helmut Krausnick (eds), *'Es spricht der Führer'. Sieben exemplarische Hitler-Reden*, Mohn, Gütersloh, 1966.

Lochner, Louis (ed.), *The Goebbels Diaries*, Award Books, New York, 1974.

Maschmann, Melita, *Account Rendered*, Abelard-Schuman, London, 1965.

Mason, Timothy W., *Arbeiterklasse und Volksgemeinschaft. Dokumente und Materialien zur deutschen Arbeiterpolitik 1936–1939*. Westdeutscher Verlag, Opladen, 1975.

Obenaus, Herbert and Sibylle (eds), *'Schreiben wie es wirklich war!' Aufzeichnungen aus den Jahren 1933–1945*, Fackelträger, Hanover, 1985.

Papen, Franz von, *Der Wahrheit eine Gasse*, List, Munich, 1952.

Picker, Henry, *Hitlers Tischgespräche im Führerhauptquartier 1941–1942*, Seewald, Stuttgart, 1977.

Reck Malleczewen, Friedrich P., *Tagebuch eines Verzweifelten. Zeugnis einer innern Emigration*, Fischer, Frankfurt a.M., 1971.

Richarz, Monika (ed.), *Jüdisches Leben in Deutschland. Selbstzeugnisse zur Sozialge-schichte 1918–1945*, DVA, Stuttgart, 1982.

Rosenthal, Hans, *Zwei Leben in Deutschland*, Luebbe, Bergisch Gladbach, 1980.

Scheurenberg, Klaus, *Ich will leben. Ein autobiographischer Bericht*, Oberbaum, Berlin, 1982.

Schoenaich, Paul Freiherr von, *Mein Finale. Mit dem Geheimen Tagebuch 1933–1945*, Christian Wolff, Flensburg and Hamburg, 1947.

Schoenberner, Gerhard (ed.), *Wir haben es gesehen. Augenzeugenberichte über Terror und Judenverfolgung im Dritten Reich*, Rutten-Loening, Hamburg, 1962.

Semmler, Rudolf, *Goebbels – the Man Next to Hitler*, Westhouse, London, 1947.

Seraphim, Hans G., *Das politische Tagebuch Alfred Rosenbergs*, DTV, Munich, 1964.

Smith, Howard K., *The Last Train from Berlin*, Knopf, New York, 1943.

Speer, Albert, *Spandau. The secret diaries*, Pocket, New York, 1977.

——, *The Slave State*, Weidenfeld and Nicolson, London, 1981.

Steward, John S., *Sieg des Glaubens. Authentische Gestapoberichte über den kirchlichen Widerstand in Deutschland*, Thomas, Zürich, 1946.

Thevoz, Robert et al. (eds), *Die geheime Staatspolizei in den preußischen Ostprovinzen 1934–1936. Pommern 1934–1935 im Spiegel von Gestapo Lageberichten und Sachakten*, Grote, Cologne and Berlin, 1974.

Trial of the Major War Criminals, International Military Tribunal, Nuremberg, 1949.

Vollmer, Bernhard, *Volksopposition im Polizeistaat: Gestapo und Regierungsberichte 1934–1936*, DVA, Stuttgart, 1957.

Walk, Joseph (ed.), *Das Sonderrecht für die Juden im N. S. Staat*, Müller, Heidelberg and Karlsruhe, 1981.

Weil, Bruno, *Durch drei Kontinente*, Cosmopolita, Buenos Aires, 1948.

Wiedemann, Fritz, *Der Mann der Feldherr werden wollte*, Blick und Bild, Dortmund, 1964.

Witetschek, Helmut et al. (eds), *Die kirchliche Lage in Bayern nach den Regierungspräsidenten Berichten 1933–1943*, Grünewald, Mainz, 1966–81.

BOOKS AND ARTICLES

Abel, Theodora, *The Nazi Movement. Why Hitler came to power*, Atherton, New York, 1966.

Adam, Uwe D., *Judenpolitik im Dritten Reich*, Athenäum, Königstein, 1979.

Adler, Hans G., *Der verwaltete Mensch*, Mohr, Tübingen, 1974.

Allen, William S., *The Nazi Seizure of Power*, Quadrangle, Chicago, 1965.

Allen, William S., 'Die deutsche Öffentlichkeit und die "Reichskristallnacht". Konflikt zwischen Werthierarchie und Propaganda im Dritten Reich', in Detlev Peukert and Jürgen Reulecke (eds), *Die Reihen fast geschlossen. Beiträge zur Geschichte des Alltags unterm Nationalsozialismus*, Hammer, Wuppertal, 1981, pp. 397–412.

Allport, Gordon, *The Nature of Prejudice*, Doubleday, New York, 1958.

Allport, Gordon, and Leo Postman, *The Psychology of Rumor*, Henry Holt, New York, 1947.

Arendt, Hanna, *The Origins of Totalitarianism*, Meridian, New York, 1969.

Aretz, Jürgen, *Katholische Arbeiterbewegung und Nationalsozialismus. Der Verband katholischer Arbeiter und Knappenvereine Westdeutschlands 1923–1945*, Grünewald, Mainz 1978.

Aronson, Shlomo, *Reinhard Heydrich und die Frühgeschichte von Gestapo und SD*, DVA, Stuttgart, 1971.

——, 'Die dreifache Falle', *Vierteljahrshefte für Zeitgeschichte*, 32 (1984), pp. 29–65.

Balfour, Michael, and Julian Frisby, *Helmuth von Moltke. A leader against Hitler*, Macmillan, London, 1972.

Bankier, David, 'The German Communist Party and Nazi antisemitism', *Yearbook of the Leo Baeck Institute*, 32 (1987), pp. 325–40.

——, 'Hitler and the policy-making process on the Jewish Question', *Holocaust and Genocide Studies*, 3 (1988), pp. 1–20.

——, 'Die Beziehungen zwischen deutschen jüdischen Flüchtlingen und deutschen politischen Exilierten in Südamerika', in Achim Schrader and Karl Heinrich Rengstorf (eds), *Europäische Juden in Lateinamerika*, Röhrig, St Ingbert, 1989, pp. 213–25.

Barkai, Avraham, ' "Schicksalsjahr 1938"; Kontinuität und Verschärfung der wirtschaftlichen Ausplünderung der deutschen Juden', in Ursula Büttner (ed.), *Das Unrechtsregime*, Christians, Hamburg, 1986, vol. II, pp. 45–67.

Baruk, Henri, *Psychiatrie morale expérimentale*, Presses Universitaires de France, Paris, 1945.

Baumgart, Winfried, 'Zur Ansprache Hitlers vor den Führern der Wehrmacht 22 August 1939', *Vierteljahrshefte für Zeitgeschichte*, 16 (1968), pp. 120–49; 19 (1971), pp. 294–300.

Benson, Lee, 'An approach to the scientific study of past public opinion', *Public Opinion Quarterly*, 31 (1967–8), pp. 522–67.

Benz, Wolfgang, 'Judenvernichtung aus Notwehr? Die Legenden um Theodore N. Kaufmann', *Vierteljahrshefte für Zeitgeschichte*, 29 (1981), pp. 615–30.

Berghahn, Volker R., *Der Stahlhelm. Bund der Frontsoldaten*, Droste, Düsseldorf, 1966.

Bessel, Richard, and Mathilde Jamin, 'Nazis, workers and the use of quantitative evidence', *Social History*, 4 (1979), pp. 111–16.

Bracher, Karl D., Wolfgang Sauer and Gerhard Schulz, *Die nationalsozialistische Machtergreifung*, Westdeutscher Verlag, Cologne, 1960.

Broszat, Martin, *Der Nationalsozialismus. Weltanschauung, Programmatik und Wirklichkeit*, DVA, Stuttgart, 1960.

——, 'Soziale Motivation und Führer-Bindung des Nationalsozialismus', *Vierteljahrshefte für Zeitgeschichte*, 18 (1970), pp. 393–409.

——, *Der Staat Hitlers*, DTV, Munich, 1971.

——, 'Zur Struktur der NS-Massenbewegung', *Vierteljahrshefte für Zeitgeschichte*, 31 (1983), pp. 52–76.

——, 'The Third Reich and the German people', in Hedley Bull (ed.), *The Challenge of the Third Reich*, Clarendon Press, Oxford, 1986, pp. 77–94.

——, *Nach Hitler. Der schwierige Umgang mit unserer Geschichte*, Oldenbourg, Munich, 1986.

Broszat, Martin, et al. (eds), *Bayern in der NS Zeit*, Oldenbourg, Munich, 1977–83.

Broszat, Martin, and Saul Friedländer, 'A controversy about the historicization of National Socialism', *Yad Vashem Studies*, 19 (1988), pp. 1–47.

Browning, Christopher R., *Fateful Months. Essays on the emergence of the Final Solution*, Holmes and Meier, New York, 1985.

Bruß, Regina, *Die Bremer Juden unter dem Nationalsozialismus*, Selbstverlag des Staatsarchivs der Freien Hansestadt Bremen, Bremen, 1983.

Brustin Berenstein, M., 'The process of exterminating Jewish communities in the so-called Distrikt Galizien', *Bletter far Geschichte*, 6 (1953), pp. 132–4 (in Yiddish).

Bukofzer, Ernst, *Laws for Jews and Persecution of Jews under the Nazis*, Hübener, Berlin, 1946.

Buscher, Frank M., and Michael Phayer, 'German Catholic bishops and the Holocaust', *German Studies Review*, 11 (1988), pp. 463–85.

Buzek, Anthony, *How the Communist Press Works*, Pall Mall, London, 1964.

Darnton, Robert, 'The Grub Street style of revolution: J. P. Brissot, police spy', *Journal of Modern History*, 40 (1968), pp. 301–27.

Dawidowicz, Lucy, *The War against the Jews 1933–1942*, Bantam, New York, 1976.

Deak, Istvan, *Weimar Germany's Left-Wing Intellectuals*, University of California Press, Berkeley, Calif., 1968.

Deist, Wilhelm, et al., *Das Deutsche Reich und der Zweite Weltkrieg*, DVA, Stuttgart, 1979.

Diehl, James M., *Paramilitary Politics in Weimar Germany*, Indiana University Press, Bloomington, 1977.

Diehl-Thiele, Peter, *Partei und Staat im Dritten Reich. Untersuchungen zum Verhältnis von NSDAP und allgemeiner innerer Staatsverwaltung 1933–1945*, C. H. Beck, Stuttgart, 1969.

Diels, Rudolf, *Lucifer ante portas*, DVA, Stuttgart, 1950.

Eitner, Hans J., *Hitlers Deutsche. Das Ende eines Tabus*, Casimir Katz, Gernsbach, 1990.

Emmerson, James T., *The Rhineland Crisis, 7 March 1936. A study on multilateral diplomacy*, Temple Smith, London 1972.

Encyclopaedia of the Jewish Diaspora, Encyclopaedia Co., Jerusalem and Tel Aviv, 1955.

Esch, Shaul, 'Between discrimination and extermination. The fateful year 1938', *Yad Vashem Studies*, 2 (1958), pp. 79–94.

Fisher, Conan, 'The occupational background of the SA's rank and file membership during the Depression years 1929 to mid 1934', in Peter D. Stachura (ed.), *The Shaping of the Nazi State*, Croom Helm, London, 1978, pp. 131–59.

——, *Stormtroopers*, Allen and Unwin, London, 1983.

Fleming, Gerald L., *Hitler and the Final Solution*, Oxford University Press, Oxford, 1986.

Fogelman, Eva, 'The Rescuers: a socio-psychological study of altruistic behaviour during the Nazi era', PhD dissertation, City University of New York, 1987.

Friedrich, Carl J. (ed.), *Totalitarianism*, Grosset and Dunlap, New York, 1964.

Funke, Manfred, '7 März 1936. Studie zum außenpolitischen Führungsstiel Hitlers', *Aus Politik und Zeitgeschichte*, 3 Oct. 1970.

Galante, Pierre and Eugene Silianoff, *Last Witnesses in the Bunker*, Sidgwick and Jackson, London, 1989.

Gascar, Pierre, *Histoire de la captivité des Français en Allemagne (1939–1945)*, Gallimard, Saint-Amand, 1967.

Gellately, Robert, 'German shopkeepers and the rise of National Socialism', *Wiener Library Bulletin*, 28 (1974–5), pp. 31–40.

Genschel, Helmut, *Die Verdrängung der Juden aus der Wirtschaft im Dritten Reich*, Bausteine zur Geschichtswissenschaft, Göttingen, 1966.

Gordon, Sarah, *Hitler, Germans and the Jewish Question*, Princeton University Press, Princeton, NJ, 1984.

Görgen, Hans P., *Düsseldorf und der Nationalsozialismus*, Schwann, Düsseldorf, 1969.

Gross, Leonard, *The Last Jews in Berlin*, Simon and Schuster, New York, 1982.

Gruchmann, Lothar, ' "Blutschutzgesetz" und Justiz. Zur Entstehung und Auswirkung des Nürnberger Gesetzes vom 15. September 1935', *Vierteljahrshefte für Zeitgeschichte*, 31 (1983), 418–42.

Hagemann, Jürgen, *Die Presse Lenkung im Dritten Reich*, Bouvier, Bonn, 1970.

Hagemann, Walter, *Publizistik im Dritten Reich. Ein Beitrag zur Methodik der Massenführung*, Hanseatischer Gildenverlag, Hamburg, 1948.

Hale, Oron J., *The Captive Press in the Third Reich*, Princeton University Press, Princeton, NJ, 1964.

Heiber, Helmut (ed.), *Hitlers Lagebesprechungen im Führerhauptquartier 1942–1945*, DVA, Stuttgart, 1962.

Herbst, Ludolf, 'Die Krise des nationalsozialistischen Regimes am Vorabend des Zweiten Weltkrieges und die forcierte Aufrüstung', *Vierteljahrshefte für Zeitgeschichte*, 26 (1978), pp. 347–92.

Herzstein, Robert E., *The War that Hitler Won*, Sphere Books, London, 1980.

Hey, Bernd, 'Bielefeld und seine Bevölkerung in den Berichten des Sicherheitsdienstes (SD) 1939–1942', *70. Jahresbericht des historischen Vereins für die Grafschaft Ravensberg*, 70 (1975–6), pp. 227–73.

Hilberg, Raul, *The Destruction of the European Jews*, Quadrangle, Chicago, 1961.

Hildebrand, Klaus, 'Innenpolitische Antriebskräfte der nationalsozialistischen Außenpolitik', in Manfred Funke (ed.), *Hitler, Deutschland und die Mächte. Materialien zur Außenpolitik des Dritten Reiches*, Droste, Düsseldorf, 1976, pp. 223–38.

——, 'Monokratie oder Polikratie? Hitlers Herrschaft und das Dritte Reich', in Gerhard Hirschfeld and Lothar Kettenacker (eds), *Der 'Führerstaat': Mythos und Realität*, Klett–Cotta, Stuttgart, 1981, pp. 73–96.

Hochmuth, Ursel, *Streiflichter aus dem Hamburger Widerstand 1933–1945*, Röderberg, Frankfurt a.M., 1969.

Hollander, Gayle D., *Soviet Political Indoctrination. Developments in mass media and propaganda since Stalin*, Praeger, New York, 1972.

Hüttenberger, Peter, 'Nationalsozialistische Polikratie', *Geschichte und Gesellschaft*, 2 (1976), pp. 417–42.

Inkeles, Alex, and Raymond A. Bauer, *The Soviet Citizen. Daily life in a totalitarian society*, Harvard University Press, Cambridge, Mass., 1959.

Jaeckel, Eberhard, *Hitlers Weltanschauung: Entwurf einer Herrschaft*, DVA, Stuttgart, 1986.

Jamin, Mathilde, 'Zur Rolle der SA im nationalsozialistischen Herrschaftssystem', in Gerhard Hirschfeld and Lothar Kettenacker (eds), *Der 'Führerstaat': Mythos und Realität*, Klett-Cotta, Stuttgart, 1981, pp. 329–58.

Joutard, Philippe, *Ces voix qui nous viennent du passé*, Gallimard, Paris, 1983.

Kann, Robert A., 'Public opinion research: a contribution to historical method', *Political Science Quarterly*, 73 (1958), pp. 374–96.

Kater, Michael H., 'Sozialer Wandel in der NSDAP im Zuge der Nationalsozialistischen Machtergreifung', in Wolfgang Schieder (ed.), *Faschismus als soziale
Bewegung*, Hoffmann and Kampe, Hamburg, 1976, pp. 25–67.

Kempner, Robert W., *Eichmann und Komplizen*, Europa, Zürich, Stuttgart and
Vienna, 1961.

Kershaw, Ian, 'Antisemitismus und Volksmeinung, Reaktionen auf die Judenverfolgung', in Martin Broszat et al. (eds), *Bayern in der NS Zeit*, Oldenbourg,
Munich, 1979, vol. II, pp. 281–348.

——, 'The persecution of the Jews and German popular opinion in the Third Reich',
Yearbook of the Leo Baeck Institute, 26 (1981), pp. 261–89.

——, *Popular Opinion and Political Dissent in the Third Reich*, Clarendon Press,
Oxford, 1984.

——, 'German popular opinion and the "Jewish Question", 1939–1943: some further
reflections', in Arnold Paucker (ed.), *Die Juden im nationalsozialistischen Deutschland*, Mohr, Tübingen, 1986, pp. 365–86.

——, *The 'Hitler Myth'*, Clarendon Press, Oxford, 1987.

——, 'German popular opinion during the "Final Solution": information,
comprehension, reactions', in Asher Cohen, Joav Gelber and Charlotte Wardi (eds),
Comprehending the Holocaust, Peter Lang, Frankfurt a.M., Bern, New York and
Paris, 1989, pp. 145–58.

——, *The Nazi Dictatorship*, Edward Arnold, London, 1989.

Klotzbach, Kurt, *Gegen den Nationalsozialismus. Widerstand und Verfolgung in
Dortmund 1933–1945*, Verlag für Literatur und Zeitgeschehen, Hanover, 1969.

Knütter, Helmut, *Die Juden und die deutsche Linke in der Weimarer Republik 1918–
1933*, Droste, Düsseldorf, 1971.

Kochan, Lionel, *Pogrom*, André Deutsch, London, 1957.

Krohn, Klaus D. and Dirk Stegmann, 'Kleingewerbe und NS in einer
agrarisch-mittelständischen Region. Das Beispiel Lüneburg 1930–1933', *Archiv für
Sozialgeschichte*, 17 (1977), pp. 1–40.

Kulka, Otto D., 'The "Jewish Question" in the Third Reich', PhD dissertation,
Hebrew University, Jerusalem 1975 (in Hebrew).

——, '"Public opinion" in National Socialist Germany and the "Jewish Question"',
Zion 40 (1975), pp. 186–290 (in Hebrew).

——, 'Die Nürnberger Rassengesetze und die deutsche Bevölkerung im Lichte
geheimer NS Lage und Stimmungsberichte', *Vierteljahrshefte für Zeitgeschichte*, 32
(1984), pp. 582–624.

——, 'Die deutsche Geschichtsschreibung über den Nationalsozialismus und die
"Endlösung"', *Historische Zeitschrift*, 240 (1985), pp. 599–640.

Kulka, Otto D. and Aron Rodrigue, 'The German population and the Jews in the
Third Reich', *Yad Vashem Studies*, 16 (1984), pp. 421–35.

Lakowski, Richard, 'Das Ende des "Stahlhelm". Ein Beitrag zur Geschichte der
Stabilisierung der faschistischen Diktatur in Deutschland', *Wissenschaftliche
Zeitschrift der Humboldt Universität zu Berlin. Geschichte und Sprachwissenschaft*, 22
(1973), pp. 39–48.

Laqueur, Walter, *The Terrible Secret*, Weidenfeld and Nicolson, London, 1980.

Lavabre, Célestin, *Ceux de l'an 40*, Subervie, Rodez, 1981.

Lenk, Leonhard, 'Revolutionär-kommunistische Umtriebe im Königreich Bayern. Ein Beitrag zur Entwicklung von Staat und Gesellschaft 1848–1864', *Zeitschrift für bayerische Landesgeschichte*, 28 (1965), pp. 555–622.

Leuner, Heinz D., *When Compassion was a Crime*, Wolff, London, 1966.

Lindgren, Henrik, 'Adam von Trotts Reisen nach Schweden 1942–1944', *Vierteljahrshefte für Zeitgeschichte*, 18 (1970), pp. 274–91.

Liu, Alan P. L., *Communications and National Integration in Communist China*, University of California Press, Berkeley, Calif., 1971.

Lösener, Bernhard, 'Das Reichsministerium des Inneren und die Judengesetzgebung', *Vierteljahrshefte für Zeitgeschichte*, 9 (1961), pp. 262–313.

Lowenstein, Steven M., 'The struggle for survival of rural Jews in Germany 1933–1938: the case of Bezirksamt Weissenburg, Mittelfranken', in Arnold Paucker (ed.), *Die Juden im Nationalsozialistischen Deutschland*, Mohr, Tübingen, 1986, pp. 115–24.

Luchterhand, Elmer, 'Knowing and not knowing: involvement in Nazi genocide', in Paul Thompson (ed.), *Our Common History. The transformation of Europe*, Humanities Press, Atlantic Highlands, NJ, 1982, pp. 251–72.

Mammach, Klaus, *Die KPD und die deutsche antifaschistische Widerstandsbewegung 1933–1939*, Röderberg, Frankfurt a.M., 1974.

Marrus, Michael R. and Robert O. Paxton, *Vichy France and the Jews*, Basic Books, New York, 1981.

Mason, Tim, 'Intention and explanation: a current controversy about the interpretation of National Socialism', in Gerhard Hirschfeld and Lothar Kettenacker (eds), *Der 'Führerstaat': Mythos und Realität*, Klett-Cotta, Stuttgart, 1981, pp. 23–41.

Mayer, Milton, *They Thought They Were Free*, University of Chicago Press, Chicago and London, 1974.

Memorial Book for the Jewish Communities of Trembowla, Strusow, Janow and Vicinity, Survivors Organization, Benei Berak, n. d.

Memorial Book of Jezierna, Survivors Organization, Haifa, 1971.

Memorial Book Rawa Ruska, Survivors Organization, Tel Aviv, 1973.

Mommsen, Hans, 'Gesellschaftsbild und Verfassungspläne des deutschen Widerstandes', in Walter Schmitthenner and Hans Buchheim (eds), *Der deutsche Widerstand gegen Hitler*, Kiepenheuer and Witsch, Cologne, 1966, pp. 73–168.

——, 'Nationalsozialismus', in *Sowjetsystem und demokratische Gesellschaft. Eine vergleichende Enziklopädie*, Freiburg i.B., 1971, vol. IV, pp. 695–713.

——, 'National Socialism. Continuity and change', in Walter Laqueur (ed.) *Fascism. A reader's guide*, University of California Press, Berkeley, Calif., 1976, pp. 179–210.

——, 'Was haben die Deutschen vom Völkermord an den Juden gewußt?, in Werner H. Pehle (ed.), *Der Judenpogrom 1938. Von der 'Reichskristallnacht' zum Völkermord*, Fischer, Frankfurt a.M., 1988, pp. 176–200.

Mommsen, Hans, and Dieter Obst, 'Die Reaktion der deutschen Bevölkerung auf die Verfolgung der Juden', in Hans Mommsen and Susanne Willems (eds), *Herrschaftsalltag im Dritten Reich. Studien und Texte*, Schwann, Düsseldorf, 1989, pp. 374–427.

Morstein Marx, Fritz, 'State propaganda in Germany', in Harwood L. Childs (ed.),

Propaganda and Dictatorship, Princeton University Press, Princeton, NJ, 1936, pp. 11–34.

Mosse, George L., 'Die deutsche Rechte und die Juden', in Werner E. Mosse (ed.), *Entscheidungsjahr 1932*, Mohr, Tübingen, 1966, pp. 183–238.

Müller Claudius, Michael, *Der Antisemitismus und das deutsche Verhängnis*, J. Knecht, Frankfurt a.M., 1948.

Nies, Erich, *Politisches Tagebuch 1935–1945*, Ebner, Ulm, 1947.

Niethammer, Lutz, 'Heimat und Front. Versuch zehn Kriegserinnerungen aus der Arbeiterklasse des Ruhrgebietes zu verstehen', in Lutz Niethammer (ed.), *'Die Jahre weiß man nicht, wo man sie heute hinsetzen soll.' Faschismus-Erfahrungen im Ruhrgebiet*, Dietz, Berlin and Bonn, 1983, pp. 163–232.

——, *Lebenserfahrung und Kollektives Gedächtniss*, Suhrkamp, Frankfurt a.M., 1985.

——, 'Juden und Russen im Gedächtniss der Deutschen', in Walter H. Pehle (ed.), *Der historische Ort des Nationalsozialismus*, Fischer, Frankfurt a.M., 1990, pp. 114–34.

Niewyk, Donald L., *Socialist, Antisemite and Jew*, Louisiana State University Press, Baton Rouge, 1971.

Noakes, Jeremy, and Geoffrey Pridham, *Nazism 1919–1945*, University of Exeter, Exeter, 1984–8.

Orlow, Dietrich, *The History of the Nazi Party*, University of Pittsburgh Press, Pittsburgh, 1969.

Pätzold, Kurt, *Faschismus, Rassenwahn, Judenverfolgung*, Deutscher Verlag der Wissenschaften, Berlin, 1975.

Peukert, Detlev J. K., *Inside Nazi Germany*, Penguin, Harmondsworth, Middx, 1989.

Phayer, Michael, 'Margarete Sommer, Berlin's Catholics and Germany's Jews 1939–1945', *Remembering for the Future*, Pergamon, Oxford, 1988, vol. I, pp. 112–20.

Plum, Günter, 'Staatspolizei und innere Verwaltung 1934–1936', *Vierteljahrshefte für Zeitgeschichte*, 13 (1965), pp. 208–22.

Pye, Lucian W. (ed.), *Communication and Political Development*, Princeton University Press, Princeton, NJ, 1963.

Rauschning, Hermann, *Gespräche mit Hitler*, Europa, Zürich, 1940.

Robertson, Esmonde M., 'Zur Wiederbesetzung des Rheinlandes 1936', *Vierteljahrshefte für Zeitgeschichte*, 10 (1962), pp. 178–205.

——, *Hitler's Prewar Policy and Military Plans, 1933–1939*, Longman, London, 1963.

Robinsohn, Hans J., 'Ein Versuch sich zu behaupten', *Tradition*, 3 (1958), pp. 197–206.

Rogowski, Ronald, 'The Gauleiters and the social origins of fascism', *Comparative Studies in Society and History*, 19 (1977), pp. 399–430.

Roon, Ger van, 'Widerstand und Krieg', in Jürgen Schmädeke and Peter Steinbach (eds), *Der Widerstand gegen den National Sozialismus*, Piper, Munich, 1986, pp. 50–73.

Rosenfeld, Elsbeth, *The Four Lives of Elsbeth Rosenfeld as Told by her to the BBC*, Gollancz, London, 1964.

Rürup, Reinhard, 'Das Ende der Emanzipation: die antijüdische Politik in Deutschland von der "Machtergreifung" bis zum Zweiten Weltkrieg', in Arnold

Paucker (ed.), *Die Juden im nationalsozialistischen Deutschland*, Mohr, Tübingen, 1986, pp. 97–114.

Rürup, Reinhard and W. Kaiser, 'Sozialismus und Antisemitismus in Deutschland vor 1914', *Jahrbuch des Instituts für deutsche Geschichte*, 2 (1977), pp. 203–25.

Saldern, Adelheit von, *Mittelstand im 'Dritten Reich'. Handwerker-Einzelhändler-Bauern*, Campus, Frankfurt a.M., 1979.

Sänger, Fritz, *Politik der Täuschungen. Mißbrauch der Presse im Dritten Reich, Weisungen, Informationen, Notizen, 1933–1939*, Europa, Vienna, 1975.

Schadt, Jürgen, *Verfolgung und Widerstand unter dem Nationalsozialismus in Baden*, Kohlhammer, Stuttgart, 1976.

Schmidt, Matthias, *Albert Speer. The end of a myth*, Harrap, London, 1985.

Schoenbaum, David, *Hitler's Social Revolution*, Anchor, New York, 1967.

Scholl, Inge, *Die weiße Rose*, Frankfurter Hefte Verlag, Frankfurt a.M., 1952.

Schultheis, Herbert, *Juden in Mainfranken 1933–1945*, Rötter, Bad Neustadt a. d. Saale, 1980.

Schumann, Hans G., *Nationalsozialismus und Gewerkschaftsbewegung*, Norddeutsche Verlagsanstalt, Hanover, Frankfurt a.M. and Hamburg, 1958.

Shoham, Giora S., 'German socialism and antisemitism; social character and the disruption of the symbiosis between Germans and Jews', *Clio*, 15 (1986), pp. 303–20.

Silberner, Edmund, *Sozialisten zur Judenfrage*, Colloquium, Berlin, 1962.

Spector, Shmuel, 'Operation 1005. Effacing the murder of millions', *Yahadut Zémanenu*, 4 (1987), pp. 207–25 (in Hebrew).

Stegmann, Dirk, 'Antiquierte Personalisierung oder sozialökonomische Faschismus-Analyse. Eine Antwort auf H. A. Turners Kritik an meinen Thesen zum Verhältnis von Nationalsozialismus und Großindustrie vor 1933', *Archiv für Sozialgeschichte*, 17 (1977), pp. 175–206.

Steinberg, Hans J., *Widerstand und Verfolgung in Essen 1933–1945*, Verlag für Literatur und Zeitgeschehen, Hanover, 1969.

Steinert, Marlis, *Hitler's War and the Germans*, Ohio University Press, Athens, Ohio, 1977.

Stern, Frank, *The Whitewashing of the Yellow Badge. Philosemitism and antisemitism in West Germany 1945–1952*, Pergamon, Oxford, 1991.

Stern, Fritz, *Dreams and Delusions. The drama of German history*, Knopf, New York, 1987.

Stokes, Lawrence D., 'The Sicherheitsdienst (SD) of the Reichsführer SS and German Public Opinion, September 1939 – June 1941', PhD dissertation, Johns Hopkins University, Baltimore, 1972.

——, 'The German people and the destruction of the European Jews', *Central European History*, 6 (1973), pp. 167–91.

——, 'Otto Ohlendorf, the Sicherheitsdienst and public opinion in Nazi Germany', in George L. Mosse (ed.), *Police Forces in History*, Sage, London, 1975, pp. 231–61.

Storek, Henning, *Dirigierte Öffentlichkeit. Die Zeitung als Herrschaftsmittel in den Anfangsjahren der nationalsozialistischen Regierung*, Westdeutscher Verlag, Opladen, 1972.

Talmon, Jacob L., *The Myth of the Nation and the Vision of Revolution*, Secker and Warburg, London, 1980.

Thamer, Hans U., *Verführung und Gewalt. Deutschland 1933–1945*, Siedler, Berlin, 1986.

Tomaszewski, Jerzy, 'The situation of the Jews in Germany in spring 1933 as reflected in reports of the Polish Republic Legation and Consulate General in Berlin', *Biuletyn Żidowskiego Instytutu Historycznego*, 139–140 (1986), pp. 131–42.

Treue, Wilhelm, 'Hitlers Denkschrift zum Vierjahresplan 1936', *Vierteljahrshefte für Zeitgeschichte*, 3 (1955), pp. 184–210.

Trevor-Roper, Hugh R., *Hitler Table Talk 1941–44*, Weidenfeld and Nicolson, London, 1973.

Uhlig, Heinrich, *Die Warenhäuser im Dritten Reich*, Westdeutscher Verlag, Cologne, 1956.

Unger, Aryeh, 'The public opinion reports of the Nazi Party', *Public Opinion Quarterly*, 29 (1965), pp. 565–82.

Volkov, Shulamit, 'The written matter and the spoken word', in François Furet (ed.), *Unanswered Questions*, Schocken, New York, 1989, pp. 33–53.

Wall, Donald D., 'The reports of the Sicherheitsdienst on the Church and religious affairs in Germany 1939–1944', *Church History*, 40 (1971), 437–56.

Warburg, Gustav, *Six Years under Hitler*, Allen and Unwin, London, 1939.

Weinberg, Gerhard L., *The Foreign Policy of Hitler's Germany*, University of Chicago Press, Chicago, 1970.

Welch, David, 'Propaganda and indoctrination in the Third Reich: success or failure?', *European History Quarterly*, 17 (1987), pp. 403–22.

Weltsch, Robert, 'First of April 1933', *World Jewry*, 1 (1958), pp. 11–12.

Wenke, Bettina, *Interviews mit Überlebenden*, Theiß, Stuttgart, 1980.

Wessel, Nils H., 'The credibility, impact and effectiveness of the Soviet non-specialized newspaper', PhD dissertation, University of California, 1972.

Wiesemann, Falk, 'Judenverfolgung und nichtjüdische Bevölkerung', in Martin Broszat et al. (eds), *Bayern in der NS Zeit*, Oldenbourg, Munich, 1977, vol. I, pp. 427–86.

——, 'Juden auf dem Lande: die wirtschaftliche Ausgrenzung der jüdischen Viehhändler in Bayern', in Detlev Peuckert and Jürgen Reulecke (eds), *Die Reihen fast geschlossen. Alltag im Nationalsozialismus*, Hammer, Wuppertal, 1981, pp. 381–96.

Wilhelm, Hans H., 'The Holocaust in National Socialist rhetoric and writings', *Yad Vashem Studies* 16 (1984), pp. 95–128.

Winkler, Heinrich A., 'From social protectionism to National Socialism. The German small-business movement in comparative perspective', *Journal of Modern History*, 48 (1976), pp. 1–18.

——, 'Der entbehrliche Stand. Zur Mittelstandspolitik im Dritten Reich', *Archiv für Sozialgeschichte*, 17 (1977), pp. 1–40.

Witetschek, Helmuth, 'Die bayerischen Regierungspräsidenten Berichte 1933–1939', *Historisches Jahrbuch*, 87 (1967), pp. 355–72.

Wolfson, Manfred, 'Der Widerstand gegen Hitler. Soziologische Skizze über Retter von Juden in Deutschland', *Aus Politik und Zeitgeschichte*, 10 Apr. 1971, pp. 32–9.

Young, Arthur P., *The 'X' Documents. The secret history of Foreign Office contacts with the German Resistance 1937–1939*, André Deutsch, London, 1974.

Zeman, Z. A. B., *Nazi Propaganda*, Oxford University Press, London, 1973.

Zimmermann, Michael, 'Die Deportation der Juden aus Essen und dem Regierungsbezirk Düsseldorf', in Ulrich Borsdorf and Mathilde Jamin (eds), *Überleben im Krieg*, Rowohlt, Hamburg, 1989, pp. 126–42.

Zipfel, Friedrich, *Gestapo und Sicherheitsdienst*, Arani, Berlin, 1960.

Zollitsch, Wolfgang, *Arbeiter zwischen Weltwirtschaftskrise und Nationalsozialismus*, Vandenhoeck and Ruprecht, Göttingen, 1990.

Index